OAKLAND COUNTY

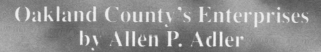

Oakland County's Enterprises
by Allen P. Adler

Produced In Cooperation with Daniel T. Murphy
Oakland County Executive

and the
Department of Community and Economic Development
County of Oakland, Pontiac, Michigan

Windsor Publications, Inc.
Chatsworth, California

Seen here appearing to rise from a field of yellow flowers, Troy has become a mecca of corporate strategy and brainpower behind the auto industry. Photo by Balthazar Korab

Making It Work In Michigan

OAKLAND COUNTY

A Contemporary Portrait
by Trout Pomeroy

Windsor Publications, Inc.—Book Division

Managing Editor: Karen Story
Design Director: Alexander D'Anca
Photo Director: Susan L. Wells
Executive Editor: Pamela Schroeder

Staff for *Oakland County: Making It Work In Michigan*
Manuscript Editor: Michael Nalick
Photo Editor: Lisa Willinger
Senior Editor, Corporate Profiles: Judith L. Hunter
Editor, Corporate Profiles: Melissa Wells Patton
Production Editor, Corporate Profiles: Justin Scupine
Proofreaders: Mary Jo Scharf, Michael Moore
Customer Service Manager: Phyllis Feldman-Schroeder
Editorial Assistants: Elizabeth Andersen, Dominique Jones, Kim Kievman,
    Michael Nugwynne, Kathy B. Peyser, Theresa J. Solis
Publisher's Representatives, Corporate Profiles: John Cornies, Harriet Hess,
    Kelly Lance
Designer: Thomas McTighe
Layout Artist, Corporate Profiles: Lisa Barrett
Caption Writer: Ursula Marinelli, Oakland Co., MI

Windsor Publications, Inc.
Elliot Martin, Chairman of the Board
James L. Fish III, Chief Operating Officer
Michele Sylvestro, Vice President/Sales-Marketing
Mac Buhler, Vice President/Acquisitions

Library of Congress Cataloging-in-Publication Data
ISBN: 0-89781-361-8
Pomeroy, Trout, 1945-
    Oakland County: making it work in Michigan/Trout Pomeroy.
        p. 192 cm. 23x31
    Includes bibliographical references and index.
    ISBN 0-89781-361-8
    1. Oakland County (Mich.)—Civilization. 2. Oakland County
    (Mich.)—Description and travel—Views. 3. Oakland County
    (Mich.)—Economic conditions. 4. Oakland County (Mich.)—
    Industries.
    I. Title.
    F572.02P66   1990
    977.4'38—dc20   90-12896
                                                              CIP

Anachronisms amid the hustle and bustle of high-tech Troy, these
barns are reminders of Oakland County's rich agricultural past.
Photo by Balthazar Korab

Contents

Acknowledgments

It was a June morning in 1989, about 5:30 a.m. Thin splashes of maroon and blue played off the eastern sky, a flock of geese sailed out toward Luna Pier, and *a group of early Oakland County settlers was standing off to the side of M-59.*

There was authenticity in the colors in the sky. But the settlers? Well, they were a mirage, by-products of historic overload. I'm seeing things, I thought. Beautiful things.

Looking back on months of immersion in the Oakland County story, that fleeting moment with "the settlers" stands above all the others. There was, I realize now, something deeply moving about the images of people on the edge of the road . . . on the edge of one man's imagination. Their body language conveyed "the settlers" knew they didn't belong here—not in this day and age. Yet there they were, in their buckskin coats and cotton dresses, standing humbly by a highway entrance ramp as mist rose off a darkened field.

Real people weren't standing by the road. But seeing them, if only in my mind, became the source of enormous comfort as I pushed this project along. And with friends like those "settlers," I was prepared to encounter the ghosts of other legendary Oakland County characters like Lewis Cass, George Booth, and Woody Varner.

People from different eras, with diverging dispositions.

People whose lives shared but one common thread—each contributed greatly to the development of Oakland County.

Accordingly, this work is dedicated to those who came before, to those who are here now, and to all who will follow. It's also for my wife, Bonny, and our boys, Garrett and Fraser, for tolerating a mind focused on imaginary settlers instead of true-to-life diaper duty.

On the editorial side, muchas gracias to Tom Walsh, Mary Lu Voelpel, Paul Dahlmann and Dave Nash, who carefully eyeballed the work, and to researcher Jackie Richardson. Special thanks also to Richard B. Jones and Duane Utech, Jr.

Thanks as well to editor Mike Nalick at Windsor Publications in Los Angeles, for letting me write about the Detroit Pistons and for all his masterful input, and to the excitable staff of the Oakland County Department of Community and Economic Development, especially Marlys Vickers. To both parties I offer my special thanks . . . for trusting me with the project and for providing gallant assistance during its creation.

If there's still room, I'd like to thank my parents, Fraser and Margaret Pomeroy, for choosing Oakland County as our home and for encouraging my development as a writer.

David Trout Pomeroy
Jan. 24, 1990
Rochester, MI

Southfield's biannual Michigan Outdoor Sculpture Exhibit gives exposure to approximately 30 Michigan sculptors at each event. The exhibit is funded by the Business Consortium for the Arts, the City of Southfield, and corporate sponsors. Photo by Balthazar Korab

Making It Work

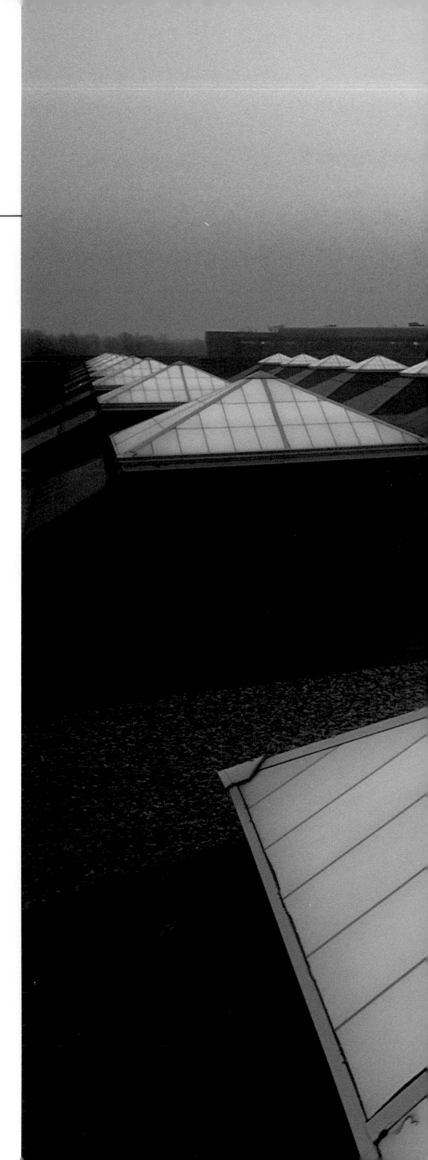

This sci-fi scene is not a futuristic vision of some space age energy source but rather the top of Rochester Hills' GMF Robotics building taken at dusk when the work day has ended. Imagine that the glow inside represents the restless untapped energy of a community whose true economic potential has only just begun to surface. Photo by Balthazar Korab

The Early Days

Long before 1817, when pioneer settlers improvised their first log huts on the shores of Paint Creek in what they would call Rochester, the entire vicinity of Oakland County was covered by seawater. This startling theory wasn't arrived at casually.

Rather it was confirmed by the presence of fossils in the area. The discovery of layers of limestone furthered the suggestion. And the great salt beds that lie beneath Detroit advanced the truth beyond a doubt.

Gradually the oceans receded and swamps appeared, followed by trees and other forms of plants and new animal life. In the 900-square-mile area that would become Oakland County, the land was flat to the south, gently rolling in the north, and blessed throughout with hundreds of fine lakes.

The shape of the region was forged by a long period of intense glacial activity that took place more than 12,000 years ago. Great masses of ice and water—originating in the Hudson Bay vicinity of Canada—heaved slowly in a southwesterly direction across Michigan, forming valleys and depressions.

The hollows filled with water, pocketing Oakland County with a truly unique concentration of lakes and rivers. About 450 of those lakes remain. The count may not be exact; some county sources refer to 500 lakes in the area, others mention 407. One man's lake, in this case, may be another man's pond—or, as one historian wrote, "some lakes are thus called only by a generous stretch of the imagination."

Whether 400 or 500, state water resource officials say Oakland County has more lakes larger than 50 acres in size than any other county in Michigan. Lakes comprise 20,000 square acres of county land and drain into the Great Lakes through the Rouge, Huron, Shiawassee, and Clinton rivers.

A PROUD PAST

Oakland County's first human inhabitants were descendants of the Six United Nations of Indians. They shared links to the nomadic people who are believed to have entered Michigan after crossing the Bering Strait land bridge. For the Indians as well as the Europeans who followed, vast water resources were the area's main attraction; Oakland's ubiquitous lakes and rivers provided fishing as well as mobility in a heavily forested land that defied other forms of travel.

Indians roamed the area for about 12,000 years. When French explorers seeking a route to China (and Jesuit fathers seeking lost souls) first visited the region in the early seventeenth century, about 15,000 Indians remained in Michigan—and only a small number in Oakland County. The major tribes were Chippewa, Potawatomi, Ottawa, Miami, Sauk, and Fox. All spoke a dialect of Algonquian.

Before settlers arrived, most Indians dwelling in Michigan had migrated on—first to Indiana and Wisconsin, then to other points south and west. The westward migration of Indians accelerated with the arrival of the first French visitors. Later, disputes between the French and British created further confusion and discontent among the Indians.

For as long as the two European powers vied for supremacy in North America, the Indians were courted by both sides. The defeat of the French

Facing page: Pictured here in ceremonial dress, Chief Pontiac visited the Oakland area and is rumored to be buried on Apple Island in Orchard Lake. The city of Pontiac was named for this Indian leader. Courtesy, State Archives of Michigan

This page: General Motors' Proving Grounds in Milford are shown here in an early promotional montage produced by the company. Courtesy, Underwood Photo Archives

left the Indians at the mercy of the British, and with the American victory over the British, the future of all remaining Indians in the area was in doubt.

The final chapter of Indian life in southeast Michigan commenced in 1701, when French trader and soldier Antoine de la Mothe, Sieur de Cadillac, established Fort Ponchartrain in the name of the governor of the French colonies in Canada. Soon after, Cadillac began offering farmland around the fort to French settlers. For those hoping to settle in the Detroit region, this gesture represented a leap forward.

When an Indian seige of Fort Ponchartrain failed in 1764, the interior of southeast Michigan became more appealing to pioneers seeking homes. Immigration to the state became even more probable in 1783 when a peace treaty signed by England and the new American government granted Michigan to the United States of America. Congress passed an act authorizing the Michigan Territory in 1805, and Detroit was declared its capital. Two years later the Treaty of Detroit gave ownership of most land in southeast Michigan—including Oakland County—to the United States.

Under the agreement as ratified, some small reservations in Oakland County remained under Indian control. One end of Apple Island on Orchard Lake was not sold by the Indians until 1827. Indians also kept two large reservations along the shores of the River Rouge in what is now Southfield. With the Indian presence in the area greatly diminished and the War of 1812 nearing resolve, Oakland County was ripe for development. By the early 1820s it had begun. From a historical perspective the intervening period was of pivotal importance to the development of the county.

CHARTING THE WILDERNESS

Commander Oliver Perry's fleet defeated the British in the Battle of Lake Erie in 1813. The British pulled out of Detroit and, by Christmas Eve 1814, the war had ended in what essentially was a draw. No boundaries had been changed;

Michigan remained a part of the United States.

Surveying efforts began in southeast Michigan in 1815 and similar undertakings commenced in Louisiana and Illinois. In all, 6 million acres of what the government called "bounty lands"—2 million acres in each of the three states—were set aside for veterans of the war.

The first surveyors to branch out into what is now Oakland County found themselves pitted against what one writer called "the rigors of the vast uncharted wilderness." They faced many inhospitable factors, including an unusually wet winter and terrain more suited to animals than men. Early surveyor Captain Herve Parke recalled encountering "thick, dark forest, quaking marshland, buzzing mosquitos, and packs of wolves" during the period. "I suffered more than my pen can describe," he wrote.

In 1816 U.S. Surveyor General Edwin Tiffin received the surveyors' report from the area that comprises the 10 westernmost townships of present-day Oakland County. In the report, surveyors noted "low wetland" and spoke negatively of the stands of beech, cottonwood, and oak they found in the area. "It is with utmost difficulty that a place can be found over which horses can be conveyed in safety," the report read. "Most places are literally afloat."

The report described the county as one-half lakes and marsh and the other half poor, barren, sandy soil. "The country is so altogether bad that not more than an acre out of a hundred if one acre out of a thousand would be fit for civilization," the report added.

The reputation of Michigan's interior took another hit later that year when respected geographer Jedediah Morse described the area as generally bare and "thrown by the winds into a thousand different shapes."

Another impediment to progress was a swamp that existed at the northern edge of Detroit, in the vicinity of Highland Park and Royal Oak. Surveyors deemed the huge bog impassable; settlers found it impossible. One historical

Facing page: Millponds were scattered throughout the early land-scape of Oakland County. This pond was created by a dam built in the late 1850s to produce power for milling operations and street-lights in the city of Rochester. It has since been filled to accommodate development. Courtesy, Rochester Historical Commission

Right: Chippewa Indians roamed through the county toting their children and belongings and leaving little evidence of their presence. This illustration depicts a mother and child dressed in winter garb that was typical of Indians with access to goods from explorers and settlers. Courtesy, State Archives of Michigan

account read: "Many a venturesome pioneer who had perhaps found his way from New York or New England has had the last atom of faith in the new country taken from him in this indescribable morass."

Not everyone was intimidated by the swamp. In the years following the Tiffin Report, a few men found their way from Detroit out into Oakland County—often by way of Lake St. Clair and the Clinton River. And when they returned to Detroit, they spoke of beautiful, fertile, hilly land that existed beyond the marsh that surrounded the city. One who heard the message was Major Oliver Williams of the U.S. Army, who led a subsequent packhorse and river expedition out of Detroit to the northwest in 1818. When his group returned, they spoke of the potential for a frontier village at the point where the old Saginaw Trail met the Clinton River—known today as Pontiac.

At the same time, the government opened a land office in Detroit to sell unsurveyed land: the minimum sections available were 320 acres. While this size of land parcel was beyond the budget of many a would-be pioneer/farmer, the mere existence of a land office set development in motion.

Lewis Cass, the territory's new governor, advanced the momentum. The ambitious Jeffersonian wanted to attract new settlers to the area to meet statehood population requirements and he argued that settlement of Michigan's frontier would divide the British and their erstwhile supporters, the Indians. Cass also had a problem with the Tiffin Report; he could not believe it. "The quality of the land in this territory has been grossly misrepresented," Cass complained to Congress. In the face of resistance Cass resolved to build up the territory "one person at a time, if necessary." He never let up on federal authorities in his quest to bring people to the territory. And when it came to disproving the Tiffin Report, Cass took on the load personally.

In 1818—the same year the Williams party ventured north—Cass and a small group set out from Detroit on the old Indian trail to Saginaw to see the land in question for themselves. They followed the trail north to where Cass and his group encountered "heavy marshland" that ended up being six miles across. With much effort, the group traversed the six-mile bog. Then, about 12 miles from the city, the marshland ended. Actual ridges in the land appeared. Cass and his party rejoiced.

Ridge Road, which ends today at the Detroit Zoological Park, received its name from its place on the ridge bordering the old swamp. The place where the Cass party discovered improving terrain was beneath a massive swamp oak tree in what would become the city of Royal Oak. The exact location is now part of the Oakview Cemetery, at Catalpa and North Main streets, where Rochester Road begins.

From there, Cass and his group journeyed northwest, toward what is now Birmingham and Pontiac. With each mile they traveled, their hopes increased. Their eyes beheld oak groves, rich soil, oak openings, plentiful stone, and a succession of sparkling bodies of water. Cass bestowed his name upon the largest lake, and named another for his wife, Elizabeth. And for good measure Cass named a lake near Birmingham after a member of the expedition, Lewis Wing.

After five days on the "road," Cass and his party made their way back to Detroit. Upon their return the *Detroit Gazette* printed Cass' report:

The flat land in the rear of our city which has been a barrier to explorers is not a swamp but rich land. It is covered with timber and though in certain seasons is wet, is now dry. A good road can be made across it. At a distance of about 12 miles from this city you come upon white oak ridges affording excellent grounds for sale. On the whole, it may be said, much of the lands travelled over were excellent. A considerable amount is good and the poorest land could be cultivated for profit.

From that point on a new attitude emerged about "the lands behind Detroit." Eastern speculators began buying up large tracts, some up to 10,000 acres. A flow of new settlers was about to be unloosed upon the county. Those with the greatest advantage were former surveyors who had seen the county's beauty firsthand.

EARLY SETTLEMENTS

The county's first settlement was established in 1817 by one of those surveyors, James Graham, who borrowed the name of his wife's hometown in New York: Rochester.

Settlements also began in Pontiac (named after the famous Indian chief, Pontiac, who visited the area) in 1818, and in Birmingham, Waterford, and Troy in the years shortly thereafter. Pontiac's prime mover was Stephen Mack, a native of

Facing page: Gravel from Oxford to build Detroit was shipped along this railroad, which was the main link from Detroit to Mackinac City via Bay City. Courtesy, Rochester Historical Commission

Below: After the Ottawa, Chippewa, and Huron tribes agreed to relinquish southeast Michigan to the U.S. government in 1807, the Indian presence in Oakland County greatly diminished. These Indians on an unidentified Michigan reservation are shown weaving baskets for their livelihood in the early 1800s. Courtesy, Grand Rapids Public Library

Vermont who was engaged in business in Detroit when the War of 1812 ended.

Mack and a company of 14 men developed a settlement on a 180-acre site located at the point where the Pontiac Trail met the Clinton River. Mack and his partners built a dam on the river and erected a sawmill, blacksmith shop, and flour mill. The last development was of such significance that the townspeople's merriment could hardly be contained. The enthusiasm was understandable. Since mills provided the power to operate machinery, they were an important asset in pioneer days. Though crude in form, often with overshot or undershot waterwheels, mills sprang up around the county wherever there was sufficient waterpower to drive their huge wooden wheels.

There were also mills in such flourishing areas as Waterford, Clarkston, Drayton, Milford, Holly, Lakeville, Rochester, Birmingham, Southfield, Franklin, and Bloomfield Hills—32 mills in all, more than in any other county in the state.

Mills of all kinds weren't the only signs of progress in the area. Doctors and other professionals began to arrive, and the variety of commerce expanded. The area was gaining identity. All this was made easier in early 1819 when Governor Cass established Oakland as a county. At the time there were 60 families residing in the area. By that same year Oakland had assumed jurisdiction over land ceded by the Indians in the Treaty of Saginaw, and county boundaries extended well into northern Michigan.

In 1820 Pontiac was selected as the county seat, and the city experienced steady growth in the years that followed, particularly as a trading center for surrounding hamlets. Land was becoming more affordable in the area—the price had dropped from two dollars per acre, with terms, to $1.25 per acre, cash.

Smaller parcels than before were offered, which meant prospective settlers could acquire an 80-acre parcel for around $100—enough land to support a family.

Settler John M. Norton arrived in Oakland in the spring of 1824 and staged an open house at his cabin, "as evidence that industry, integrity and 'pluck' are sufficient for success in this fertile and free country," wrote early Oakland County historian Thaddeus S. Seeley.

SETTLERS FLOCK TO OAKLAND

Many of Oakland County's first residents came from New York on steamships by way of Lake Erie, and the flow of new arrivals increased with the completion of the Erie Canal in 1825. The 363-mile-long waterway between Utica and Buffalo connected Michigan, by way of Lake Erie, with the Hudson River and points east. The canal provided people in congested New England with a new way to move west and opened Eastern markets for Michigan produce.

The Clinton River Navigational Company was formed in 1827 to improve and render navigable the Clinton River from Mt. Clemens to Pontiac. The project was completed only as far as Rochester. Remains of the canal project are visible today in Bloomer State Park #2, near Rochester, where a state historic marker has been erected.

The river improvement projects were stalled by the advent of another form of transportation—the rails. Railroads were cheaper to build, offered faster service, and reached more points than the rivers did.

The Pontiac & Detroit Railroad Company was chartered in 1830, then reborn four years later as the Detroit & Pontiac Railroad Company. Early track systems between the towns were built on wooden rails. Trains were pulled by horses because the swampy base of the rails offered insufficient support for the heavy locomotives.

Within a few years the iron-stripped rails would extend 16 miles from Detroit to the tavern stop at Royal Oak; by 1843 the tracks extended into Pontiac. This was a breakthrough, Seeley wrote. "Previously in Detroit's hinterland, overland travel was a test of dogged strength and plodding determination." Completion of the railroad to Pontiac replaced the 10-hour journey by horseback with a five-hour trip by horse-drawn train.

Early rail systems in the county were developed between Pontiac and Sylvan Lake, Detroit and Pontiac, and various points north and west, including Flint, Orion, and Milford. These new systems connected the rich farm lands of Oakland with Detroit and allowed city people to visit the country.

In 1837 Pontiac was incorporated as a village—and its regional notoriety increased. On the East Coast, immigrants reported, Pontiac was better known than Detroit. The boundaries of the county were finalized in 1838 when Holly became the 25th and final township to join the county.

REBOUNDING FROM DISASTER

In 1840 a fire destroyed most of Pontiac's downtown. Twenty-five buildings were lost; damages were $25,000. "The spectacle was truly awful and sublime," the *Jacksonian* of Pontiac reported in describing the scene of the fire.

Some of the city remained, including the famed Hodges Hotel and county offices. Pontiac was quickly rebuilt, enhancing its reputation as an important hub of county activity.

An unnamed man who arrived in the city in 1850 painted this picture in papers on file with the County Pioneer Society: "There were runners everywhere and every kind of conveyance . . . horse stages, two horse wagons, open busses running to hotels, ready to go to Flint, Saginaw, Lapeer, Commerce, Rochester. When we left New York we thought we were coming to the woods. It proved to be a lively woods."

Pontiac was becoming an advanced municipality. Bridges were built, a village fire department was added, a gas works was inaugurated in 1860, and, in 1861, Pontiac became a city.

As the pages of American history sadly recall, 1861 was also the year when the Civil War erupted in the land. Some 400 "Oakland boys" lost their lives during the war; more than 3,700 served, mostly in volunteer regiments. One of them was Colonel Moses Wisner, an early political leader in the county who died of typhus in 1863 in Lexington, Kentucky. He was the son of a farmer in Auburn, New York. After immigrating to Michigan, Wisner became an

Below: Downtown Pontiac, the center of commerce in the county through the 1960s, was the setting for early automobile development and manufacturing in the early nineteenth century. The emerging automobile, interurban system, and horse-drawn carriages all converged from 1915 to 1920, as shown in this view north of Saginaw Street. Cupolas of the county courthouse are visible above the roofs. Courtesy, State Archives of Michigan

attorney and served as prosecuting attorney of Oakland County, as a judge, and as governor of Michigan. The Wisner residence north of Pontiac now houses the local historical society.

Wisner wasn't the only early political leader in Oakland with New York roots; onetime judge, Pontiac mayor, and state legislator Augustus Baldwin came from Syracuse and another county leader, Alfred Hanscom, was a native of Rochester. This was typical; of Oakland's original landowners, a third hailed from western New York. Ontario County in New York supplied Oakland with 185 settlers over a 10-year period. Most of them took up land in Farmington, Novi, or Troy townships. After the New Englanders, German and Irish settlers followed.

By the late 1800s political leadership began to reflect the ranks of the locally born: Lapeer native Henry M. Look was elected prosecuting attorney in 1871, and the area's state senator at the time, Mark S. Brewer, was a native of Addison Township.

Oakland County was known throughout Michigan at the turn of the century as a leading agricultural producer. The county boasted more farm acreage than any other county in the state; in fact, farms covered 80 percent of the

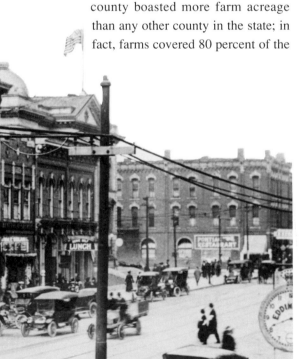

land until 1920, and as late as 1870, 35,000 of Oakland's 40,000 people were still living on farms. Oakland was a leading producer of wheat, potatoes, wool, cheese, butter, and pork, and as early as 1873, the county's orchards were also producing apples and cherries for the region. Many small farmers went on to become prosperous landowners.

Summer cottages began to attract more and more Detroiters to the county in the late 1800s—first in the summer and eventually on a more permanent basis. "The lakes are so near Detroit, and the metropolis of Michigan is so conveniently connected with the larger lakes by electric lines, that Detroit people have not been slow to see the advantages," the *Pontiac Press* reported.

From 1860 to 1870 Pontiac's population doubled from 2,575 to 4,872, and the production of flour, shoes, and woolen products kept the local economy viable. In 1870 there also were 10 small carriage-making shops in Pontiac, employing 70 craftsmen. However this early economic momentum was short-lived.

GROWING PAINS
Financial panic swept the area in 1873, reflecting the basic immaturity of the region's fragile banking structure. For the infant carriage industry and the economy in general, the result was stagnation. Many Pontiac residents either returned to the farms or fled to larger cities like Detroit and—to the consternation of Pontiac—Flint, which had become a significant outstate center while Pontiac floundered.

Even little Holly in northern Oakland County rivaled languid Pontiac for economic development during the 1870s. Citing their proximity to Flint's lumber-driven economy, investors in Holly lured railroad interests to the small village at the time when major rail routes were being established in the state. Overall, trackage in Michigan increased sevenfold from 1863 to 1883, during which time six railroads crossed Oakland County.

New hamlets arose at isolated stations along the routes. By 1883 two lines entered Holly, Oxford, Rochester, South Lyon, and Wixom; three went into Pontiac, making Pontiac more attractive to industry. New materials flowed in; locally manufactured goods flowed out.

THE CARRIAGE INDUSTRY
The first factory to build carriages for wholesale distribution came to Pontiac in 1886. The local citizenry helped pool funds to erect a facility large enough to house the new factory, and the investment paid off as other large carriage-makers located in the city. With the demand for carriages great, Pontiac led the way in developing mass-production techniques to keep up with the public's desire for the vehicles.

Large factories sprang up, their craftsmen specializing in axle-making, body-building, cushioning, painting, and other specific functions. By 1900 Michigan had become the fourth-largest carriage-making state, and Pontiac and Flint had become the two most productive towns in the state. Buggy-makers from Ontario, Ohio, and other surrounding areas began moving their operations to Pontiac, and specialty manufacturing related to the industry took a strong foothold in the city.

By 1900 carriage-making dominated the local economy, employing more than 1,000 men in the area, or 75 percent of the city's male work force. Ten years later, however, the industry would be virtually dead . . . replaced in toto by the new automobile industry. Pontiac, in any event, had become an established "vehicle center."

OAKLAND'S ECONOMIC BASE SOLIDIFIES
Another area of Oakland County enjoying economic development at the turn of the century was Rochester, home of the state's third-leading producer of woolen goods, Western Knitting Mill. The D.M. Ferry Seed Company and the Parke-Davis pharmaceuticals company also opened sizable operations in the Rochester area.

The first year of the twentieth century was a milestone in Oakland County for one other important reason: by this time Pontiac had two new connecting streetcar links with Detroit. Faster and more in tune with the times than the horse-drawn railcars of the previous era, the electrically operated trolleys began to link Oakland County's outlying towns with the metropolitan area to the south. The names of the railways described their routes: the Pontiac and Sylvan Lake Railway, the Oakland Railway (linking Pontiac and Royal Oak), the Grand River Electric Railway. A line was built connecting Rochester to points east, and when that line was later extend-

Well into the twentieth century many a Detroiter's idea of a good time was taking a trolley ride, either on the Grand River line to a connecting line into the lake country of northwestern Oakland County, or out through Rochester to Lake Orion. Getting out of the city was a high priority because it was getting crowded. Industrialization had packed Detroit to the bursting point with factories and people. There were businesses and laborers' homes everywhere. Detroit manufacturers began spreading their

ed to Lake Orion, the northern Oakland County resort fell into the expanding sphere of the Detroit metropolitan area.

Above: Owned by the Detroit United Railway, the Pontiac Division operated the Royal Oak to Pontiac line on which this electric trolley ran. Additional routes from north Pontiac to Orchard Lake and back to south Pontiac operated along the route through Sylvan Lake and Keego Harbor. As the combustion engine grew in popularity, the Pontiac Division became the Eastern Michigan Railway which eventually became the Eastern Michigan Bus Company, later purchased by Greyhound. Courtesy, State Archives of Michigan

Left: The Barkum Mill was built around 1870 and produced flour. It was driven by waterpower from the Clinton Kalamazoo Canal. The Western Knitting Mills purchased this facility in 1914 for a warehouse, which eventually burned down in the 1930s. Courtesy, Rochester Historical Commission

bases of operations into the northern village of Highland Park and beyond as space became harder to find.

Royal Oak had attained electric rail service in 1896, a development which helped to stretch the definition of the expanding business and residential corridor north of Detroit. Birmingham started gaining population, as did the burgeoning Bloomfield Hills, which began to rival Grosse Pointe for luxury homes by the early twentieth century.

THE GROWTH OF TRANSPORTATION

Roads were a new priority, especially in Pontiac, an area that

Above: Harness show-ponies were a passion with Matilda Dodge Wilson, who sought breeding and show animals around the world. She is shown here with her prize winning pony, "Small Wonder," on the grounds at Meadow Brook Hall. Courtesy, Meadow Brook Hall

Right: Built by Matilda Dodge Wilson in the 1920s to resemble a great English country home, Meadow Brook Hall is one of four auto baron estates in southeast Michigan. Bequeathed to the state of Michigan as the site for Oakland University, the hall and outbuildings comprise an elegant part of the entire development which includes a championship golf course, the Meadow Brook Theatre, and the campus of Oakland University. Courtesy, Meadow Brook Hall

was emerging as one of the nation's primary automobile production centers. The Rapid Motor Company became the city's first auto factory when it moved from Detroit in 1905, three years after its founding by Max Grabowski. In 1908 the company merged with the General Motors Company, later the General Motors Corporation.

A former buggy-maker, Edward J. Murphy, founded the Oakland Motor Car Company in 1907, and two years later Flint businessman William Crapo Durant bought that company, making it the fifth acquisition of his General Motors Company. Durant then bought Pontiac's three other automakers, making the city virtually a one-company town. In 1912 Seeley wrote: "The automobile industry of Pontiac is less than a decade old but it is a lusty youngster."

The city was producing 1,600 vehicles—gas and elec-

tric—per month. In all there were 40 auto-related shops in the city, employing 5,000 workers and credited with generating five-sixths of the local economy.

In 1913 Durant founded the General Motors Truck Company in Pontiac. The firm established an appreciable presence in the marketplace, a situation that improved significantly with the advent of World War I, when GM directed nearly all of its efforts toward the war.

Pontiac experienced its greatest population explosion between 1910 and 1920, when 20,000 new residents moved into the city. During the same time, the suburbs between Pontiac and Detroit were also experiencing growth—much of it spurred by Henry Ford's decision to manufacture the Model T in Highland Park, two miles south of Oakland County.

AN ATTRACTIVE ALTERNATIVE

Soon Highland Park's congestion problems rivaled those of nearby Detroit. But people had an out: the train lines that ran north from the center of the jam. Realtors platted land first in Royal Oak Township, then in Ferndale, and both communities were certified by the state by 1920. During the 1920s, 40,000 acres were platted in Oakland—more than twice the amount laid out prior to 1920. By 1930 nearly 75 percent of Royal Oak's acreage had been subdivided. New municipalities were established during this period; Detroit, Royal Oak, and Pontiac were extended by annexations; and industrial facilities began springing up throughout the county, from South Lyon to Ferndale.

In 1915 there were fewer than 2.5 million cars registered in the country; by 1925 that figure reached 20 million cars, and more than 200 firms were making them. Within another 10 years, only a few dozen manufacturers remained. And General Motors had emerged as the industry's leading producer.

Adding to its headquarters in Detroit and major plants in Pontiac, in 1924 GM instituted an industry-first proving ground in Milford on a 4,000-acre site. In 1925 GMC Truck merged with Yellow Cab Company of Chicago; later, that enlarged company entered the bus-making business. The first Pontiac was built in 1926, designed to fill the price gap between Chevrolet and Oldsmobile.

"The Pontiac more than exceeded in popularity even General Motors' expectations," wrote legendary GM chairman Alfred Sloan, Jr., who took control of the automaking firm in

Typical of the fine craftwork throughout Meadow Brook Hall, the dining room is a treasure trove of antiques and exquisite plaster work. Lunch is served daily and many organizations utilize these unique facilities. Courtesy, Meadow Brook Hall

the early 1920s. "In the first year of Pontiac production, GM had to appropriate an extra $5 million so that Pontiac capacity could be met."

Population in the tri-county area (Oakland, Macomb, and Wayne counties) increased by 600,000 in the 1920s with the expansion in auto manufacturing and related industries; 100,000 of those newcomers settled in Oakland.

By the late 1920s Oakland County had begun to take on a look that has lasted through the years. In 1929, for example, the 16-story Pontiac State Bank Building was built. Consid-

ered a remarkable accomplishment in its time, the building remains the tallest structure in Pontiac. The Cranbrook Foundation in Bloomfield Hills was established in 1927 by philanthropist George Gough Booth. The foundation's 135 beautifully landscaped acres featured schools, an Episcopal church, an institute for botanical and zoological science, and an academy of art. The White Chapel Memorial Park cemetery in Troy was begun in 1925. In 1928 the Detroit Zoological Society (later Detroit Zoological Park) began on a 125-acre site in Royal Oak.

DEPRESSION HITS HARD

The Depression years had a severe impact on Oakland County because the auto industry suffered more than other industries during that period. But even in 1933—the worst year of the Depression—General Motors still managed to net $165,000 after taxes. GM's Oakland line of cars disappeared during this time, along with other cars like the Kissel, Peerless, Du pont, Marmon, and Stutz. This weeding out of nameplates helped concentrate the automobile business into the control of the Big Three; of every 10 cars manufactured in 1935, GM, Ford, and Chrysler made nine.

"The Depression ruthlessly extirpated whatever was weak, inefficient, surplus or declining," Arthur Hagman wrote. "One of its victims was the Detroit United Railroad. No other major city's interurban network was swept away so early, so completely." But even as the electric railroad faded into history, the automobile held on with steely resistance. The country and Oakland County may have been in a slump . . . but people were still driving automobiles.

Between 1935 and 1940 Detroit experienced an out-migration of 90,000—with most of those people moving to other parts of the tri-county area. Pontiac's relationship to the rest of the county began declining in terms of population and economic influence. The 1930s were also a period of labor union growth and a time when GM began its decentralization of assembly facilities.

THE WAR YEARS

The coming of World War II led to the construction of giant new factories in the area, like the Chrysler Tank Arsenal in nearby Warren, and the location of many small tool and die shops in Ferndale and Hazel Park. War conversion left 200,000 industrial workers unemployed. But Michigan became "The Arsenal of Democracy," and war production kept the plants relatively busy. Between 1940 and 1945 as many factories were established in Ferndale as in the 20 years before the war. In total some 350 light industries sprang up in Bloomfield Township, Troy, Royal Oak, and Southfield—all war-related. Already equipped to mass-produce steel-fabricated parts, the auto industry played a large role in the war, con-

By 1925 there were 20 million cars registered in the United States, and Americans hit the road in droves. The flourishing automobile industry attracted scores of new residents to Oakland County. Courtesy, Underwood Photo Archives

tributing more wartime materiel (from bombs to helmets to aircraft engines) than any other industry, according to the Automobile Manufacturers Association.

The post-World War II period brought a large demand for housing in Oakland. In the process of meeting that demand, some of the best farmland in the county began to feel what one historian called "the bite of bulldozer blades." In spite of the growth, more than 100,000 acres of fertile farmland remain in the county today, making it one of the best farming areas in southeast Michigan.

Most of the growth took place in unincorporated township areas. Nearly twice as many acres were subdivided during the 1940s as had been in the previous decade; much of this activity took place in Southfield and Troy.

A BOOMING POPULATION

During the 1950s Oakland County experienced the greatest rate of population growth of any county in the state—an increase of 300,000. The suburban movement spread into the far corners of the county. By 1967 about one-quarter of the county's land area had become homesites; 15 new municipalities were established between 1953 and 1967. County government also expanded, increasing the number of its employees from 373 in 1950 to 1,558 by 1965.

Many wartime plants closed in Pontiac, but General Motors' Truck and Coach Division continued to build nearly 10 percent of the nation's trucks and buses, and its Pontiac Division remained the nation's third-largest producer of automobiles. By 1958 more production workers were employed in suburban Oakland than in Pontiac, including thousands with jobs at the Ford Tractor Division in Birmingham and Ford's Lincoln-Thunderbird plant in Wixom.

Between 1954 and 1967 at least 21 new shopping centers opened from Southfield to Bloomfield. The largest was the 162-acre Northland Shopping Center in Southfield, called a milestone in shopping center history, with nearly 1.5 million square feet of floor space. In 1961 the city of Pontiac erected its fifth and current courthouse complex on Telegraph Road and annexed part of Waterford Township.

In the 1960s only 12 other counties in America grew at a faster rate. By 1970 Oakland's population was just 100,000 shy of one million, and by 1976 Oakland was the eighth-wealthiest county in the country, with a median family income of $20,000.

Somerset Park in Troy opened in the early 1960s. The 300-acre development was conceived by the Biltmore Development Company and became the largest complex of its kind between New York and Chicago. Somerset today includes a 6.5-acre shopping mall, parks, golf courses, pools, and 2,226 multiple-dwelling units. Biltmore also acquired 600 acres on the north side of Big Beaver Road—where work was begun in

Facing page: Wholesale baker Sophie Gauss, a Pontiac resident, turned out 15,000 loaves of bread daily, as well as cakes, pies, cookies, and other pastries, at her Pontiac and Ann Arbor plants. During the 1920s she employed more than 100 people in her baking operations. Courtesy, Underwood Photo Archives

the 1960s on the 500,000-square-foot headquarters building of the K mart Corporation, which has become the second-largest retailer in the country.

BUSINESS HITS HIGH GEAR

Detroit ad agency MacManus, John and Adams moved its headquarters to Bloomfield Hills in the late 1960s. Major developments followed, and soon southern Oakland County was peppered with new office buildings. Companies such as Reynolds Metals, IBM, Michigan Bell, Eaton Yale & Towne, and Federal Mogul placed major offices in the area. Southfield reaped major benefits from this expansion. In the late 1980s significant new clusters of high-rise buildings were still appearing in Southfield—giving the suburban hub more office space than downtown Detroit.

Troy and Farmington Hills also began to take on new looks of their own in the 1980s, with substantial office growth in each area. From 1983 through 1987 Farmington Hills issued 122 office building permits, Troy issued 102, and Southfield, 97.

Completion in 1975 of the Pontiac Silverdome on Opdyke Road lured two Detroit-based sports franchises and brought new attention to the county. By the mid-1980s the area surrounding the Silverdome in what had become Auburn Hills and Rochester Hills was in a state of profound transformation; Opdyke Road was becoming a high-growth corridor, with new offices and businesses springing up along its path. M-59, extending through the area in an east-west direction, also began to emerge as a major corridor of Detroit-area business growth. The Palace of Auburn Hills, a major sports and entertainment facility, opened its doors three miles north of the Silverdome in 1988.

From 1983 to 1988 Michigan gained 538,000 new jobs—the fourth-largest net job increase of any state in the nation. Most of those jobs came to the tri-county area, with Oakland County the very strong leader, said Doug Ross, director of Michigan's Department of Commerce. "Pontiac is situated in the middle of one of the biggest boom areas in America," he added.

Ross said Oakland County is adding "world-class" industry—industry that operates in an international marketplace. These firms create a demand for skilled local people and at the same time serve as "a magnet" for skilled people from around the world. The result, Ross said, is and will continue to be "a more prosperous and competitive Oakland County."

firms," said University of Michigan business professor Daniel Denison. In many cases small companies expand by using the expertise and experience of people who grew up in the auto industry.

HIGH TECH TAKES THE LEAD

Oakland County currently is home to 40 percent of the nation's robotics industry and to 40 percent of Michigan's top 50 high-tech companies.

Joseph D. Joachim, director of the Oakland County Department of Community and Economic Development, expects economic growth in the county to accelerate in the early 1990s as new activities begin generating in and around the 1,800-acre Oakland Technology Park in Auburn Hills. The park is expected to add 52,000 new jobs and $2 billion to $3 billion in new business development before the turn of the century. It will operate in conjunction with nearby Oakland University; the two will exchange educational programs, research, and technology.

Chrysler Technology Center will be an anchor tenant in the technology park when Chrysler moves its research operations from Highland Park to Auburn Hills in the early 1990s; others already in place include Comerica, Electronic Data Systems (EDS), and GMF Robotics. The automotive headquarters and technical centers of General Motors, Ford, Chrysler, Saturn and Volkswagen of America are also located in proximity to the area.

Oakland County in 1980 had a population of more than one million, and its income level and manufacturing base each ranked sixth nationally. The end of the 1980s found Oakland County on the verge of becoming "the new center of gravity" for the auto industry—particularly in the areas of research, distribution, product development, advertising, and marketing. Add the fact that one-half of the dollar volume of U.S. auto production is located within a 70-mile radius of Oakland, and the gravity reference rings true.

While approximately half of Oakland County remains undeveloped, growth will surely continue—for the same reasons it has since James Graham and his family set up shop on the shores of Paint Creek, kicking off one of the major county success stories in America today.

In all, Oakland County added 160,000 new jobs in the years following the early 1980s recession—a 48-percent increase. Building permits for office construction also steadily increased during the late 1980s.

Oakland's economy was also spurred by the entrance of research and development facilities in the area. In the late 1980s a number of new hotels appeared in the center of the county, enhancing Oakland's tourism industry. The medical industry and retail business also were on the upsurge countywide, and there was major economic growth in southern Oakland County with the completion of a 7.9-mile stretch of Interstate 696 (I-696) from Interstate 75 (I-75) to Lahser Road—the final link in the metro area's east-west freeway system.

Surveys reveal a fertile atmosphere in Oakland for entrepreneurs. Today most jobs are being created in companies engaged in business services, including accounting, law, and engineering. "Oakland's economy is still dominated by the auto industry, but most jobs are created by small, growing

Skyscrapers in the Cornfields

There is no geographic ambiguity: the center of Oakland County lies in Waterford Township. Yet when it comes to defining the county's "working center," agreement on an actual economic midpoint doesn't come as quickly . . . or with as little margin for error.

Some say the city of Southfield forms the "essential core." Their perspective is based on the fact that 300,000 people come to the city every day to do business, rendering Southfield one of the busiest hubs in the state and certainly in Oakland. Whether calculated on a three-county or seven-county basis, Southfield—that is, southeast Oakland County—is at the population center of the Greater Detroit region, said Jack Driker, special projects coordinator for the Oakland County Department of Community and Economic Development.

From a strictly Oakland County perspective, though, Southfield forms more of a southern anchor than a central focus point.

Northeast of Southfield there is Troy, home to 80,000 residents and 100,000-plus daytime workers . . . home to more than one dozen industrial parks and the "Golden Corridor"—1,500 acres of office and commercial land located on Big Beaver Road. No less a source than the *Wall Street Journal* called Troy "one of the hottest corporate boomtowns in America." Like Southfield, Troy has become a major retail center, with the Somerset and Oakland malls. It is also home to K mart's world headquarters and is the operations base for dozens of other major corporations.

Then there is Auburn Hills—formerly Pontiac Township—where the emergence of dozens of new research facilities reflects the increasingly global nature of the county's economy. This up-and-coming city is home to the Oakland Technol-

ogy Park—established in the 1980s and already one of the nation's most important research and technology centers. The "Oak-Tech Park" has among its tenants Chrysler Motors Inc., EDS, and ITT. Support industries lured by the park continue to spring up around this primary research center, furthering the startling transformation of the area from sparsely settled woodland into one of the nation's new high-tech citadels.

Astounding accolades accompany the name Auburn Hills—a name that didn't even exist until the mid-1980s. Auburn Hills is a high-tech boomtown. At its western border it· abuts the 80,000-seat, larger-than-life Pontiac Silverdome. It is also, as America's basketball fans have come to know, home of the Palace of Auburn Hills—hence, home-court for a local upstart bunch, the 1989 and 1990 National Basketball Association champion Detroit Pistons.

Big-league and big-time, Auburn Hills is but one of several new "exurban job centers" that has surfaced on the new Oakland County economic map during the final third of the twentieth century. So are Southfield and Troy, for that matter. The same applies on a smaller scale to Farmington Hills, Novi, and Rochester Hills—areas in which new office and retail developments form small centers unto themselves.

There is no exact logic to such a situation. And the result may be, as in Oakland's case, "skyscrapers in the cornfields." Exact or not, the forces that created Oakland County's high-growth economic centers have been certain . . . and certainly well documented.

FREEWAYS INCREASE ACCESS TO SUBURBS

The list of forces begins with the growth of Detroit—from a community of farmers and traders into a city known throughout the world for its manufacturing might. That growth

This view from above the Prudential Town Center reveals the lush green residential countryside of one of Oakland County's busiest hubs—Southfield. The contrast between peaceful, semirural residential areas and bustling economic pockets of activity, which permeate Oakland County, is truly amazing. Photo by Beth Singer

pushed people and places out in a northwesterly direction, from the shores of the Detroit River to the woods and fields of Oakland—and points beyond. The suburbs grew, first in the southeast along the Detroit border, and eventually into the central reaches of the rolling hills and lake country.

After the people and their passion for Oakland County arrived, the need for freeways to connect them with Detroit and its mid-century job base was clear . . . and soon accommodated. By the late 1950s superhighways began providing fast, direct access between Detroit and its northerly suburbs. Within the next decade a slew of additional futuristic roads—freeways that most people's grandparents could never have imagined—were either in place or on the engineer's desk.

The region's first "freeway"—the Davison Expressway in Wayne County—was built during World War II to facilitate the movement of materials between the city's war production plants. The Lodge Freeway (U.S. 10) followed in the late 1950s, providing an important new link between Detroit, Southfield, and outstate Michigan. The Chrysler Freeway (I-75) followed, opening up Troy and eventually Auburn Hills and Rochester Hills. Southfield, however, was the jumping-off point for development in the county.

SOUTHFIELD: WHERE FREEWAYS MEET

During the Civil War there were 1,500 residents in the Southfield area—including farmers, mill operators, cheese factory workers, tavern owners, and storekeepers. Southfield retained its rural character well into the twentieth century; until the post-WWII development of the Northland Shopping Center, the city's east-west roads remained in primitive condition.

"There wasn't much going on here," said Tod Kilroy, Deputy Director of Southfield's Planning Department. "Telegraph Road and Northwestern Highway were paved but the mile roads were still dirt." However, in the eyes of the region's leading retailer, J.L. Hudson, the future of Southfield seemed surely paved in gold.

In 1950 Hudson informed a startled Detroit area of plans for a $20-million development—Northland Center. For the average citizen of Oakland County, Hudson's vision of an enormous department store as the core of a vast shopping center at the virtual edge of suburbia was nearly incomprehensible. It was one thing for Hudson's downtown store to prosper. But a Hudson's in the northern suburbs during the Eisenhower years was a unique and novel concept.

Nevertheless Northland opened in the early 1950s, and its

*The sun sets on the Spec Office Building, a glass high rise located in Troy along Big Beaver—the road known as "the Golden Corridor."
Photo by Balthazar Korab*

very existence changed the way people thought about Oakland County. For one thing they began to realize they could shop there. Soon they would realize they could work there as well.

The emergence of new land uses and new suburban lifestyles took root initially in Southfield, in the area surrounding Northland. The vicinity enlarged in scope and importance with the construction of Northland Towers in the mid-1960s. The dual buildings offered amenities unheard of in the area, including underground parking and 90 executive commercial offices. Subsequently Stouffer's Northland Inn opened for business in the Northland complex, adding luxurious hotel accommodations and dining facilities to the area.

Voters approved a plan in 1958 to make Southfield a charter city. By then areas once a part of Southfield Township, like Lathrup Village, Franklin, and Beverly Hills, had incorporated, becoming independent entities. Political boundaries around Southfield have remained intact since then. And Southfield itself has blossomed into rich maturity.

The arrival of Northland Center in Southfield did not happen by accident, Kilroy said. Rather the major development occurred as a result of the existence of basic utilities in the area. "If sewer and water systems hadn't been provided, then obviously things would have been a lot different than they are now," he said. "Development would have been more scattered."

The decision to route essential services to the north was made in the late 1940s by the Detroit Water Board, giving great impetus to suburban growth. In the next decade sewer capacities were extended to Southfield and adjoining suburban areas. "Those are the kinds of things people just take for granted today," Kilroy said. "But they set the whole thing in motion."

In Southfield that motion took the form of a master plan, developed in 1967. In the plan various land uses were determined for the area bordered by Eight Mile Road to the south, Thirteen Mile Road to the north, Inkster Road to the west, and Greenfield Road to the east. "Twenty years ago the city had a vision," Kilroy said. "Now it's been implemented. Southfield's about 90 percent developed. The decisions they made in the late sixties have come true."

Southfield today consists of six major pockets of economic activity, including Northland, Prudential Town Center, City Center, First Center Complex, American Center, and the area adjacent to Galleria Silver Triangle. Altogether there are more than 6,000 businesses in the 27-square-mile city, including the offices of 86 of America's *Fortune* 500 companies.

BASF Corporation, Inmont Division; Nippondenso America Ltd.; and Automotive Sector World Headquarters, Allied Signal, Inc. are among the top companies with offices in Southfield. High-profile firms such as Standard Oil, Reynolds Aluminum, IBM Corporation, Boron Oil, and Federal Mogul Corporation also have general, regional, or research offices in the city. And their number is growing. In 1988 alone 1.8 million square feet of new office space came to Southfield, which reported an occupancy rate of 87 percent for that year. "There is more office space here than anywhere else in Michigan," Kilroy said.

Already Southfield has surpassed Detroit for having the largest concentration of office buildings in the region, said Douglas Winkworth, vice president of project development with Kirco Realty & Development, Ltd., which has constructed and now manages nearly 10 million square feet of executive office space in southeast Michigan. In the next 20 years another 9.2 million square feet of office space is slated to be added to the existing 22 million.

Paradoxically Southfield is highly residential in character. "Fly over the city and all you see is a sea of greenery," Kilroy remarked. "When you drive through, you tend to see the high-rise buildings and retail complexes. But what we really have here are hundreds of fine neighborhoods." Further into the fabric of the community, Kilroy said, parts of Southfield "look like someplace up north." A few sections west of Telegraph Road remain semirural in character. "You still have small, five-acre farms out there and people with horses. It's hard to believe." Within sight of Southfield's lingering farm anomalies are new office complexes, magnificent shopping centers, busy freeways, and countless subdivisions.

Kilroy said Southfield's mix of office buildings, retail centers, and residential areas emerged as a result of the city's proximity to Detroit's northern freeways. "It's like they say, 'location, location, location,'" he said. "This is where the expressways meet. If Interstate 275 had been continued up to Flint, it would have been different."

Instead environmental concern in the 1960s forced highway planners to stop construction of I-275 immediately below western Oakland County's wetlands—in the southwest corner of Farmington Hills.

While Southfield is located on the lower rim of the county, Oakland's southern border is now more closely associated with the I-696 link between I-75—at Oakland's eastern extreme—and I-275, at the western end of the county. The final 7.9-mile stretch of freeway was completed in 1989. It extended the freeway from Lahser Road across Farmington, Southfield, Lathrup Village, Royal Oak, Oak Park, and Pleasant Ridge to where it now intersects I-75—near Ten Mile and John R roads.

In its entirety I-696—which carries some 130,000 cars each day—runs from I-275 in Farmington Hills to Interstate 94 (I-94) in St. Clair Shores and forms a "circumferential beltway" that connects all of the Detroit area's major freeways. As a result, Driker

Pages 32-33: The Excello Building on Big Beaver in Troy, taken at night when the city is quiet, is part of "The Golden Corridor"—a stretch of commercial development that's proven to be gold in the hands of the businesses that touch it. Photo by Balthazar Korab

Below: Just a few minutes from the whirlwind of corporate activity, and the geographic junction that unites three major expressways, business continues as usual on small farms. Photo by Ulrich Tutsch

Facing page: The interior of the First Center Building in Southfield provides the building's occupants with lunchtime art exhibits and concerts by local musicians. First Center houses offices, restaurants, shops, and service-oriented businesses. Photo by Balthazar Korab

said, intercity through traffic "is offered more alternatives" than were available before the completion of the final freeway link. Those alternatives are expected to stimulate significant economic growth in the Southfield and south Oakland County area. "The marketplace will be more competitive, fluid, and dynamic," the respected county planner said.

I-696 east of I-75 was constructed in the mid-1970s, without meaningful delays; the westerly section, on the other hand, was held up in communities along its proposed course by prolonged debate and arbitration related to its development. The delays were confounding to some, but by-products included a number of unique enhancements along the I-696 route across southern Oakland County.

These "mitigating elements" include the heavy application of screen and sound walls, greenbelts, and extensive landscaping. The Michigan Department of Transportation also built three plazas along the final link of the new freeway, as well as a state-of-the-art, three-level interchange at Woodward Avenue that provides for a smooth flow of traffic.

The real story behind the completion of the final link of I-696 has a purely Southfield theme: If not the actual center of Oakland County, Southfield emerged stronger than ever as a result of its prime access to this enormously important new freeway extension.

Though the community is 90 percent developed, the City of Southfield registered twice as many new building projects in 1988 as in the previous year. "It was the busiest year in 20 years," Kilroy said. Single-family homes continued to give way to condominium projects. And the growth of small new office developments and shopping centers kept pace.

Winkworth said Southfield's explo-

Facing page: Condominiums in Oakland County can be just as ele-gant and spacious as any traditional home, as is apparent by this beautiful Bloomfield Hills condominium, located in a neighborhood called Hickory Grove Hills. Photo by Beth Singer

Right: Companies and businesses locate in Oakland County to be near their markets and to be a part of the technological brainpower that drives the automotive industry. Photo by Balthazar Korab

Below: The gleaming Liberty Center, located in Troy, is one of Oakland County's many striking examples of corporate architecture. Photo by Balthazar Korab

sive growth as a new urban center was fueled originally by the availability of land, access to transportation, and proximi-ty of good housing for the work force. The same favorable forces, he said, applied equally to the city of Troy.

TROY: THE GOLDEN CORRIDOR

The development of Troy as a world-class office and retail center is closely associated with four events: the opening in 1964 of I-75; the 1968 opening of the Oakland Mall, one of the first enclosed malls in the county; the development of the upscale Somerset Mall in 1969; and the establishment of sev-eral enormous corporate headquarters, with the K mart inter-national headquarters being most prominent.

Located on 45 acres of land on Big Beaver Road, the 910,000-square-foot K mart building—which has nearly dou-bled in size since it was first built in the late 1960s—features 22 modules of office space, plus 30 towers that serve as core units. In 1972, six years after its sales topped the one-billion-dollar mark for the first time, K mart—known then as the S.S. Kresge Company—moved into the new building. K mart is now the nation's second-largest general merchandise retailer; in 1987 its 2,200 stores had sales of $25.6 billion.

Troy's office growth has climbed steadily upward since K mart arrived, and the city has ranked a consistent second to

Southfield in new construction starts. In 1988 Troy boasted 11 million square feet of office space, with more than one million additional square feet in construction.

Columbia Center, located near the I-75/Big Beaver Road interchange, is among Troy's newest high-profile business centers. Since the first of two proposed towers was built in the late 1980s, the facility has been recognized as one of the state's definitive business environments. High-profile companies with headquarters or major facilities in Troy include Standard Federal Savings, Uniroyal-Goodrich Tire, Ford New Holland, Sears Roebuck & Co., Kelly Services, and Ameritech Publishing Inc., which moved to the city in 1984.

General Motors' Saturn Corporation headquarters is also located in Troy, and Saturn's Engineering Center is in nearby Madison Heights. The primary Saturn facility is situated on Stephenson Highway, near the operations of such well-known firms as General Dynamics and the highly advanced Du pont Tech Center. According to the Michigan Department of Commerce, there are 47 foreign firms doing business in Troy, including automotive enamel manufacturer BASF-Inmont.

Jack P. McAndrews, head of Du pont Company's automotive operations, told the *Wall Street Journal* that companies related to the auto industry are drawn to Troy by the presence of similar businesses, not to mention the access to a large number of customers. "This is the nerve center of the

Facing page: This dramatic sculpture graces the K mart corporate headquarters located in Troy on Big Beaver Road. K mart is the nation's second-largest general merchandise retailer. Photo by Balthazar Korab

Below: Here robotics are assembling an automobile body at the General Motors Lake Orion Assembly Plant. With 3.3 million square feet, the plant is one of the world's largest factories under one roof. Photo by Beth Singer

automotive industry, worldwide," McAndrews said.

Troy planning director Laurence Kiesling said the 34-square-mile city was 70 percent developed by the late 1980s. As is the case in Southfield, Troy is also intensely residential; in fact, only 1,500 of Troy's 21,000 acres are zoned office or commercial. Conversely more than 80 percent of the city is zoned residential and there were more than 25,000 dwellings in the city by the mid-1980s. About 1,800 of the city's 2,000 acres of industrial-zoned land were developed at the time.

INFRASTRUCTURE AND CONSOLIDATIONS FOSTER BOOMTOWNS

As was the case in Southfield, the presence of sewer interceptors and water systems played a pivotal role in the development of Oakland County's other boomtowns, including Troy and Auburn Hills, said Roger Marz, professor of public administration at Oakland University and a former county planning commissioner. "That's what's really astonishing," Marz said. "That's why you can put a skyscraper in a cornfield. Don't forget: They use a lot of water in a skyscaper. That's why you can't put one in Almont . . . or just anywhere like that."

The decisions of many corporations to select Southfield and Troy as sites for their national or regional headquarters also drove the development of the two cities as major Oakland County centers. "Prospective tenants look at the profile of who's here, see these high-caliber corporate tenants and the commitment they've made to the area, and decide on that basis," said Winkworth.

Another important factor, he added, has been a high level of managerial competence in the respective cities. "Both Southfield and Troy have demonstrated an interest in attracting good quality corporate neighbors. They've had sophisticated, knowledgeable staffs . . . individuals who clearly recognize the importance of attracting

development. They worked responsibly to foster that. They've been forward-looking communities that have given us good, professional, fair treatment."

In addition a substantial amount of the new business activity in Southfield and Troy has come in nonautomotive areas such as insurance, high tech, and computer service. Another factor is an improved understanding among corporate decision makers of what Michigan has to offer in terms of quality of life—or what Winkworth called "a breaking down of boardroom mentality."

When all is said and done, perhaps the greatest catalyst to the growth of Oakland County's new boomtowns has been the large number of corporate consolidations in the county. In the years immediately following the early 1980s recession, major companies servicing the Big Three automakers elevated their commitment to service this market and to conduct research and development work here . . . as well as to maintain their sales operations in the suburbs north of Detroit.

In any discussion of the amazing growth of Southfield, Troy, and Auburn Hills, the "new identity of auto suppliers" topic surfaces quickly. "We came out of the early 1980s recession and General Motors, Ford, and Chrysler began telling

Facing page: This newly constructed building is the first of two towers in Troy known as the Columbia Center. The bulldozer is making way for a three-level, 2,000-space parking garage for the building's occupants—including Transamerica, NEC Electronics, Great Lakes Insurance, and others. Photo by Balthazar Korab

Below: A firm believer in the integration of the university's life with the community at large, Dr. Joseph Champagne, president of Oakland University, played a critical role in the development of Oakland Technology Park. Courtesy, Oakland University

their suppliers they had to get more competitive with the imports," explained Joseph D. Joachim, director of Oakland County's Department of Community and Economic Development.

"They were getting leaner and meaner, skimming back overhead and beginning to out-source functions like research, development, and engineering to this new structure of supplier industries they'd created, where suppliers are chosen in terms of their cost-effectiveness and quality," Joachim said. "It all sprouted up from what were before just sales offices for these suppliers. Now they're offering engineering and research as well.

"The Big Three said, 'Do it close to home.' So the companies grew, right here in Oakland County. Companies like ITT, Du pont, General Electric . . . doubled in size and increased their research activities. When it came to out-sourcing, the Big Three found a highly qualified technical labor pool in their own backyard. This is where all the technical knowledge is . . . the talent to help these companies become more competitive. It's been a big eye-opener for everyone."

AUBURN HILLS: ON THE HIGH-TECH EDGE

One whose eyes were already focused on the future was Dr. Joseph Champagne, president of Oakland University. Champagne's role in the conception, birth, and development of the Oakland Technology Park in Auburn Hills was critical. Champagne came to Oakland County from Texas, where he had begun to ponder the idea of establishing a linkage between

Saturn Corporation has located its headquarters in Troy. Called
"the new brain center of the automotive industry" by Roger Smith,
chairman of General Motors, Oakland County provides a wealth of
talented people for projects such as the new Saturn car, which made
its debut in September 1990. Photo by Balthazar Korab

educational communities and economic development activities in their areas.

Champagne came to Michigan in 1981, in the midst of what he called "a depression in the state." At the same time, then-governor William Milliken established a High Technology Task Force and empowered its representatives to identify possible locations for intensive development of high-technology, high-growth industries. Within a year Champagne happened to attend a function where he met a representative from Michigan's Department of Commerce. The two struck up a conversation and agreed to spend an hour together later that day touring the land west of the university.

"It all clicked at that meeting," he said. "We were talking about land use and industrial development and I thought, hey, what about putting some type of research development here near Oakland University . . . the I-75 corridor, where we already have thousands of acres of land, gas lines in, railroad tracks across M-59, a river running through, water mains in, and everything here, along with the university. I thought, My God, dummy Joe, look what you've got right here in your own backyard."

"You're right," the Commerce Department representative told Champagne after touring the tree-studded acreage west of Oakland University. "What a magnificent parcel you've got here." Soon Al Bogdan, the newly appointed chief of staff of the High Technology Task Force, learned of the situation surrounding the university and visited its campus. "We talked the same language," Champagne recalled. Within 18 months Bogdan had endorsed the site as being "truly worthy of sincere development." Events then developed at a rapid pace.

Realizing a private concern had to take a lead position in the development of the area, Comerica Bank jumped in first. Comerica bought the original 210-acre setting in the park and constructed a $40-million operations center that now employs 1,800 workers.

Enter Schostak Brothers & Company, the largest commer-

The Chrysler Technology Center, scheduled for completion in the early 1990s, occupies 3 million square feet and has a price tag of about $2 billion. The facility is expected to employ approximately 5,000 workers. Photo by Gary Quesada/ Korab, Ltd.

cial real estate firm in southeast Michigan, which teamed up with Champagne, representatives from nearby Oakland Community College, and the primary landowners in the area to think through the expansion of the park. Comerica eventually acquired another 800 acres in the park and asked Schostak to help plan its development.

Outside contractors were hired to design and market the park. A decision was made to aim marketing efforts at attracting foreign firms as well as firms already in Michigan "to help prevent them from leaving the state," Champagne said.

The ball was rolling. It picked up enormous momentum in 1984, when Chrysler Motors Corporation announced it would purchase 500 acres in the park. Today Chrysler is in the process of building its $2-billion, 3-million-square-foot Chrysler Technology Center. Due for completion in the early 1990s, it

is expected to employ 5,000 by 1993.

Following Chrysler, one of the early companies to locate in the Oakland Technology Park was EDS, which hired 8,900 new employees and put them to work in buildings that house two information processing centers described by Auburn Hills mayor Robert Grusnick as being "beyond *Star Wars*."

EDS alone has brought a tremendous amount of recognition to the new technology park. EDS vice president James P. Buchanan said his company also improved its access to automated manufacturers by locating in Auburn Hills. "When EDS first began moving here, we knew the impact would be significant but we didn't imagine just how significant," Oakland County executive Dan Murphy told *Fortune* magazine. "The impact has done more than just create jobs. It has reinforced our image as a center for automated manufacturing technology and strengthened our bid for other high-tech companies."

The list includes companies like ITT Automotive Inc., which began construction of a 270,000-square-foot research campus on a 35-acre site in the park in 1988. Other projects were more speculative. Near the Oakland Technology Park,

but west of the I-75/University Drive interchange, Schostak Brothers & Company also established 46 lots for development in the Auburn Centre Industrial Park. And other spin-off projects multiplied along the once-remote Opdyke corridor.

Overall the pace of development in this 1,500-plus-acre park has been a source of amazement for local political officials. Auburn Hills city manager Leonard Hendricks said more than 65 percent of the buildings that will ultimately comprise the Oakland Technology Park were already in place by 1989. "What was supposed to be a 20-year development scenario has become more like a 10-year scenario," he said.

"Nobody knew it would be of this magnitude and nobody knew it would happen this fast."

Development in Auburn Hills stretches from the southeast corner of the city, near the GMF Robotics facility in Rochester Hills, all the way north to the front yard of the GM Orion Plant in Orion Township. Along its route this extension of stunning new office and research buldings dots nearly every hillside and intersection. The emphasis at most of these modern facilities is on robotics, computer operations, engineering automation, and advanced manufacturing applications.

The area has also become the new address of several

With 22 million square feet of business real estate, Southfield boasts the largest concentration of office space in Michigan. The city has attracted 86 of America's Fortune 500 companies, including Nippondenso America Ltd., whose uniquely shaped building is pictured here. Photo by Balthazar Korab

hotels, office buildings, and research and engineering facilities, including the American home of GKN, a British automotive supply firm.

Nearly 100 new buildings—most of them 100,000 square feet or larger—are also nestled throughout Auburn Hills. Clusters of new offices and research facilities sit atop hills, beside flowing rivers, in groves of protected walnut trees,

and alongside obscure roads that until the late 1980s were unpaved vestiges of a time when townships were still townships and potholes reigned supreme.

Prepare to encounter EDS' computer center, or Secure Data Corporation's breathtaking headquarters, where employees on breaks can watch deer grazing along the Clinton River, or the sprawling Chrysler Technology Center.

Nearby, 80 acres of land are being developed as a supplier park, of sorts, for the Chrysler facility. "Chrysler's going to have a lot of impact here, but with I-75 going through, much of what we're getting is also related to GM, because it's easy to get from here to their tech center in Warren and their plants north of here," Hendricks said.

Grusnick, who served the area as supervisor when it was Pontiac Township, said the dramatic development of the Oakland Technology Park occurred as a result of the efforts of the coalition comprised of Champagne and representatives of Comerica, Oakland Community College, and primary landowners in the area.

Grusnick said the growth of the Oakland Technology Park also gathered momentum when the voters of then-Pontiac Township voted to adopt cityhood and change the name of the community in the early 1980s. "That had a big impact," he said. "I don't think we would have seen all this growth . . . to this extent . . . without those changes. Now we've gone from having dew in the grass to having cushioning in our beds."

The numbers support Grusnick's statement: Auburn Hills' assessed property value nearly tripled, from $131 million in 1984 to $330 million in 1989; and the number of people working in the city increased from 4,000 in 1980 to 16,000 in 1990.

The Oakland Technology Park is expected to employ between 12,000 and 15,000 people within its base area. But those numbers may only represent part of the employment picture. Studies conducted by the University of Michigan for the Southeast Michigan Council of Governments (SEMCOG) indicate that base will in turn generate as many as 52,000 additional jobs by 1995.

As of 1990 buildings under construction or completed in and around the park totaled 9.4 million square feet of floor area.

"It will be a center of technology which I don't think is going to be repeated anywhere in the Midwest," Joachim said. "It firmly establishes Oakland County as being the technology center of this region."

Southfield. Troy. Auburn Hills. The names connote astonishing development. And indeed their transformation has changed Oakland County, casting it into the future with absolute certainty. Any lingering doubts about the economic fate of the area have been put to rest with the sustained growth of Automation Alley.

Commerce and Communities

From Saskatoon to Scandinavia the game is the same: it's called economic marketing. Since participation is essential for success, most communities have at least some hand in the all-important business of "self-promotion."

Oakland County is no exception—on the surface, at least. Emissaries from Oakland travel the globe promoting the county's high-tech environment and business-friendly public infrastructure. The message is simple and universally understood: Oakland County's successful track record distinguishes its efforts from the efforts of other communities worldwide that toot their own civic horns. When it comes to attracting new businesses, corporations, facilities, or whatever is needed for economic growth, few cities, states, or communities in the late twentieth century can match the performance of Oakland County.

Credit this success to the quality of the area. Developers, adopting mercantile parlance, refer to Oakland as "an easy sell." Government officials sound a similar note. "People outside Oakland County often say, 'Gee, what kind of magic do you have?'" said Joseph Joachim, director of Oakland County's Department of Community and Economic Development. "The answer is, there is no magic . . . we just happen to have the best product around. Companies come here, first for the proximity to their markets, and second, for the next important reason—quality of life. It's something we have an abundance of."

Quality of life in Oakland County is expressed in the area's healthy employment base, strong educational institutions, outstanding housing, modern roads, and exceptional recreational opportunities. In all categories Oakland is flourishing—particularly on the job front. Unemployment in Oakland dropped to the six-percent range in 1989—three points below the state average and down from 17-percent unemployment seven years earlier.

BOUNCING BACK FROM TROUBLED TIMES

Ten years earlier, however, during the late 1970s, a profound feeling of angst had permeated the American automobile industry. Nowhere was this collective concern felt greater than in Michigan, and specifically in Oakland County, where the car business has traditionally been everyone's business, directly or otherwise. Once dominant in the international automobile marketplace, Michigan's Big Three automakers began to face a greater degree of competition from foreign automobile manufacturers in the 1970s. By the early 1980s Americans were nearly as apt to buy a car made in Sweden, Germany, or Japan as they were to "buy domestic." This change in buyer mood took its toll locally. Auto industry production dropped from a peak average of 15 million new cars per year to less than 10 million in the early 1980s.

Domestic loyalty continued to wane as overall production numbers fell off and imports captured increasingly large chunks of many buyer groups—from economy-minded consumers to performance enthusiasts to luxury car buyers. For the Big Three the choices were limited: Respond intelligently or decidedly die. Fortunately for the region, Detroit's automakers opted for the first alternative, and by the mid-1980s the leaner and presumably meaner Big Three were on the ascent.

This "smart response" did not come without pain, for blue-collar workers, white-collar managers, suppliers, and sons of suppliers alike. But come it did, and with it came a remarkable revival of the region, the industry, and Oakland County's

Oakland County has mastered the art of attracting new businesses, corporations, facilities, and housing developments. Here, workers erect the skeleton of a new home in West Bloomfield. Photo by Beth Singer

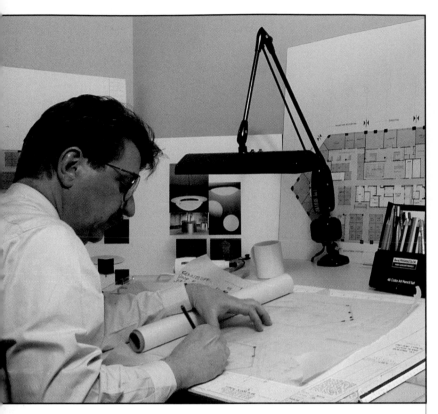

health services. Of the county's 33,000 businesses, 2,800 firms participated in manufacturing activities; Oakland County ranked 19th among U.S. counties in dollar value of manufacturing shipments.

The "new diversity" took physical root in the high-tech corridors that developed north of Detroit in Oakland County. In 1988 a University of Michigan survey of 33,000 new workers—employed by 300 companies providing automation and technical support to Michigan manufacturers—found that more than a third of those new jobs were in Oakland. Local surveys, meanwhile, indicated the number of Oakland County workers in the service sector increased from 23 percent in 1979 to 34 percent in 1990.

"That's been a huge leap," Joachim said. "It signals many things, including a greater independence here from the automobile industry. Our goal is to have 50 percent of our work force involved in nonautomotive industries. When you think it used to be 90 percent automotive, you realize what a difference that changing pattern represents."

While the nature of Oakland County's jobs has been changing, the intelligence level of those doing the work has been on the uprise. Extensive retraining programs, funded by the Governor's Office for Job Training and jointly operated by the United Auto Workers and General Motors, have targeted displaced autoworkers and have resulted in a smarter work force . . . and a new face on the area's automobile industry.

On the eve of the twenty-first century, there is also a new face on each of Oakland County's four primary geographic areas. The fresh look extends from the "circumference communities," including:

- The old-line edge of Detroit, from Royal Oak across Pleasant Ridge, Ferndale, and Hazel Park;
- West to Northville, Novi, Wixom, Farmington, and South Lyon;
- North, through Milford, Highland, and into the semirural townships of Rose, Holly, Springfield, and Groveland;
- Then, completing the county, to its northeastern reaches and the land north of Rochester, including Oxford, Orion, Addison, and Oakland townships.

Within these "circumference communities" there is also a new look to the heart of the county. Oakland's historic interior is up-to-date, rejuvenated, and thriving—from the highly populated city of Pontiac and Waterford Township to newer people-centers like Rochester Hills and Clarkston, from Birmingham and the Bloomfields to Commerce, Keego Harbor, and the lake country beyond.

From corner to corner and end to end, Oakland County is

economy. Michigan's auto industry lost 130,000 blue-collar jobs from 1978 to 1988—dropping from 935,000 durable goods manufacturing jobs to 710,000. But many former autoworkers survived, and even flourished, making the transition from the manufacturing plant to the new age.

At the same time the number of automotive supply firms in Oakland County skyrocketed, to approximately 2,000 in 1990. "As the industry changes, so do suppliers themselves," the *Oakland Press* reported. "New techniques and attitudes make it imperative large suppliers work more closely than ever before with major manufacturers." With the new suppliers came new jobs and opportunities. In spite of sizable auto manufacturing job losses, Michigan managed to add more than a half-million new jobs between 1982 and 1988.

The nature of those jobs also began to change. Between 1970 and 1980 the number of people in the state earning a living in factories dropped from 30 to 23 percent. Later reports revealed the direction taken by some of those exiting the auto industry. For example University of Michigan economist George Fulton said 2,000 new Oakland County jobs were created from 1986 to 1989 in chemicals, plastics, printing, stone, clay, and glass industries.

This new diversity also came in the service and retail sectors, as well as in engineering and applied technologies. By the late 1980s, according to county sources, about 22 percent of Oakland's residents worked in manufacturing, 33 percent in service businesses, 21 percent in retail businesses, and the rest in wholesale trades—finance, insurance, real estate, construction, transportation, utilities, government, education, and

The increased cash flow that accompanies economic upswings in Oakland County is managed by hundreds of financial advisors and stock traders like these two in Troy. Photo by Balthazar Korab

presently an exceptionally vital montage of commerce and communities, of rolling land and beautiful lakes, of forests and freeways, of fascinating people and formidable places.

SOUTHEAST OAKLAND COUNTY

Living in southeast Oakland County means easy access to the full range of metropolitan Detroit's many diverse institutions, including shopping centers, central business districts, hospitals, new and modernized offices, industrial parks, factories, colleges, schools, and churches—not to mention the fabulous Detroit Zoological Park.

Small industrial facilities line the mile roads in southeast Oakland, particularly east of Woodward Avenue, which continues to be an important commercial corridor. In fact Woodward Avenue from Ten Mile Road to Fourteen Mile Road is considered one of the busiest shopping areas in the state. The types of businesses in the area range from light manufacturing and industry to materials suppliers and distributors, from retail and service to vocational and professional schools.

With the completion of the last link of the I-696 freeway, the area is situated within a 45-minute drive of most of the jobs in metro Detroit, according to the Oakland County Economic Development Division. Royal Oak stands poised to ride the new wave of development triggered by the completion of I-696. Concept plans that call for a core area bounded by Main Street, Woodward Avenue, and I-696 offer a breathtaking view of Royal Oak's future. The plans seek to link the Detroit Zoo to Royal Oak's central business district by establishing new hotels, conference centers, and offices, with a support mix of commercial and residential facilities. As envisioned the new Royal Oak will include Habitat Village, a wildlife interpretive center, and Royal Plaza, a collection of hotels and high-rise apartment buildings.

Outdoor cafes lend to the eclectic atmosphere of downtown Royal Oak, which was transformed in the mid-1980s with the renovation of key city buildings. Prominent among these undertakings was the $6-million rebirth of the six-story Washington Square Plaza at Fourth and Washington streets. "We feel the downtown area in Royal Oak is poised for a big surge in the marketplace," plaza developer Jay Hanna told *Crain's Business Detroit*. The building is less than one mile

from I-696. Planners expect the stretch of I-696 between Lahser Road and I-75 to become the metropolitan area's virtual hub of surface transportation, which should attract considerable commercial development.

SOUTHWEST OAKLAND COUNTY

Southwest Oakland County is the airport side of town, offering the county's best access to the Detroit Metropolitan Airport. But that only begins to tell the story. Some of southeast Michigan's most exclusive residential developments are also in the Farmington area, as are dozens of high-tech industrial settings and prestigious office centers.

The growth of the southwestern corner of Oakland County was prompted initially by the development of the Ford Wixom Assembly Plant—still one of the county's largest employers, with 3,730 workers. Here the Ford Motor Company annually

builds in excess of 200,000 luxury cars, including Lincoln Town Cars, Continentals, and Mark VIIs. Growth in this region also resulted from the early 1980s development of the 1.2-million-square-foot Twelve Oaks Mall, which features 180 stores and has attracted multiple spin-off shopping plazas in the surrounding area.

New projects in this area include the Lake Pointe Office Center, the Novi Town Center, and the Novi Hilton hotel on Haggerty Road. By the mid-1990s the Haggerty corridor—from Eight Mile Road north to Pontiac Trail in West Bloomfield Township—is projected to have more than 1.5 million square feet of office space. Population in this corner of the county is expected to exceed 150,000 by the year 2005, and plans are under way to expand the road system to accommodate expected development.

As is the case with the Hazel Park-Royal Oak area in the southeast corner of the county, the southwest area is reaping significant benefits from the newly completed final link of the I-696 freeway—known as the Uptown Beltway. In all, the new superhighway provides 27 miles of freeway service through areas where potential growth has been restrained by congested mile roads and generally poor access. The area abutting the new freeway is acknowledged to be the largest corridor of commerce and industry in Macomb and Oakland counties. With the new roadway open, shipping and delivery times across southern Oakland are reduced, and employment opportunities are growing dramatically. "The I-696 Uptown Beltway offers a quantum of opportunities for businesses,

This majestic tiger basks in the snow at the Detroit Zoo, located in Oakland County just off of I-696. Pedestrians strolling the streets of nearby Huntington Woods need only to close their eyes and listen to imagine they've wandered into the wilds of Africa. Photo by Dwight Cendrowski

industries and residents of south Oakland County," the Oakland County Economic Development Division proclaimed in referring to south Oakland as "southeast Michigan's new center of gravity."

Nearly 70 percent of the county's office space is located in the area between Novi and Madison Heights—with a majority of that space in Southfield. The corridor is also home to more than half of the county's hospital and shopping center space. Retailing and service activities are expected to increase along Eight Mile Road as traffic patterns shift onto the new freeway.

Farther to the northwest, former General Motors chairman Alfred P. Sloan put Milford on the map in 1924 when he inaugurated the GM Proving Grounds on a 4,000-acre site outside the rural village. The facility encompasses six square miles and contains a road network of 128 miles, including test roads, an oval test track, circular test tracks, and extensive straightaways.

At its 60th anniversary the Proving Grounds—by that time a state-of-the-art test facility—employed more than 2,500 engineers, test drivers, scientists, mathematicians, computer technicians, and other professionals. "When requirements arise for test equipment not available from

Right, above: The Detroit Metropolitan Airport in Romulus is easily accessible via one of Oakland County's many expressways. For many travelers the airport is no more than a half hour away. Photo by Balthazar Korab

Right, below: Travelers leaving from the Detroit Metropolitan Airport have hundreds of flights to choose from, and airport-related businesses offer many overnight, long-term parking facilities, as well as hotels, restaurants, and taxi services. Photo by Dwight Cendrowski

commercial suppliers, Proving Grounds' specialists design and build it," GM proclaims.

Even with the busy test site on its periphery, a relaxed, semirural ambience still characterizes Milford, which is linked to the heart of Oakland County by M-59 and Commerce Road.

NORTHWEST OAKLAND COUNTY

Northwest Oakland County remains essentially undeveloped in 1990, from Holly to Groveland, Brandon, Rose, Springfield, Independence, Highland, and White Lake townships. Farms, in some instances, have given way to residential developments.

Highland and White Lake townships are essentially residential, with small pockets of service-related activities and a few manufacturing concerns.

Rose Township and its easterly neighbor, Springfield Township, have retained much of their rural-agricultural character throughout the late twentieth century—a trend experts predict will continue well into the future. About half of Oakland County's 900 square miles are yet undeveloped . . . and most of that natural territory is in this area. County officials say highway systems in the region are not conducive to growth, which suggests the northern reaches of Oakland County will retain their rural character for at least the next 20 years.

Former county planning commissioner Roger Marz agreed: "Only the far northwestern corner of the county will remain sacrosanct, compared to all other areas. It will be a long time before you see any dense filling of places like Rose Township. I can't see it right now. What drives development is a perception that you can make money building and selling. I don't think that perception exists out there." Many observers think the final completion of I-696 in south Oakland County will check urban sprawl in north Oakland. They theorize that I-696 will serve to focus reinvestment dollars in the established areas, where needed roads and utilities are already in place.

Holly, at the northwest corner of Oakland County, is an important regional center with a diverse retail district, city services, a healthy job base, and proximity to I-75 and major rail lines. East of Holly, in Groveland and Brandon town-

ships, agriculture dominates light industry as the prevailing business.

The tranquil nature of life across Oakland's northern tier would change to some extent with the completion of a proposed high-speed trunk line that would cross northern Oakland County, linking Genesee and Macomb counties. The future of the project—tentatively called the North Oakland County Parkway—is unclear, although reports indicate the new road,

In the early 1980s the sleepy town of Novi was transformed by the development of the 1.2-million-square-foot Twelve Oaks Mall, offering shoppers 180 stores including J.L Hudsons, Lord & Taylor, Sears, and J.C. Penney. Photo by Jim West

if approved, would be built at least 12 miles north of M-59 and 26 miles north of I-696. If this were the case, the road would pass through Addison, Oxford, Brandon, and Groveland townships.

NORTHEAST OAKLAND COUNTY

From the quiet farm country north of Oxford to the busy industrial activity of Orion Township, northeast Oakland County offers a variety of faces. For the most part this corner of the county is largely residential, with accompanying retail development located primarily along the the four-lane Michigan 24 (M-24) corridor that connects Pontiac and Lapeer.

Orion, on the northern edge of Auburn Hills and the city of Pontiac, is home to General Motors' 3.3-million-square-foot Orion Assembly Plant, one of the largest factories under one roof in the world. South of the giant auto plant are dozens of automotive supplier firms and various light industrial concerns. Orion also serves as a primary regional recreational base, with Lake Orion as the center of activity.

Oakland County's northeastern townships—Addison and Oakland—have a distinctive identity. These areas are heavily wooded and rolling; not surprisingly, the townships have retained a rural ambience, but with an upscale tone. Lavish horse farms near Leonard, for example, are the norm rather than the exception. And executive homes on large four- and five-acre parcels coexist with the area's old farms.

Oakland Township has become a rural extension of sorts to the city of Rochester, as evidenced by the preponderance of elaborate homes in the area and the working and social relationships those homeowners maintain with the metropolitan area to the south. For a city still boasting a downtown feed and grain store in 1989, Rochester has an upscale business flavor. The same applies to its neighboring community, Rochester Hills—known until the mid-1980s as Avon Township. Both Rochesters have new office centers and extensive commercial developments that complement the hundreds of upscale subdivisions nestled in what the Indians called "The Heart of the Hills."

CENTRAL OAKLAND COUNTY

As the legal and geographic center of Oakland County, Pontiac and Waterford Township play an important role in county affairs. Employment in the area exceeded 70,000 at the end of the 1980s; more than 40 percent of those jobs were in automobile manufacturing. The two centers of automotive activity are the headquarters and factory of the Pontiac Motor Division of General Motors and GM's Truck and Bus Plant, located on the north and south ends of Pontiac, respectively. Altogether GM accounts for 39 percent of Pontiac's $780 million worth of equalized property value.

Of equal importance is the effect the growth *around* Pontiac is expected to have on the city within. City officials hope that influence will lure companies into downtown and the surrounding area where more than 1,500 acres are available for development.

Below: Rochester Feed and Grain, also known as Rochester Elevator, has occupied the same downtown structure since 1872. The owners sell agricultural products, pet supplies, and salt for melting ice on the roads. Photo by Gary Quesada/Korab Ltd.

Facing page, top: In the past 15 years the Pontiac Silverdome has been the site of countless events, from Super Bowl XVI to the historic visit by Pope John Paul II. Photo by Santa Fabio

Facing page, bottom: The $56-million Pontiac Silverdome, completed in 1975, seats more than 80,000 people. Home to the Detroit Lions, the Silverdome was also at one time the place to see the Detroit Pistons weave their magic. Photo by Balthazar Korab

The key to that possibility is the existence of Wide Track Boulevard, the north-south version of Woodward Avenue that in 1961 became a beltway of sorts, surrounding downtown Pontiac. In the following years important city institutions like the police headquarters, the city library, and the Pontiac School System located along Wide Track. Private enterprise followed suit.

General Motors Truck & Bus Group Worldwide headquarters became the lead tenant in Pontiac's elaborate Phoenix Center, completed at the south end of the Wide Track Loop in 1981. Known originally as the Pontiac Plan, the development was built on a cleared, 20-acre site and today consists of more than one dozen buildings, including a senior citizens tower, parking structures, and an open-air park—atop the parking area and overlooking the city.

Pontiac received a significant boost in 1975 with the completion of the $56-million Pontiac Silverdome. The 80,000-seat facility was originally called the Pontiac Metropolitan Stadium. The Silverdome sits near the I-75/M-59 intersection, on what was once called Tomahawk Hill—a hilly playground for area motorcyclists. In its 15-year history the Silverdome has attracted everything from rodeos to political rallies to religious crusades, from professional basketball and soccer to top entertainers and religious leaders. In addition to being the home of the Detroit Lions football team, the Silverdome also hosted Super Bowl XVI in 1982. Although the game between the San Francisco 49ers and the Cincinnati Bengals only lasted a few hours, its impact was felt for years to come.

By the time the Super Bowl took place, more than 10 million fans had visited the unique stadium. And selection of the Silverdome as the site of the National Football League championship game brought wider recognition to Oakland County. The stadium had become "a beacon to the entire state that Pontiac is a leader, a community that is a place to be, an area on the grow," wrote former chamber of commerce official James Stone. "The Silverdome is the foundation upon which the 'New Pontiac' will be built," he said. Today the Silverdome remains the world's largest stadium with an air-supported dome. It is clearly visible from downtown Pontiac, two miles away—thanks largely to its 10-acre, Teflon-coated, fiberglass dome that "floats" like a cloud in the sky, more than 200 feet above the stadium's playing field.

New recognition meant new growth on the periphery of the city in the mid-1980s and within its core at the end of the decade. In total the thrust of Pontiac's renaissance has been to rejuvenate the entire core contained within the Wide Track Loop. Former GM executive Louis Wilking, who has directed Pontiac's Commercial and Industrial Development office, worked to revitalize theaters in the city's downtown area. Other organizations have followed the entertainment cue, including the Pontiac Development Foundation, a nonprofit group of business owners and officials which was formed to help the city develop. The foundation's mission has also included strengthening Saginaw Street's nucleus of night spots, restaurants, and specialty stores.

Where growth is real, yet not sought, is along Elizabeth Lake Road at the northwest edge of the city, where the Trammel Crow Company began developing the Oakland Pointe Office Park and the Oakland Pointe Shopping Center in 1986. The office buildings and the 50-store, open-air mall

brought hope to Pontiac as the projects represented what the *Oakland Press* called "the first new major commercial development in the city in many years."

Trammel Crow remains the key player in the conversion of a 400-acre site from the grounds of a state psychiatric facility to retail centers and offices for service-related businesses. Beyond that site is the massive Summit Place Mall, surrounded by many smaller commercial developments and the Oakland County government center.

The county government complex is of critical importance to the business and legal community. In addition to being the county's judicial center, "1200 North Telegraph"—as the county complex is known locally—is also home to the coun-

An older community, Bloomfield Hills was established as a city in 1932. Its winding, rolling streets, lush foliage adorning weathered trees, and beautiful homes built in a grand tradition make Bloomfield Hills a great place to call home. Photo by Balthazar Korab

ty executive's office, which oversees the department of Community and Economic Development.

The department grew out of the Oakland County Economic Development Group and has been a full-fledged division of county government since 1988. It helps companies secure public contracts, offers financing assistance and small business loans, and markets the county internationally.

While Pontiac and Waterford Township make up the governmental center of the county, Oakland's most prestigious residential area lies to its south, in Birmingham and the Bloomfields: Bloomfield Township, Bloomfield Hills, and West Bloomfield Township. Together these four communities form a notably exclusive residential core where home prices and properties are rarely less than magnificent.

Birmingham, with 24,000 residents, is the retail center of the area, although a number of successful shopping centers have also emerged in the surrounding townships. New low-density office complexes and hotels joined the mix in the 1970s and 1980s, particularly along the Woodward Avenue and Telegraph Road corridors and—more recently—along Long Lake Road, east of Woodward in Bloomfield Hills.

Birmingham, with 4.2 square miles of mostly residential area, is more diverse than the others; Bloomfield Hills, a city since 1932, has homes with an average value of more than $300,000 and was rated second nationally in 1989 in terms of annual income per person ($59,830); West Bloomfield Township has the county's greatest concentration of lakes—and the area's most expensive lakeside properties.

Oakland County's prime residential areas extend north of Birmingham and the Bloomfields, through Troy, Rochester Hills, and the City of Rochester. Upscale housing also characterizes Orion Township, Clarkston, and the lake country north and west of Waterford Township.

FROM BEDROOM COMMUNITY TO EMPLOYMENT CENTER

Joe Joachim refers to Oakland County as a work employment center—"the new American city"—with a greater day population than night population. "We've completely turned around. Now we have in-migration for employment, which is totally contrary to past patterns," he said. Southfield, Joachim said, is a good example of the new two-way pattern: The city has a daytime population of 300,000 and a nighttime population of 80,000. Similar disparities between night and day populations exist in Troy and Auburn Hills.

The character of each of Oakland County's job centers is directly related to its proximity to what some call the GM/Chrysler Corridor and others call Automation Alley. In its most literal sense this "alley" is more like "a twisting artery." However categorized, this spiraling line of high-tech businesses extends between Detroit and Ann Arbor, up and

down the I-75 Corridor, and southward across I-696 through Southfield, connecting Troy and Auburn Hills with Farmington Hills and Novi.

Within the corridor's boundaries exist 36 percent of all Michigan's automation supply companies. Over 40 percent of all robotics sales in the country are generated there, and nearly all of the 60-plus U.S. robotics companies operate plants or offices within Greater Detroit's high-tech corridor. Contrary to some reports robots mean jobs; county officials said automated manufacturing system companies generated more than 10,000 jobs in Oakland County in 1984 and 1985, and it is estimated that another 40,000 people will join those ranks by 1995.

"Oakland County has been laying claim to being the real center of Michigan's Automation Alley, with considerable support," Joachim said. "Whereas across the country everybody wanted to become big tech-centers, this place succeeded at it. We're at the center of the country's automated manufacturing industry which puts us in a prime position to attract

Above: Lakefront properties in West Bloomfield Township are among Oakland County's most desirable real estate. Photo by Balthazar Korab

Facing page: Rochester Flower Day, held in June in the heart of downtown Rochester, is an opportunity for Oakland County residents to enjoy the flowers and fresh crops from each other's backyard gardens. Photo by Gary Quesada/Korab Ltd.

support and service industries related to the existing core." Oakland County's hired hands aren't the only ones praising the area's success in matters related to national and international economic growth. The prestigious British publication, *The Economist,* referred to southeast Michigan's Automation Alley as "the fastest growing high-tech region in the U.S., if not the world."

Born of necessity in the early 1980s, when domestic automakers committed themselves to extensive automation, the robotics industry in Oakland County is implementation-oriented. The same industry in the Ann Arbor area is geared toward conceptualization. "The term 'technology-based' is different here than it is in Ann Arbor," Joachim said. "In Ann Arbor, they invent it; but it's applied here." Throughout the county technology is becoming a new fact of life. "It's foremost on most people's minds," Joachim said. "It's like what [General Motors chairman] Roger Smith said when they [GM] dedicated the new Saturn headquarters in Troy—that Oakland County is 'the new brain center of the automotive industry.' It's all happening here . . . we're at the heart of it."

Oakland County's economic future, according to Roger Marz, should eclipse anything seen so far. "The indicators are positive," Marz said. "For example, we haven't even touched the surface yet on what we'll see as a result in southeast Michigan of the trade agreement between the United States and Canada. This is, after all, one of only two places along the entire border where you have major industrial complexes on each side, with major connections and experience in dealing with each other. The new agreement should generate a tremendous amount of commercial development . . . and southeast Michigan will be a logical place for it to happen."

As the twenty-first century approaches, Oakland County's economic indicators point toward a positive future—for its people, its businesses, and the metropolitan region at large. This healthy outlook bodes well for quality of life . . . a concept that finds true definition in what continues to be Michigan's most dynamic setting—Oakland County.

Taking Care of People

Rich in history and economic vitality, Oakland County has also gained stature as an important regional hub of medical and educational activities. The development of these essential units of county life has brought balance to the area; Oakland, in effect, has become more than a suburb. Like the quintessential politician, Oakland County now manages to be all things to all people—especially the more than 1.1 million people who live here. Little wonder many of metropolitan Detroit's important institutions have set up shop in what was until the early 1900s little more than quiet lake country.

Throughout the county today more than a dozen general medical and surgical hospitals and satellite centers of large Detroit hospitals offer a full complement of health services, as do two psychiatric hospitals. In all, Oakland County hospitals have 4,227 beds.

At the same time, hundreds of excellent educational programs are available to county residents through several accredited institutions of higher learning. In addition there are 28 public school districts in the county and more than 100 private and parochial schools.

The establishment of Oakland's medical and educational centers has coincided with the county's changing population patterns. The centers were located first in Royal Oak and Pontiac; then in Troy, Rochester, and West Bloomfield Township; and, finally, in the rolling hills of Milford, Highland, and Oxford townships.

HOSPITALS

A close-up look at Oakland County's hospitals, universities, colleges, and other centers of learning reveals three common strains: a meaningful connection to the past, a solid role in the present, and a deep commitment to the future.

Providence Hospital, Southfield

A small group of nineteenth-century women known as the Daughters of Charity of St. Vincent de Paul founded what became Providence Hospital in Detroit. The hospital, which moved to Southfield in the 1950s, originally provided maternity services, and that emphasis continues today. Presently Providence Hospital offers more birthing options than any other hospital in Michigan. In 1989 the hospital recorded 4,600 births.

In addition to having noteworthy cardiology and cancer-care programs, Providence is also affiliated with the Michigan Ear Institute, an otology/neurotology facility in Farmington Hills. The hospital has also been a pioneer in outpatient ear surgery and is one of only a few hospitals in the country performing laser surgery for disease of the middle ear.

Providence Hospital has been a leader in establishing various care centers throughout Oakland County, including medical service facilities in South Lyon, Milford, and Novi. The hospital employs 3,338 people and has a medical staff of 610 physicians.

Botsford General Hospital, Farmington Hills

Botsford General Hospital serves Farmington Hills and surrounding communities. The 336-bed osteopathic health-care facility is a nationally recognized teaching facility where interns and residents train in 16 specialties and sub-specialties. The hospital was founded by Dr. Allen Zieger as Zieger Osteopathic Hospital in Detroit in 1944; in 1965 it expanded and moved to its present location on Grand River Avenue. Since then the hospital has acquired and renovated buildings

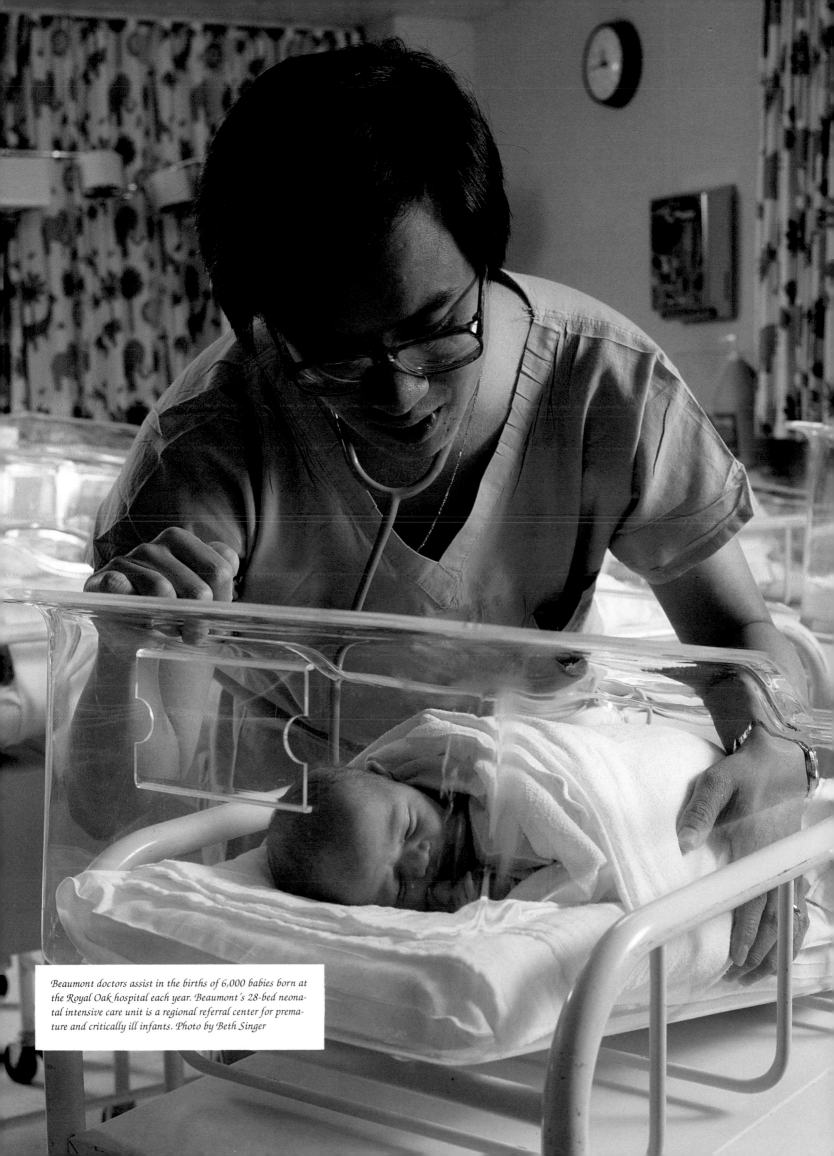

Beaumont doctors assist in the births of 6,000 babies born at the Royal Oak hospital each year. Beaumont's 28-bed neonatal intensive care unit is a regional referral center for premature and critically ill infants. Photo by Beth Singer

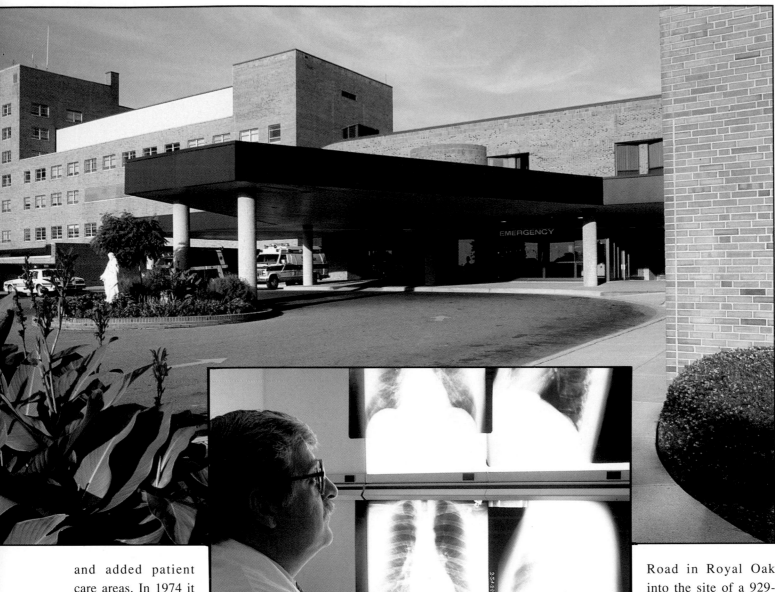

and added patient care areas. In 1974 it took its current name, Botsford General Hospital.

Among Botsford's areas of specialty is the hospital's Gero-psychiatric Services Program, which is designed to meet the psychological and medical needs of older adults. The program also provides assessment, diagnosis, and treatment of psychiatric problems affecting this age group. Botsford Family Services also provides rehabilitation programs in the area of chemical addiction. The hospital is an affiliate of the Zieger Health Care Corporation.

William Beaumont Hospital, Royal Oak

William Beaumont Hospital was named after one of America's great pioneer physicians. The hospital opened its doors in 1955, completing the transformation of what were 105 acres of farmland at Woodward Avenue and Thirteen Mile Road in Royal Oak into the site of a 929-bed hospital—one of the busiest in the country in the number of inpatient admissions. Beaumont serves as a regional referral center in emergency medicine, neonatal intensive care, kidney transplants, and cardiology. As a teaching hospital Beaumont maintains residency programs with more than 200 physicians in training. Its programs cover nearly all medical specialties, from obstetrics and gynecology to pediatrics, and from radiation and oncology to ophthalmology. Beaumont Hospital also operates a separate 189-bed hospital in Troy, a preventative health center in Birmingham, a health clinic in Ferndale, and medical buildings in Royal Oak, Troy, West Bloomfield, and Rochester Hills. In all, Beaumont has a medical staff of more than 1,000 attending physicians. With 6,000 full-time employees the hospital is the third-largest employer in Oakland County.

Pontiac General Hospital, Pontiac

Founded as the Oakland County Hospital in 1910, Pontiac General Hospital (PGH) is the regional center for neonatal intensive care and radiation therapy. The original hospital was built on three Huron Street lots that were purchased in 1906 for $500. Seed money for the hospital project was raised by a group of local women who formed the Pontiac Hospital Association and staged rummage sales, bake sales, and other events to fund what was, in effect, a grand civic venture; in 1906 Pontiac's nearest hospital was in Detroit. When the Pontiac Hospital Association bequeathed the 30-bed hospital to the city of Pontiac in 1915, it became known as Pontiac City Hospital. Since then the hospital has grown steadily. It took its current name in 1931, when an east wing was completed. By 1958 the original building had been razed and the hospital's current 389-bed structure was in place. PGH established an emergency department and a physical medicine and rehabilitation center in 1969.

Today PGH offers medical education programs and maintains an ambulatory services division, a community mental health center, and two satellite centers—the Waterford Ambulatory Care Center and the Pontiac General Health Care Center. PGH's residency programs are enriched by the hospital's membership in the Oakland Health Education Program (OHEP), a consortium of five major county hospitals. Through this arrangement member hospitals cooperate in research and educational activities, thereby reducing individual costs.

Pontiac Osteopathic Hospital, Pontiac

From the early 1950s, when the 32-bed facility was founded, to the present, Pontiac Osteopathic Hospital (POH) has provided service to residents of central Oakland County. As a primary medical care center, the hospital delivers a full range of health programs. It began in 1953 when three area osteopathic doctors converted a clinic on Auburn Avenue in Pontiac into an osteopathic hospital. Within two years POH moved into the seven-story Pontiac Hotel on North Perry Street in down-town Pontiac; in 1961 the hospital signed an option to buy the Central Methodist Church on East Huron Street. Eventually the old building was renovated, and a new three-story, 276-bed hospital was built on surrounding property. Other additions followed in the 1960s when POH established its well-known emergency trauma center.

Today the hospital is the fourth-largest osteopathic hospital in Michigan. The 308-bed facility has a staff of more than 165 doctors, 700 nursing personnel, and 1,000 employees. In addition to its main Pontiac center, POH also operates the Community Health Center in Oxford, a satellite center that provides urgent care and family practice to the citizens of northern Oakland County. POH interfaces with the community on a number of other fronts, through programs such as the Diabetic Education Series, prenatal education classes, hypertension clinics, bereavement assistance, and CPR training. Its division of occupational medicine has designed programs that creatively address the needs of area businesses. One such program, known as Workwize, offers reconditioning for injured workers.

Huron Valley Hospital, Milford

This relatively new 153-bed facility was established in 1986 to serve the needs of the people of western Oakland County, as well as Livingston County to the west. Osteopaths, dental surgeons, and more than 250 medical doctors—including specialists in areas such as cardiology, radiology, and medical imaging—staff Huron Valley Hospital (HVH). Therapists and other specialized professionals are also a part of HVH's staff. Many physicians are on the staffs of teaching and research hospitals, and HVH is linked in research, resources, and technology with the world-class Detroit Medical Center and the Academic Health Center of Wayne State University. As a community hospital HVH offers life-style improvement programs, support and self-help groups, behavior therapy programs, and training classes in first aid, CPR, and sign language.

Crittenton Hospital, Rochester

Crittenton Hospital came to Oakland County in 1967, following 130 years of service in Detroit. Originally known as the Florence Crittenton Mission, the hospital was established as a home for destitute women. In 1907 the mission became known as Florence Crittenton Hospital and began to provide hospital care for its patients. In 1923 it changed from a private to a public hospital, and residency programs in obstetrics and gynecology were developed. Crittenton continued to grow and in the 1950s changed its name to Crittenton General Hospital. Later in that decade its board of trustees realized that the suburbs were in severe need of hospital beds and embarked on a mutual venture with the Bertha Van Hoosen group in Rochester to develop a hospital in northeastern Oakland County. The Rochester unit of Crittenton opened in 1967—the same year that "General" was deleted from the hospital's name. With demand for its beds decreasing, the Detroit unit closed its doors in 1974; during the same time the Rochester hospital was experiencing growing pains. Construction of a second tower of the Rochester hospital was completed in 1977. A 50,000-square-foot south wing was added in 1985, providing physicians and staff with new, state-of-the-art equipment.

Today Crittenton is a 250-bed community hospital with a medical staff of more than 270 medical doctors who practice in more than 30 specialties. Crittenton is one of the Rochester area's largest employers, with a staff of more than 1,300. The hospital maintains a detoxification unit, an occupational medicine program, and a women's center that has become widely known for its educational excellence. Crittenton also offers CAT scanning and a full range of rehabilitation and therapy programs.

St. Joseph Mercy Hospital, Pontiac

St. Joseph Mercy Hospital was established in 1927 and is governed by three entities: a divisional board representing the community, the medical staff, and the Religious Sisters of Mercy—Province of Detroit. The hospital is one of 23 divisions of the Sisters of Mercy Health Corporation, the largest multi-hospital system in Michigan and one of the largest not-for-profit health-care systems in the United States. It is designated as the regional referral center for pediatric intensive care and also provides leadership in the treatment of psychiatric problems. "St. Joe's," as it's known, has more than 450 physicians on its medical staff, spanning more than 65 specialty and sub-specialty areas. The hospital is a progressive teaching and research facility, offering undergraduate, graduate, and continuing medical educational programs. Outpatient programs at St. Joseph Mercy Hospital include care centers offering dental, pediatric, and surgical care and other services ranging from diabetic self-care to cardiac rehabilitation.

In 1987 the hospital opened the first laser-surgery center in Oakland County, and in recent years St. Joseph Mercy Hospital has opened MercyCare Family Medical Centers in Union Lake, Birmingham, and Rochester Hills. The hospital also sponsors progressive programs with seniors groups, economically disadvantaged people, and area public schools.

Henry Ford Hospital—Royal Oak, Southfield, Troy, Rochester, West Bloomfield, and Waterford

In total, 33 such outpatient centers encircle Henry Ford Hospital's Detroit "campus" and serve, in effect, as "feeders" to the main hospital. The centers provide health care in both primary- and specialty-care areas and share access to Henry Ford Hospital's 550-member, multi-specialty physician group practice, the second-largest group practice in the nation.

From Royal Oak to Rochester and across the central expanse of Oakland County, first-rate health care has become the norm rather than the exception. Following the same geographic pattern, educational excellence has also emerged as a new standard of quality of life.

Above: With more than 1,300 employees, Crittenton Hospital provides employment to more people in the Rochester area than any other organization. Photo by Beth Singer

Right: Pontiac General Hospital went from a 30-bed hospital in 1915 to today's 389-bed health-care facility. It was originally built in response to the lack of health-care facilities outside of Detroit. Times certainly have changed. Today, Oakland County offers a total of 4,227 hospital beds. Photo by Balthazar Korab

UNIVERSITIES AND COLLEGES
Oakland University, Rochester Hills

Evidence of Oakland's increasingly multipolar makeup is manifest throughout the county—most strikingly, perhaps, at Oakland University (OU), in Rochester Hills. Michigan State University Oakland, as OU was known in its infancy, opened its doors in 1959 to 570 curious freshmen. Today OU is poised to enter the twenty-first century as one of Michigan's most highly respected centers of learning, and as a key player in the Oakland Technology Park—the overtly ambitious high-tech development surrounding the university.

The university was born of the desire of the Oakland County Planning Commission to create a college and the imaginations of Alfred and Matilda Wilson, upon whose expansive estate OU was founded. That estate was known as Meadow Brook Farms. It was established at the turn of the century by Mrs. Wilson's first husband, John Dodge—one of the Dodge brothers who founded the Ford Motor Company and, later, the Dodge Motor Company. In its early years the "estate" was actually nothing more than an old country farmhouse along

Adams Road. The Dodges spent quiet weekends there, away from the industrial clamor of Detroit—25 miles to the south. In time the Dodges established a golf course and clubhouse on the 1,400-acre property. Next came an indoor swimming pool and, eventually, a network of farm buildings that provided the ways and means for Meadow Brook Farms—a local landmark inhabited mostly by cows, chickens, and herds of Mrs. Wilson's prize Belgian draft horses.

Four years after John Dodge died in 1920, Matilda Dodge married lumberman and political activist Alfred G. Wilson. Between 1926 and 1929 the Wilsons toured Europe and England in search of architectural concepts for Meadow Brook Hall, the mansion they were building on the lavish property. One week following the October 1929 stock market crash, the Wilsons opened the $3-million, 200-room, Tudor- and Jacobean-inspired home (complete with 26 fireplaces, 13 sets of chimneys, two elevators, and a secret staircase). The American economy was on the rocks, but Alfred and Matilda Wilson managed to carry on at Meadow Brook, where they raised prize-winning animals and sustained the splendid grounds for what would become greater purposes.

Wilson counted among his affiliations involvement with the Michigan State College of Agricultural and Applied Sciences—the East Lansing-based college that pre-dated Michigan State University (MSU). His wife was a board member of that institution in the 1930s and played a key role in linking the interests of MSU and Oakland's planning commission—each of which sought to establish a college in the burgeoning county. In 1957 the Wilsons formally offered their property to MSU (though they did retain the right to use Meadow Brook Hall and the 127 adjoining acres). In addition to donating the beautifully wooded grounds to the college, the Wilson estate contributed $2 million to help launch the new educational venture.

OU in its early years was strictly a commuter school, and the first courses offered in 1958 were of the noncredit, continuing education variety. Classes, according to both legend and fact, were conducted in a converted chicken coop. Inauspiciousness was plainly inscribed upon OU in its primitive form. But it was counterbalanced by the leadership of Durward B. (Woody) Varner, the school's first chancellor. Varner's high-profile, larger-than-life image overshadowed the

chicken coop factor as he guided OU through the process of establishing an identity of its own—in a county not traditionally known as an educational center. To help shape the university Varner brought together 50 community leaders and a committee comprised of many of the country's leading academic thinkers. To them Varner posed this question: Given a clean slate, how would you build an ideal university for this age? The committees agreed on almost every issue, including what was considered to be the key point—that Oakland should stress the liberal arts and avoid proliferating courses.

Varner and his successor, Donald D. O'Dowd, progressed significantly on all fronts. Business administration, education, and engineering were selected as OU's primary academic specialties. Other policies were established, including the concept that continuing adult education should be closely associated with the university's credit-bearing curriculum. Varner, O'Dowd, and other early administrators "fostered a faculty ethos and motivated students to accept a mystique of uniqueness, which, while expressing more an aspiration than a reality, provided a self-confident energy which sustained the institution for more than a decade," wrote the editors of an internal university planning document.

In 1963, on the eve of its first commencement, Oakland University assumed its current name and began to shy away from its original identity as a MSU clone. Since then, expand-

Oakland University campus includes the music pavilion, an 18-hole golf course, as well as athletic and recreational fields. In recent years the university has gained notoriety for its fine soccer team. Photo by Jim West

ing enrollments and an increasingly diverse student body have brought other changes to the university, and OU has fixed its attention on developing professional, career-oriented undergraduate and graduate programs. University policies regarding the importance of general education in the context of professional programs have also continued to undergo scrutiny and revision . . . while the university's mission has continued to expand. With many of the older students attending night classes at OU, the number of re-entry students has come to equal the number of newly recruited high school graduates among the student body.

Today OU is one of 13 autonomously governed public state colleges and universities in Michigan—and the only such institution in Oakland County. Located between Pontiac and Rochester, OU's campus is comprised of two dozen buildings, including estate buildings left from the old Wilson farms; new, glistening academic and activities buildings; a music pavilion; an 18-hole golf course; and athletic and recreation fields. The university offers academic programs ranging from baccalaureate to doctorate levels.

OU's curriculum and broad range of cultural, athletic, and intellectual programs reflect the greater agenda of the area. A mix of outreach activities, such as adult counseling centers, continuing education courses, and early childhood programs, addresses that agenda. So does the commitment of OU president Dr. Joseph Champagne to bold ventures like the $4-billion Oakland Technology Park, located adjacent to the OU campus.

Buoyed by OU's growth and the university's role in rapid development of the high-tech park, Champagne said the university's relationship with Oakland County is entering a new level of maturity. New programs are intensifying, as are imaginative collaborations with local school districts in areas like curriculum development. Financial grants are flowing in, triggering what Champagne called "a major expansion outward" in programs and facilities, including OU's new Health Enhancement Institute, which provides services in remodeled Meadow Brook stables to area adults.

Champagne said OU's first chancellor, Woody Varner, brought "a cultural vision" to the university. Champagne said he, himself, has tried to bring "the economic dimension." For all practical purposes he has succeeded. Thirty years after its founding, Oakland University now has a binding relationship with the county that bears its name. Seen in its totality the university has emerged as the regional interactive center of education, as well as the area's ultimate think tank. OU's often-visionary programs have branched out and touched the lives of tens of thousands of students and other members of the community.

Its developing relationships with the dozens of high-tech businesses that have established offices, laboratories, and research facilities around the edge of OU's campus promise more of the same. The university is taking on additional research contracts with its new neighbors, a process that is expected to accelerate when OU completes construction of a science and technology building in the early 1990s. With an international faculty and an enrollment of more than 12,000 students from throughout southeast Michigan, the university effectively mirrors Oakland County—what it is now and will be in the future. Future plans call for accommodating the growing enrollment while preserving the campus' rural atmo-

sphere. Planners hope to unify the four sections of OU's 1,600-acre campus—currently divided by open space and wetlands—while maintaining a landscaped buffer around the grounds.

Oakland Community College

Grand Rapids had a junior college. So did Flint, Port Huron, and Jackson. In Oakland County, however, the emergence of the community college concept came relatively late . . . and methodically. Not until the early 1960s did county educational

officials authorize a study to make recommendations regarding the establishment of a local community college. In any event the wheels were in motion. In 1963 voters agreed, by a very close margin, to establish a community college system in Oakland County. But a one-mill tax proposal attached to that bill failed, and it took an additional year of effort by the pro-college group called Oakland County Community College Citizens Advisory Council for the millage to pass. Having cleared that hurdle Oakland's community college network selected its first president, Dr. John E. Tirrell, and chose three initial sites for classes: In Auburn Hills (then Pontiac Township) board members purchased a 247-acre former military base at the intersection of I-75 and M-59; in Union Lake they established the Highland Lakes Campus on the 160-acre site where Oakland County TB Sanitarium and a onetime nursing home had been located; a third site consisting of 149 acres in Farmington Hills was subsequently acquired and became the Orchard Ridge Campus. Classes commenced on the first two campuses in 1965.

Oakland Community College (OCC) in its current form offers a wide range of credit and noncredit courses on five campuses and a mini-campus to more than 27,000 full- and part-time students. OCC's curriculum offers something for practically everyone. At the core of OCC's mix of courses are 102 associate degree programs.

The community college system is now spread throughout Oakland County, from the Orchard Ridge Campus in Farmington Hills to the Highland Lakes Campus in Union Lake, from the Southeast Campus Center in Royal Oak to the Auburn Hills Campus on Featherstone Road. In addition OCC has campuses in Southfield and at the Pontiac Center in downtown Pontiac; it also offers courses at high schools around the county.

As is the case with Oakland University, OCC's Auburn Hills campus is contiguous with the Oakland Technology Park, making it a logical focus point for technological training

SCHOOL BUS

35

Facing page, inset: St. Mary's College in Orchard Lake offers programs in business administration, general studies, and human services. Photo by Erdvilas Bankauskas/The Michigan Stock Shop

This page: In 1990 alone, Oakland County educated an enrollment of 200,000 primary and secondary education students in both private and public schools. Photo by Balthazar Korab

These two Bloomfield Hills students pose proudly in front of the tiles they and their classmates designed and created. The tiles were built right into the wall and will be a tribute to the young artists long after they have graduated. Photo by Gary Quesada/Korab Ltd.

in fields like computer-integrated manufacturing and robotics systems. OCC built a high-technology building at its Auburn Hills campus for these new programs. It also teamed up with International Business Machines (IBM) and Cross & Trecker Corporation to provide new equipment and other resources for OCC's computer-integrated manufacturing program. "Partnership with industry is essential if we are to utilize all available resources," former OCC chancellor R. Stephen Nicholson said.

The school sponsors seminars with various corporations in its new technology center, where it has become increasingly involved in the operation of corporate training programs and in helping to effect "technology transfer"—the integration of technological processes. "The different technologies are here in southeastern Michigan and all of it has to be integrated— the electronics, the metallurgy, the design—all have to come together in terms of the automobile industry," Nicholson told *Oakland Business Monthly.* "If America is going to be competitive and globally effective, we're going to have to utilize high technology . . . If we can't find the answers to that in Oakland County, I don't think it can be solved anywhere in America. I think we have an immense concentration of talent, labor, capital, technology, and organizational skills here . . . and all these things are emerging in the college."

While the Auburn Hills campus is caught up in the promise of the Oakland Technology Park, OCC's other campuses are focused on offering programs in areas like the health sciences (Highland Lakes and Southfield) and liberal arts and pre-professional courses (Orchard Ridge and Royal Oak). In Pontiac the community college offers basic education classes, seminars, and retraining programs to displaced auto workers. Similar services are available to businesses seeking employee retraining assistance. Nicholson told *The Motor City News* that the college's focus in the future will continue to be on the development of human resources, economics, and the community. "We feel the future of the college will be more with people who are in the mainstream of life," he said. Consistent with national trends, the average age of OCC students has risen. Nicholson said the college's role is changing as it seeks to maintain relevance in what has become "a lifetime learning society."

Lawrence Technological University, Southfield

Lawrence Institute of Technology (now Lawrence Technological University) was founded in Highland Park in 1932, during the Great Depression. Its programs were—and are now—geared toward working students. Classes, mostly in engineering, were held in an old Ford Motor Company trade-school headquarters until 1955, when the school moved to its current 100-acre site—formerly a General Mills research farm—on the banks of the Rouge River in Southfield.

Lawrence Tech, as it's known in the area, has become an integral component in the county educational picture. The independent, coeducational university is composed of colleges of architecture and design, arts and science, engineering, and management. Day programs enroll more than 3,500 students seeking bachelor of science degrees. And Lawrence Tech is one of only a few universities in the country that offers such programs on a regularly scheduled basis entirely in the evenings. Nearly 2,000 students are enrolled in the night program.

Lawrence Technological University was named for its founders. Russell E. Lawrence started the school in 1932 but died only two years later. His brother Ellsworth George Lawrence stepped in and served as president until 1964. By then the university was rapidly expanding its physical plant, which now includes nine major buildings. Through the 1980s Lawrence Technological University convincingly outgrew its earlier image. As its graduates surfaced throughout the upper leadership ranks of area businesses, the old perception of a

West Bloomfield elementary schoolchildren wait impatiently to be picked up from their extracurricular activities after school. Photo by Beth Singer

technical school that provided training merely "to keep the wheels of industry turning" gave way to a broader appreciation of Lawrence Tech's contribution to Oakland County and the Detroit area. While its academic reputation has grown, the university has maintained its close relationship with the Detroit area's expanding business community. For example the university's well-known Industrial Research and Development Program continues to be vital in helping industry develop solutions to problems, as well as new processes and products; other academic programs analyze specific industrial problems and focus on areas like fastener research and vehicle dynamics.

Located off the Lodge Freeway (Michigan 10) at the intersection of West Ten Mile Road and Northwestern Highway, Lawrence Technological University is positioned near the

exact population center of Oakland County, which the university considers an asset. "It's the center of the world of real work, real problems to be solved and real possibilities for a full professional and cultural life," reads a catalog description of the campus location.

Walsh College Of Accountancy and Business Administration, Troy

With its main campus in Troy and extension programs in Port Huron, Macomb County, and Detroit, Walsh College has become a vital part of southeastern Michigan's unique and vital mix of higher educational institutions. Walsh College grants undergraduate degrees in the fields of accountancy and business administration and graduate degrees in accountancy, finance, and taxation. Founded by Dr. Mervyn B. Walsh in 1922 as the Walsh Institute of Accountancy, the school altered its educational structure in 1968 and became Walsh College of Accountancy and Business Administration.

Today it is the only degree-granting institution of its kind in the United States. Day and evening classes convene on the college's 20-acre campus, located on Livernois Road in Troy, about 17 miles north of Detroit. On the average more than 2,000 students per semester attend Walsh College, which seeks to provide "personalized education" that benefits students while also enhancing "the spirit of free and individual enterprise," according to a passage in the college catalog. College president Jeffery W. Barry said "specificity of purpose and quality education" are the cornerstones of the Walsh College educational experience.

Michigan Christian College, Rochester Hills

Like many of Oakland County's colleges, Michigan Christian College has a Detroit origin. Lay leaders from Churches of Christ in the city formed a committee in the early 1950s to develop guidelines for a Christian school. Through their efforts the North Central Christian College was created, and in 1957 its board purchased a 37-acre estate near the corner of Livernois and Avon roads. Various fund-raisers were conducted in the ensuing years to build a campus on the site, and classes began in 1959 when 54 students enrolled in the college's pioneer class. Since then the campus has acquired additional land and now includes 15 buildings on 91 acres of forested land surrounding Lake Norcentra.

Saint Mary's College, Orchard Lake

Part of the Orchard Lake Schools, Saint Mary's College offers night and weekend programs, geared toward adult commuters, in business administration, general studies, and human services. Saint Mary's College shares it origins with Saints Cyril and Methodius Seminary, a Roman Catholic educational institution built by Polish immigrants in Detroit. The seminary originated in 1885 under the direction of Father Dabrowski, its first rector. Early programs focused on the training of seminarians in traditional programs; yet Dabrowski also insisted that students study physics, chemistry, mechanics, and other pursuits he called "required of our times." According to today's campus leaders, Father Dabrowski's legacy of spiritual, intellectual, and practical values "continues to energize" the college and forms the basis of its programs. In 1909 the seminary moved to the former site of Michigan Military Academy, on the high ground between Orchard and Pine Lakes, seven miles west of Pontiac. In 1927 three separate institutions were created: Saint Mary's Preparatory; Saint Mary's College, a four-year liberal arts college; and Saints Cyril and Methodius Seminary, a four-year graduate theologate. The college was incorporated under state laws in 1942, and title of ownership passed from the Archdiocese of Detroit to a corporation and board of trustees.

Since then, Saint Mary's College has evolved, both in terms of its student body and its curriculum. Its traditional strengths in areas like philosophy, theology, and languages have been broadened to include programs in fields like communication arts, the social and natural sciences, business administration, and computer science.

Cranbrook Schools in Bloomfield Hills provide the ideal setting for impressionable young minds to enjoy nature, beauty, art, and architecture in an educational and artistic environment. Photo by Ulrich Tutsch

Siena Heights College, Southfield

Siena Heights College was formed by the Adrian Dominican Congregation in 1919. Today the independent, coeducational institution—with its main campus in Adrian and a degree-completion program in Southfield—is designed to meet the needs of working adult students. Siena Heights offers junior/senior-level courses to associate degree graduates as well as to students seeking to complete bachelor degree requirements in business administration, allied health, general studies, and many trade and industrial areas.

PUBLIC AND PRIVATE SCHOOLS

Arriving in 1940 from the Oakland County prosecuting attorney's office, a notice proclaimed that the county had attained a population of 250,000 residents. County commissioner of schools E.J. Lederle quickly realized the implications of the document. State law required that counties with more than a quarter-million population create county school districts. And so followed the formation of the Oakland Schools, an intermediate school district that exists "to help the county's 28 local school districts do a better and more cost-effective job in educating the children of each community," according to a passage in the district's *Report on Corporate Objectives 1987-88.*

The district encompasses 900 square miles and a total of 360 public school buildings; another 120 nonpublic school buildings strengthen the county's educational base. In 1988 officials said there were 23,573 students enrolled in Oakland County's nonpublic schools; public enrollment exceeded 175,000.

Oakland County's public school districts range in size from Clawson, with less than 2,000 students, to Pontiac, with nearly 17,000 students. Other districts with enrollments of more than 10,000 students include Farmington, Rochester, Troy, and Waterford. In 1988 a total of 14,604 students were enrolled in public school kindergarten classes in Oakland County, and 12,707 students had reached the 12th grade. According to the State of Michigan, nonpublic schools in the county with the largest enrollments in 1988 included Detroit Country Day School, one of 10 private schools in Birmingham, with 1,221 students; Cranbrook Schools in Bloomfield Hills, with 1,256 students; and Bishop Foley High School in Lamphere, with 954 students.

In total Oakland County's public and nonpublic schools enroll nearly 200,000 students and offer a collective variety of programs that would rival any county in the state, said Oakland Schools public information director Nancy Stark. "This is boom city," she said, "both in terms of economic development and educational development. At this point, we can offer just about everything in the way of communities and schools, from sophisticated city settings to lake country to semirural areas . . .

with a lot of suburbia in between. Without exception, we have excellent districts in the county and the educational momentum is great, throughout the area."

Certain strains run through each of the 28 public school districts, Stark said. "High parental expectations are the norm and that translates into high performance. The ability of children here is higher than state and national averages. And it keeps going up."

The county's private schools tend to complement the public system, she added. "I can't think of a place in the county where there isn't a good relationship between the two. The communities that support these nonpublic schools obviously favor the diversity they offer . . . and we have a lot of that."

Dr. Rebecca Rankin, director of the Oakland Schools' Division of General Education, said diversity is one of the primary themes as Oakland County enters the 1990s. "The changing racial and ethnic mix in the county is astounding," she said. "A number of different groups are burgeoning and we're predicting we'll be the most ethnically mixed county in the United States by the mid-1990s." Part of the new ethnic mix derives from the county's increasingly international workplace, Rankin said. Other forces driving this trend have more to do with the broader demographic changes taking place in the region. Particularly in south Oakland County school districts are experiencing notable growth in the enrollment of students with ethnic backgrounds representing Latin American, Asian, Middle Eastern, and Russian roots. "We have an increasingly rich ethnic mix, and that new diversity alone brings strength to the county, and amazing opportunities," Stark said. "It's evidence of changing times, circumstances, and needs."

At the same time, the Oakland schools are piloting programs intended to electronically link the county's 28 districts. "The technologies are changing as rapidly as the ethnic mix," Stark said. "We've already established an information network that connects coaxial cable systems two ways, which enables us to conduct two-way voice and video communications throughout the county. For example, they can teach Japanese in one setting and we can beam it anyplace else we want." Such breakthroughs, she said, benefit school districts as well as municipalities, which will use the technology to train firemen and for other purposes. "The possibilities are infinite," Stark said.

Detroit Country Day School, the Roeper City & Country School for the Gifted, and Cranbrook Schools have the highest enrollments of the county's private schools and have earned widespread acclaim for their excellent academic programs. While these institutions have attracted much of the attention, Oakland is home to dozens of highly respected nonpublic schools, from the elementary level through senior high, both religious and nonreligious. From secular to secretarial, Oakland County's educational opportunities are virtually limitless.

One example of Oakland County's vast educational resources can be seen in Pontiac's ability to overcome adversity. Pontiac's local school district suffered severe economic problems in the mid-1980s because of diminishing revenue from auto manufacturing facilities in the community, but by the end of the decade, fortunes were improving . . . and improving radically. As the 1990s begin the Pontiac schools are seeing the first of what is expected to be a significant flow of fresh revenue from the nearby Oakland Technology Park. Auburn Hills assessor Victor Bennett said that by 2003 the school district will be taking in twice as much revenue as it did in late 1989—all because of the presence of the massive park. "We will have more money than we know what to do with," a district official told *The Oakland Press*.

More than dollars are involved in the arrival of the Oakland Technology Park—the largest high-tech research facility in the Midwest. Educational observers in Oakland see the emergence of the park as an auspicious development that will impact the county's educational structure, at all levels and in all forms. Curriculum decisions will take into account the nature of jobs opening up in the area's increasingly demanding, high-tech employment environment. And new employers in the county will look increasingly to the local schools—public and private—for the kinds of highly skilled technical workers they need. Such trends are already noticeable, and consequently the educational structure of the county has gained national attention. Marcia Baum, an economic liaison officer with Michigan's Department of Commerce, said political leaders are depending on the area's educational sector to help perpetuate the high-tech development that is fueling Oakland County's future. "We're depending upon our community colleges to reeducate and retrain the unskilled and on our universities to provide the newly skilled labor force and the research tools necessary to continue to attract new technologies," Baum told the *Wide Track News*.

Labor and industrial relations specialist George A. Fulton from the University of Michigan said firms from around the country and the world are settling in Oakland County because of its high level of educational attainment. Fulton said "the marriage" of good employment opportunities and people who are qualified to take advantage of them is what makes Oakland County one of the strongest local economies, not only in Michigan, but in the entire United States.

It's a heady concept. And it's all in place in Oakland County. Leading hospitals. Leading universities, colleges, and schools—both public and private—all lead to the conclusion that something special has happened in this region north of Detroit. And when Oakland's cultural strengths are factored into the equation, the county's awesome ascent toward civic integration is nearly complete.

The Finer Things in Life

It probably isn't fair for any one county to be blessed with as many cultural attributes as Oakland County is blessed. Although *not quite* criminal it is suspiciously unjust. You could spend the rest of your life driving around America looking for another place like Cranbrook, for example, and probably not find it. In Oakland County, on the other hand, Cranbrook is available 365 days a year, eager to take you in and share with you its ubiquitous cultural splendor.

On its own Cranbrook comes close to equating cultural overkill. Its 300 acres of architectural and horticultural glory are certainly enough to overwhelm the hungriest of aesthetic appetites. For Oakland County, though, one enormous cultural entity just isn't enough . . . not in a world where there is also a Meadow Brook, the living vision of Matilda Dodge Wilson, on the Oakland University campus in Rochester Hills.

Together Meadow Brook and Cranbrook form the cultural heart and soul of Oakland County. The "Body Art" is not without its other organisms, in the form of galleries, theaters, entertainment venues, bookstores, museums, and the like. But its pulse and rhythms flow from Cranbrook and Meadow Brook—each totally unique in its respective context.

HELLO, CRANBROOK

In the early 1900s, to the average eye, there wasn't much hope for Samuel Alexander's old farm on dusty Lone Pine Road. The apple orchard was in fair shape, but the peach trees were fading. And the grapevines had definitely seen better days. In spite of the poor condition of the turn-of-the-century spread, newspaper baron George Gough Booth and his wife, Ellen Scripps Booth, sensed its potential.

Wise to real estate opportunities, as well as the finer things in life, Booth purchased the property in 1904 for $85.71 an acre. Originally the Booths used the 175 acres of rolling terrain as a summer residence and recreational playground for family and friends, but during their visits they also set about improving the property—first on their own, and later with the help of teams of landscape architects, farmers, gardeners, and laborers. In 1908 the Booths moved into a new home—an Albert Kahn-designed dwelling that the Booths called Cranbrook House (named for the village birthplace of Booth's father in Kent County, England). It was built with the first concrete blocks cast in Oakland County.

Surely there was nothing ordinary about George Booth. In addition to being a successful publisher and a loving father, he was actively committed to three major fields in his lifetime: art, education, and architecture. Among his multiple distinctions Booth was the first president of the Detroit Society of Arts & Crafts, founded in 1906 "to promote the revival of artistic handicrafts and encourage good and useful work as applied to useful service." An artisan at heart, Booth "had a strong desire to develop Cranbrook's natural beauty," wrote Arthur Pound in *The Only Thing Worth Finding: The Life and Legacies of George Gough Booth.*

To realize his desires, Booth and his family busied themselves building roads and planting greenery. Pound wrote, "Cranbrook has seldom been free of workmen building roads, ponds, fountains, farming structures, faculty houses and gardens . . . George Booth was obsessed by a love of building."

Beginning in 1915 when the Booths erected an open-air Greek theater on Lone Pine Road, dedicated to the performing arts, the family's country estate was steadily and systematically transformed into what is now known as Cranbrook Educa-

Listed on both the Michigan and national registries of historic
places, Meadow Brook Hall was the realization of a dream home for
the late Matilda Dodge Wilson. Meadow Brook Hall is one of the
most magnificent examples of residential architecture in existence.
Photo by Balthazar Korab

of Cranbrook's major buildings and was the first president of what is now Cranbrook Academy of Art. Saarinen referred to one of those buildings—Kingswood School—as his masterpiece. "Vision and an enlarged sense of possibility brought Booth and Saarinen together," wrote the editors of *Design in America: The Cranbrook Vision 1925-1950*. Their union left an indelible mark on Oakland County. In tandem Booth and Saarinen created a community that attracted the world's leading painters, writers, designers, architects, and other artists.

The Booths formed the Cranbrook Foundation in 1927 to perpetuate the multiple institutions on their beloved property. "We were unwilling to go through life with our aim centered mainly in the pursuit of wealth and with devotion wholly to the ordinary opportunity for social satisfaction," the Booths said at the time. Instead they sought to "give tangible expression to new adventures" at Cranbrook. To assure the foundation's success George Booth committed nearly all his net worth to it; income from Booth newspaper stocks formed the basis of the foundation's $12,000,000 endowment. At that time the Booths envisioned "a sizable academy dominating the entire scene" of his property. For Oakland County—and for artists and scholars from across the world—it was a gift of rare dimension.

True to the vision of George and Ellen Booth, the work going on at Cranbrook remains as vital today as it did in his time. The perpetuity of those efforts was assured in 1973 when Cranbrook Educational Community was established. It is comprised of three divisions: Cranbrook Academy of Art, Cranbrook Institute of Science, and Cranbrook Schools.

"We are a community that has a mixture of both private and public functions," explained David C. Hart, Jr., assistant to the president of Cranbrook Educational Community. "The art academy and Cranbrook Schools are private institutions but the campus itself and a number of programs are open to the public."

Cranbrook continues to encourage public participation by providing access to its educational programs, museums, public events, and public grounds. More than 250,000 visitors tour the densely forested Cranbrook grounds each year. "It seems to have something for everyone," Cranbrook historian George Nelson wrote. "Peaceful walks through its gently rolling acres, the stimulating experience of seeing genuinely 'human' architecture . . . a magnificent collection of sculp-

tional Community; a church, two schools (one for boys, one for girls), a natural history museum, and an academy of art were constructed.

In addition to working with Kahn on Cranbrook House, Booth came in contact with other leading architects of the time—including Finnish architect Eliel Saarinen, who taught Booth's son Henry at the University of Michigan's school of architecture. Like others who would follow, Saarinen visited Cranbrook to see the grounds and meet the family . . . and ended up staying to make history.

By the time he met George Booth in 1923, Saarinen's prodigious talent was already recognized in Finland. The two shared the philosophy that art "was not just an adornment but something that should permeate every aspect of life," according to Cranbrook planning documents. Together they developed the first comprehensive plan to deal with the entire Cranbrook site; the Finnish architect ultimately designed most

tures scattered through the grounds . . ."

Cranbrook Academy of Art is recognized as one of this country's leading schools of art, design, and architecture, and its museum hosts exhibitions that typically feature the work of Cranbrook alumni. Cranbrook Institute of Science includes two nature centers, is ranked among the important natural history and science museums in the country, and offers educational programs, exhibitions, collections, publications, and research. It includes a planetarium, an observatory, and exhib-

it halls that focus on minerals, physics, anthropology, and earth history. A building adjacent to the museum called Nature Place houses the Discovery Room where youngsters can experience hands-on contact with various intriguing objects. Cranbrook Schools consist of Brookside, Cranbrook Kingswood Middle School, and Cranbrook Kingswood Upper School and are known for the excellence of their college preparatory educational programs.

Forty acres of landscaped grounds and gardens also sur-

*Facing page: In 1927 George G. Booth set out to establish a founda-
tion for an educational community in Bloomfield Hills with its focus
on the arts. He succeeded and Oakland County still enjoys the fruits
of his dream. This is an aerial perspective of a portion of the Cranbrook Schools. Photo by Balthazar Korab*

*Right: Cranbrook is noted for containing one of the largest collections
of work by Swedish sculptor Carl Milles. More than 60 bronze stat-
ues were purchased and installed at Cranbrook, beginning in 1934.
Photo by Balthazar Korab*

*Below: Cranbrook regularly sponsors art exhibits, open for public
viewing, which typically feature work from alumni. Cranbrook's
Academy of Art is known as one of the finest schools of art, design,
and architecture. Photo by Balthazar Korab*

round Cranbrook House, comprising what *Detroit Free Press*
gardening writer Betty Frankel called "one of the finest estate
gardens in the United States." Magnificent views abound—of
generous lawns, stately and mature trees, exquisite flower
beds, and seemingly infinite rows of precisely maintained
shrubs. "Visiting the gardens, which are open to the public
from May through October, is the next best thing to a trip to
England," Frankel wrote.

When the Booths lived at the estate, it was managed by a
large staff; today that work is done almost entirely by Cranbrook House and Gardens Auxiliary volunteers. The group
also administers tours of Cranbrook House, where most of the

Meadow Brook Concours d'Elegance, a gathering of elegant cars that benefits Meadow Brook Hall, is just one of the many events held at Meadow Brook each year. Photo by Balthazar Korab

Booths' original furnishings remain in place. In 1989 the U.S. Department of the Interior designated Cranbrook Educational Community as a National Historic Landmark.

With the Booths came Cranbrook; when they departed in the mid-1900s, the cherished grounds and invaluable facilities were left behind. Cranbrook remains today, perhaps, Oakland County's greatest cultural and educational attribute—and one of America's undisputed cultural gems.

HELLO, MEADOW BROOK

The Booths had a mansion in Bloomfield; the Wilsons had a mansion in what was then called Avon Township—now Rochester Hills. In each case the same eventual questions arose: What to do with the mansion? What to do with the elaborate grounds surrounding it? And in each case a similar answer emerged: Create an institution . . . for the arts and for the people.

The Wilsons arranged for their estate to be converted into a public institution of learning—which would later become Oakland University. But there were additional elements to their vision. "One of the purposes of the Wilson grant was to develop a cultural center at Oakland University," said Jane Mosher, director of community relations and group sales for the Meadow Brook Theatre and Music Festival—a cultural program of the university. "They decided at that time that the performing arts would be to this institution what Big 10 football is to other schools."

And so it was that Oakland University (OU) made a gigantic commitment to the performing arts. In 1964 it launched the Meadow Brook Music Festival, a series of summer concerts featuring the Detroit Symphony Orchestra and other artists. Performances were held in the Howard C. Baldwin Pavilion on the OU campus. A school of performing arts joined the academic mix at OU in 1967, and the Meadow Brook Theatre opened in the same year, solidifying the university's reputation as a major state cultural center.

To say the new musical venue in Oakland County gained instant credibility might be an understatement. The *New York Times* printed several major pieces during the early years of the festival's existence, commenting on "the quality of the program, the beauty of the setting and the phenomenally great acoustics." In spite of the success of the early format, festival officials continued to explore the possibility of enlarging the scope of its musical fare. In the late 1960s, using federal grant money, the festival enlisted the assistance of a demographically mixed group of 1,600 area residents to help chart the course of future bookings. Over a four-year period members of the group attended concerts —first for free and later for reduced costs. They also filled out questionnaires, registering responses to various types of entertainment. When the study was complete, Jane Mosher said, Meadow Brook officials realized that "there were many more musical tastes out there besides classical."

Meadow Brook Theatre has become one of the country's most successful regional theaters. With more than 12,000 subscribers it regularly brings the best in classic and contemporary drama to Oakland County residents, in a theater known for its intimacy and superior performances. Critics generally applaud the professionalism of

Led by OU's first chancellor, Woody Varner, the festival began to bring in a new mix of popular performers. In 1970 acts such as Buffy St. Marie, The Guess Who, Al Hirt and Pee Wee, and The Young Set each took their turn on the Meadow Brook stage, along with the Detroit Symphony Orchestra (DSO). And even the DSO lightened up a bit, inviting mainstream extrovert Meredith Wilson to be guest conductor on one occasion. Dance programs also flourished in the Meadow Brook mix at one point, although acid rock never found a home in the Baldwin Pavilion. "We tried rock once," Mosher said. "The air was blue. We didn't do that again for a while."

In 1989, the Meadow Brook Music Festival's 26th season, acts like Perry Como, Andy Williams, and Bob Dylan were among the highlights. Meadow Brook has a seating capacity of 7,500, including 2,200 pavilion seats and 5,300 lawn seats. Meadow Brook Music Festival is one of a half-dozen major outdoor summer music festivals in the United States and shares association membership with music festivals in Illinois (Ravinia), Ohio (Blossom), New York (Saratoga), Massachusetts (Tanglewood), and Virginia (Wolf Trap). Meadow Brook is the only such venue located on a university campus. "Oakland has a tremendous outreach program, and I think Meadow Brook is just a part of that," said Mosher, who joined the staff at Meadow Brook in the early 1960s. "The university is dedicated to providing cultural enrichment to the people of the surrounding community and that's evident in everything we do."

In addition to the music festival, Meadow Brook consists of a highly acclaimed professional theater group and an art gallery. While the festival brought national attention to Meadow Brook and Oakland County, the performing arts community within OU continued to expand. Professional theater came in 1967 when the Academy of Dramatic Art was established, along with the John Fernald Company, a professional resident repertory theater group.

the theater's productions, and community sentiment mirrors that supportive attitude. "I thank you again and again for the quality of your productions, for the thought that is so evident in your choice of plays, and for gracing our community with such beauty," a Rochester area patron wrote in a letter to the theater.

In its 1989/90 season the Meadow Brook Theatre presented the Detroit premieres of Alexander Ostrovsky's "The Diary of a Scoundrel" and Tom Griffin's "The Boys Next Door." Other recent productions included Lee Blessing's "A Walk in the Woods" and the Charles Dickens classic, "A Christmas Carol." Terence Kilburn worked as artistic director on all productions.

Meadow Brook Hall, the former home of the Wilsons, also has a cultural program at OU, but it operates separately from the music festival, theater group, and art gallery.

A tremendous mix of unique cultural events characterizes the Meadow Brook calendar each year. Most functions take place in the 80,000-square-foot Meadow Brook Hall—one of the most elaborate "homes" built in twentieth-century America and one of the finest examples of residential architecture anywhere in the world. Today it serves as a conference center, hotel, and public museum. Trained volunteers guide visitors on tours of the four-story mansion that cost $4 million to build and another $10 million to furnish. To say the interior design is ornate is insufficient; the craftsmanship, appointments, and priceless art treasures reflect the ultimate in lavish expression. The buildings were turned over to Oakland University by Matilda Dodge Wilson in 1971.

Since then countless organizations have found ways to stage events at the old Wilson home—perhaps the most outstanding facility of its kind in the region. Typically visitors come for the tours, which are conducted year-round on Sundays. In July and August tours are also conducted during the week. At the hall Oakland County residents frequently attend special events, like art shows. Others anticipate annual events such as the Meadow

Brook Concours d'Elegance, a gathering of elegant cars that benefits Meadow Brook Hall. In recent years the event has been staged in conjunction with spin-off events, like the Special Automotive Fine Arts Invitational Exhibition and Sale, conducted in 1989.

ALTERNATIVE FORMS OF ENTERTAINMENT

Cranbrook and Meadow Brook are the primary jewels in Oakland County's cultural cap, but they're not the only sources of glitter. The county is home to a number of top entertainment and athletic venues, from active theaters in southern Oakland's Royal Oak and Birmingham to the Pine Knob Music Theater in Independence Township and the Pontiac area's two attractions—the Pontiac Silverdome and the Palace of Auburn Hills. While the Silverdome is home to the Detroit Lions football team and the Palace is home to the two-time NBA champion Detroit Pistons, both arenas regularly host concerts featuring top international entertainers and other cultural events.

In its first 10 months the Palace hosted 140 events—with 54 shows in its first 90 days. Included in the mix were 45 basketball games and numerous tennis and wrestling events. Among big-name entertainers appearing at the Palace were Michael Jackson, Neil Diamond, and Madonna (who attended high school in Rochester). During that same period the 80,000-seat Pontiac Silverdome hosted more than 100 events, including 10 Lions football games, motor sports, wrestling, amateur sports, rock concerts, conventions, and trade shows.

The 22,000-seat Palace of Auburn Hills, which opened on

August 13, 1988, with a concert by rock singer Sting, was built as an entertainment center as well as an arena for sports. The *Detroit Free Press* noted that it "owes its ambience as much to the Magic Kingdom as it does to Magic Johnson or the Pistons." The Palace features 180 private suites, theater-style seats, and what the *Montreal Daily News* called "razor sharp sightlines and opera-like acoustics." In its first year the $70-million Palace of Auburn Hills was voted Best New Arena by readers of *Pollstar* and *Performance* magazines, trade publications circulated primarily among entertainment executives. Additionally, a 50-acre, 17,500-seat outdoor theater called the Palace Gardens is due to open in spring 1991.

While the Pontiac Silverdome and the Palace of Auburn Hills attract considerable crowds for a variety of events, much of the county music scene continues to find its focus at Pine

Facing page: The sumptuous interior of Detroit's Fox Theatre is a conglomeration of Far Eastern, Egyptian, Babylonian, and Indian themes from various eras. The original owner, William Fox, called this style the "Eve Leo Style," a tribute to his wife who traveled around the globe assembling furniture, artifacts, and paintings to lavishly appoint the theater. Photo by Santa Fabio

Right: Each year Holly hosts the enchanting Renaissance Festival, a celebration of the fifteenth and sixteenth centuries, complete with costumes, cuisine, equestrian events, theater, and more. Photo by Gary Quesada/ Korab Ltd.

Knob in Independence Township. The 550-acre Pine Knob Complex is located immediately east of I-75 and consists of an outdoor music theater, a restaurant, ski resort, golf course, and condominium development. Pine Knob opened its 18th season in May 1989 with a performance by rock singer Eddie Money. Diverse acts followed, including Jackson Browne, Rod Stewart, and Dick Clark's "American Bandstand" concert.

"People expect diversity from Pine Knob," said publicist Simone Prince. Over the years the popular outdoor theater has delivered, featuring performers in the traditional mode like Frank Sinatra and Barry Manilow and in rock 'n' roll acts like Alice Cooper and the Doobie Brothers.

The amphitheater, owned and operated by Nederlander Theatrical Organization, features 6,646 pavilion seats and 10,000 lawn seats. Nederlander also operates the Birmingham Theatre and signed a three-year contract in the late 1980s to promote concerts at the Pontiac Silverdome.

In addition to having close access to prominent entertainment sites in Oakland County, area residents also take advantage of their proximity to the Joe Louis Arena, Fox Theatre, and Masonic Temple—all important concert venues in nearby Detroit. Combined with Oakland County's major facilities, these sites add to the region's entertainment alternatives and give the region what some are calling the largest number of concert sites in the country.

MUNICIPALITIES STAGE CULTURAL EVENTS

In downtown Pontiac, atop the Phoenix Center Plaza, festivals are scheduled during the summer—many of them with tie-ins to ethnic events that take place simultaneously. In other communities throughout the county, the pattern is the same: Summertime means entertainment-time. From Shain Park in Birmingham to the Bloomfields beyond, the emphasis is on community concerts, featuring everything from rock and reggae to highbrow classical fare.

Professional, community, dinner, and college theater groups also carry on enthusiastically throughout the county, presenting first-rate performances at numerous locations . . . and generally in an open-to-the-public context. And, on any given night, disparate settings such as the Academy of the Sacred Heart in Bloomfield Hills, the Columbiere Center in Clarkston, and the

Jewish Community Center in West Bloomfield all may be offering the public some form of intriguing cultural activities.

The popular music scene in Oakland County also has a rich tradition dating back to the 1950s, when local singer Jack Scott packed local dance halls. That good-time feeling continued during the 1960s, when Motown acts performed frequently in the area, and when Ann Arbor-native Bob Seger saturated the local pop music scene with his raucous brand of Midwest rock, on his way to international stardom with the Silver Bullet Band.

Other American pop stars share distinct Oakland County roots, including singer Marshall Crenshaw of Berkley; Noel "Paul" Stookey of the folk trio Peter, Paul and Mary, who spent his high school years entertaining his fellow students in Birmingham; and singer/actor Glenn Frey, a native of Royal Oak. Comedian Robin Williams honed his comical senses in the Birmingham area in those memorable years before Mork met Mindy. Oakland County's best-known resident artist may be Aretha Franklin, the soul singer who rose from the Detroit gospel scene to the top of her profession and resides in Bloomfield Hills—home also to Chrysler Motors Corporation chairman Lee Iacocca and Detroit Pistons star Isiah Thomas.

A VITAL ART SCENE

As measured by the number of area galleries, theaters, and art-related activities, Oakland County ranks among America's most elite counties.

Once a city known for its hardware and grocery stores, Birmingham has become Oakland County's undisputed art gallery center, with no less than a dozen such businesses operating—most of them in the company of offices, banks, and fine retailers along the city's quaint Woodward Avenue corridor. From art deco to contemporary glass, artistic expressions—in most imaginable forms and fabrics—are displayed at one time or another in Birmingham's galleries. Other finds

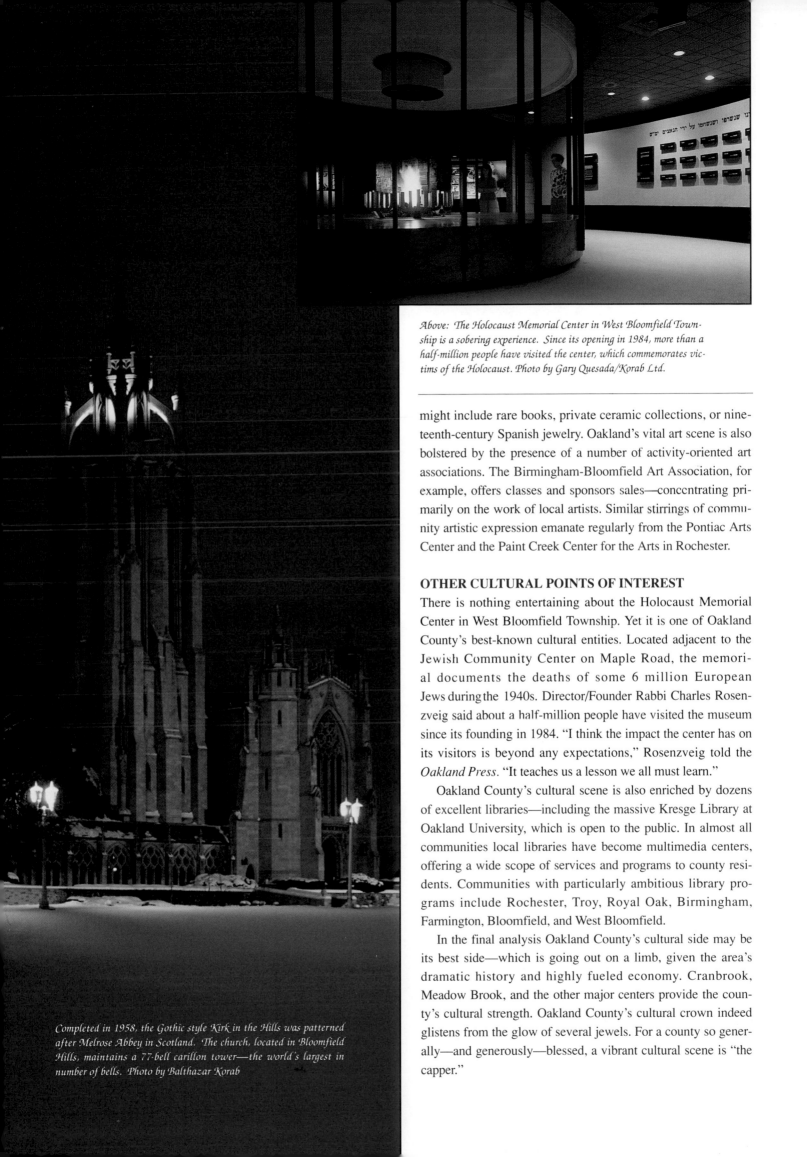

might include rare books, private ceramic collections, or nineteenth-century Spanish jewelry. Oakland's vital art scene is also bolstered by the presence of a number of activity-oriented art associations. The Birmingham-Bloomfield Art Association, for example, offers classes and sponsors sales—concentrating primarily on the work of local artists. Similar stirrings of community artistic expression emanate regularly from the Pontiac Arts Center and the Paint Creek Center for the Arts in Rochester.

OTHER CULTURAL POINTS OF INTEREST

There is nothing entertaining about the Holocaust Memorial Center in West Bloomfield Township. Yet it is one of Oakland County's best-known cultural entities. Located adjacent to the Jewish Community Center on Maple Road, the memorial documents the deaths of some 6 million European Jews during the 1940s. Director/Founder Rabbi Charles Rosenzveig said about a half-million people have visited the museum since its founding in 1984. "I think the impact the center has on its visitors is beyond any expectations," Rosenzveig told the *Oakland Press*. "It teaches us a lesson we all must learn."

Oakland County's cultural scene is also enriched by dozens of excellent libraries—including the massive Kresge Library at Oakland University, which is open to the public. In almost all communities local libraries have become multimedia centers, offering a wide scope of services and programs to county residents. Communities with particularly ambitious library programs include Rochester, Troy, Royal Oak, Birmingham, Farmington, Bloomfield, and West Bloomfield.

In the final analysis Oakland County's cultural side may be its best side—which is going out on a limb, given the area's dramatic history and highly fueled economy. Cranbrook, Meadow Brook, and the other major centers provide the county's cultural strength. Oakland County's cultural crown indeed glistens from the glow of several jewels. For a county so generally—and generously—blessed, a vibrant cultural scene is "the capper."

Taking Time Off

T he idea is to refresh the mind, refresh the body, refresh the being. That's why it's called "recreation"; you are creating anew. Recreation has always been important to Oakland County's active residents. Lately, however, the idea of getting out, shaking it loose, and diving half-mad into at least one sport or activity has gained unprecedented acceptance in this land of lakes and parks, this land of generous geographic attributes: gracious golf courses, outstanding water- and snow skiing, bountiful ballfields, herculean health clubs, Hiawathian hiking trails, and limitless recreational opportunities. If this isn't paradise, it must be paradise once-removed. And few are the souls who haven't caught onto the notion.

In Oakland County, as in the rest of the United States, recreation has taken on a high sense of purpose—a great integration into people's collective sense of what, after all, is important. And necessary. And fun.

For increasing numbers of people, being active and fit now ranks equally as high on the importance scale as having a solid roof overhead and a good accountant. Stand anywhere in Oakland on any fine afternoon, open your eyes, and you'll see people jogging, running, sprinting, galloping, dashing, walking briskly, walking backwards. Name the pace, Oakland's athletic set exudes it. "People in motion," as Mama Cass put it.

People are riding bicycles in "the darndest places." And skateboards in even "darnder" places. Folks in Oakland County are riding anything they can get their feet on: preadolescents on low-power motorized bikes, bearded men on larger ones, smiling seniors cruising along in sleek carts that enable them to be active, windsurfers skimming across on the hundreds of lakes scattered gloriously throughout the western and northern townships of the county.

Simultaneous to this glorification of perspiration, this crusade of sorts that has elevated the running shoe above peanut butter and blue jeans in the American cultural hierarchy, the county is also alive in baseball and softball. In the hearts and minds of thousands of Oakland County residents, from tiny tots to tottering grandpas with expanding stomachs, these pastimes rank highest on the list of staple American activities.

Semi-serious, semi-professional-quality baseball is played on most summer nights at sandlot fields in Pontiac and Royal Oak, before sizable local crowds of appreciative, baseball-wise partisans. Teams in other competitive leagues beat it around the base paths at commercial softball centers in Rochester Hills and on diamonds surrounding the county's hundreds of public and private schools. Some residents—men and women, boys and girls—play in multiple leagues, simultaneously. "It's like having a second full-time job," explained one woman who plays shortshop for three separate teams. The exercise imperative is full upon us . . . and nowhere more fully than in the egalitarian world of Oakland County softball.

Golfers, on the other hand, are growing radically in number every year, as more and more people catch on to the pleasure of being out on the course with friends, stretching the muscles, whacking challenging white balls up even more challenging fairways. Tennis players are also growing in number, as new initiates discover the immense enjoyment to be found in hustling soft yellow balls over a four-foot net, yet inside the baseline. Racquet clubs throughout the county offer reserved court times, instruction, and competitive events; public tennis courts are available in nearly every community.

While half the population of Oakland County is running, playing baseball and softball, golfing, or stroking tennis shots, thousands of others are out recharging mind and body on the

A child casts his makeshift fishing pole into Crooked Lake at Independence Oaks. The peacefulness of the sound of the water and the cool splashes on a hot summer day make the quality of life in Oakland County very special. Photo by Chris Boylan/Unicorn Stock Photos

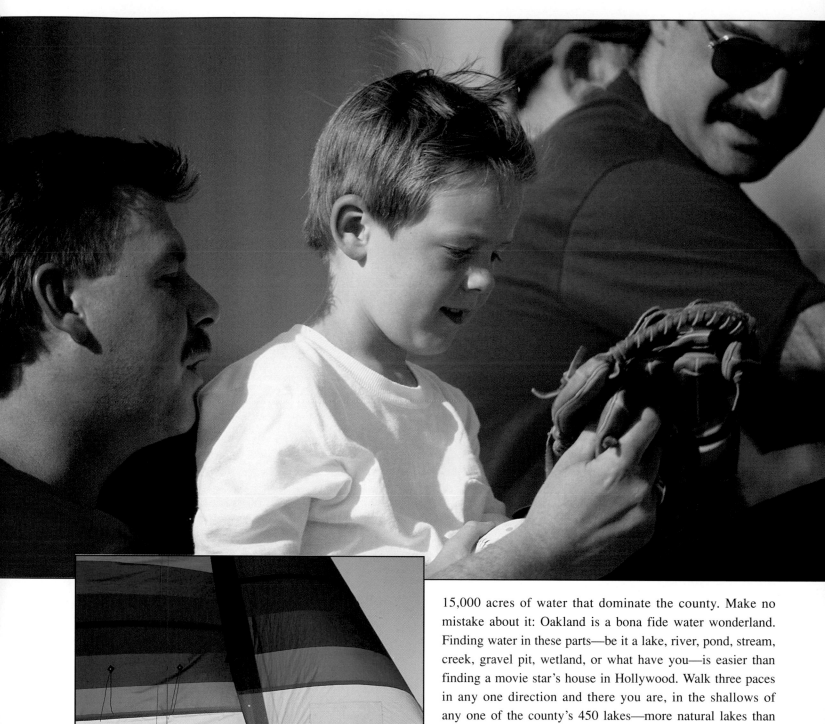

15,000 acres of water that dominate the county. Make no mistake about it: Oakland is a bona fide water wonderland. Finding water in these parts—be it a lake, river, pond, stream, creek, gravel pit, wetland, or what have you—is easier than finding a movie star's house in Hollywood. Walk three paces in any one direction and there you are, in the shallows of any one of the county's 450 lakes—more natural lakes than any other county in the state of Michigan. In Oakland neighborhoods there are boats in what seem like every other driveway . . . and more fishermen than any poor fish ever deserved to encounter.

Lake culture drew people to Oakland County. And lake culture remains Oakland's most identifying characteristic. To some, having regular access to any number of lakes means waterskiing or, at least, being pulled across the water in an old inner tube. To others it means snorkeling or scuba diving, competitive swimming, sailing, canoeing, or riding in a slow float-boat to someplace besides China. And if riding on a float-boat exceeds anyone's excitement threshold, there's always the prospect of a quiet cookout on the lakeshore.

Facing page, above: As soon as the winter is gone, players dust off their softball gloves and head out to one of Oakland County's many softball sandlot fields. Photo by Gary Quesada/Korab Ltd.

Facing page, below: Lake living and recreation on more than 450 lakes in the county is part of the four-seasons life-style enjoyed by county residents. The great lakes, located 20 miles from the county, provide significant recreation opportunities and abundant fresh water for business and industry. Photo by Balthazar Korab

Below: Men and women alike rush to Oakland County's golf courses to steal some moments of quiet on the green. Here the sun peeks through the trees as it sets over a course. Photo by Balthazar Korab

GETTING INTO IT: OAKLAND-STYLE

Downhill skiing, outsiders are often surprised to learn, is also an important recreational activity in Oakland County. While modest in comparison to, say, the Swiss Alps, Oakland's skiing areas offer a stimulating challenge to novices and a winter opportunity to stretch it out for those with more advanced skills.

Cross-country skiing opportunities, on the other hand, are available throughout the county—both on a structured, commercial basis and on a more casual, informal level. In Oakland, hills abound, as the names of numerous communi-

ties imply. Not everyone in the county can cross-country ski outside their back door, but a lot of them can. Those who can't, need only venture a short distance from wherever they live to find a splendid site for strapping on the skis.

Recreation, in general, isn't limited to the outdoors . . . or strictly to the summer and winter months. In between, among other activities, Oakland County residents and visitors venture in large numbers to the Hazel Park Harness Raceway (a major horse racing facility), the Detroit Zoological Park in Royal Oak, and to contests featuring the Detroit Red Wings professional hockey team and Detroit Tigers professional baseball team in the nearby Motor City. Countless others maintain sailboats and motorboats on waters connected to Lake St. Clair and the Detroit River—both of which are located within a short drive of Oakland County. Michigan, commonly called the "Water Wonderland," has more registered boats than any other state, and a substantial number of those boat owners call Oakland home.

Beyond the water, but not beyond the "water holes," there are some 44 public golf courses in golf-goofy Oakland County. This perfectly green county is also home to more than a dozen top private courses, including Indianwood Country

People cross-country ski throughout the county—both on structured, commercial paths and on a more casual, informal level, in their own backyard. Frozen and snow-covered lakes make excellent cross-country skiing trails. Photo by Balthazar Korab

Club in Auburn Hills, home of the 1989 Ladies Professional Golf Association Open Tournament; and Oakland Hills Country Club, in Bloomfield Township, where many national championships have been played. Orchard Lake Country Club, located in the heart of western Oakland's most concentrated lake country, has also played host to a number of important championship tournaments in recent years.

In addition the Huron-Clinton Metropolitan Authority maintains five 18-hole golf courses and two "pitch 'n putts" (three-par courses); it also has two other courses on the drawing board. Huron-Clinton is the regional park system created by a legislative act in the early 1950s. A quarter-mill tax imposed on the residents of Wayne, Oakland, Macomb, Washtenaw, and Livingston counties finances the system, which includes 13 metroparks. The 18-hole golf courses in Oakland County are at Kensington and Stoney Creek parks.

More than 250,000 golfers annually use the Oakland County Parks and Recreation golf courses, from the eminently picturesque Springfield Oaks Golf Course in Davisburg to the small-but-challenging Red Oaks course in Madison Heights. The county also manages 18-hole courses, on Thirteen Mile Road in Farmington Hills (Glen Oaks) and in White Lake Township (White Lake Oaks). Each of the county's four courses has its own personality.

Glen Oaks

At Glen Oaks the front nine are easy to walk while the back nine are hilly. At the end of the round, fortunately, refreshment awaits in the 1920s English-style, stone clubhouse, which is listed on the Michigan Historic Registry and also has a fine bar and grill.

White Lake

At White Lake the front nine are wide open while the back nine are more tree-enclosed. The entire course encompasses 140 acres and includes a magnificent clubhouse and pro shop.

Red Oaks

At Red Oaks a nine-hole executive golf course is located in a mature urbanized area. Beginners and seniors most enjoy this flat, narrow course.

Springfield Oaks

At Springfield Oaks the Shiawassee River provides a scenic backdrop for a fairly challenging 18-hole layout, with water holes, trees, and hills in full abundance. The clubhouse offers a panoramic view of the course.

AN EXTENSIVE PARK SYSTEM

Oakland County is a recreational hotbed for many of the same reasons it is economically strong and notably enriched in educational, medical, and cultural institutions and experiences. Chief among those reasons is foresight—the kind exhibited by the county's early leaders. Clearly they saw the future coming, with all its implications. And clearly they did something about it.

One date—November 8, 1966—stands as an important milestone in the chronology of Oakland County's emergence as a recreation paradise. Oakland's voters approved a special millage to acquire and develop a park system in the county. It was, Kenneth Van Natta wrote, the first time in the history of Oakland County that voters had approved a special millage "for a purpose not directly connected to education."

It was also the birth of the Oakland County Parks and Recreation Commission and all the good that would follow. "The voters and taxpayers of this county . . . saw the need and opportunity and had the willingness and courage to finance the program themselves," Van Natta wrote. It was only a quarter-mill—or 1/4th of a mill, as others might express it. Nevertheless that tax measure meant a lot to future generations.

Commissioners set about examining water resources and land amenities and began to determine where potential—and affordable—park sites might exist. Soon those options were clearly identified, and little time was wasted in launching the acquisition phase. Headwaters of rivers in the area were identified as having the cleanest water and best land resources. Accordingly some 1,600 acres of land including the headwaters of the Shiawassee and Clinton rivers and the west branch of Paint Creek were purchased for future park sites.

In all, five parks were developed on this land in the early 1970s; they became operational in 1972. Since then the growth of the county park system has been phenomenal. By 1980 annual visitorship exceeded one million, and the figure has been increasing every year since then. And throughout the years Oakland County residents have supported the park system, renewing the one-quarter mill tax every five years.

Today the Oakland County Parks and Recreation Commission operates a park system that includes nine recreational parks and encompasses 4,000 acres. The sites have been planned in such a way that they retain the natural beauty of the land, yet offer the maximum number of recreational activities.

Oakland County's park system has become known as a national innovator in leisure facilities and programs. Among its "firsts" is the country's first year-round, dome-covered driving range. Programs for seniors and the handicapped have also been advanced within the system, which has been supported since 1983 by a nonprofit foundation created by private citizens interested in preserving and enhancing parks and recreational opportunities in Oakland County.

The names of various facilities within the Oakland County Parks and Recreation system appropriately connote oak trees.

The annual Oakland County Hot Air Balloon Festival takes place at the Springfield Oaks County Park. During the festival there's plenty of excitement in the air, as well as hot air balloons. Photo by Gary Quesada/Korab Ltd.

Springfield Oaks

Located on Andersonville Road in Davisburg, Springfield Oaks totals 270 acres—170 of them donated by an individual named Manley Davis. The park includes an 18-hole golf course, recognized as one of Michigan's most popular and challenging. It also features marked cross-country skiing trails and hosts a number of cross-country ski races and special events.

The park houses a youth activities center with an 8,400-square-foot exhibit hall and an auditorium that seats 800 persons. Wedding receptions, dances, parties, and swap meets are among common activities at the center. It also features a multipurpose room, designed for business meetings, conferences, receptions, seminars, dinners, and reunions. Outside there are two riding areas—one lighted—with plentiful grandstand seating.

The outdoor center is designed to accommodate rodeos, concerts, livestock contests, tractor pulls, and demolition derbies. The golf course has its own banquet room and a clubhouse that can be rented. The Springfield Oaks County Park is also home of the annual Oakland County Hot Air Balloon Festival and 4-H Fair. The activities center is transformed into a fairground for the week-long event.

Groveland Oaks

Located east of Holly, on Dixie Highway, the Groveland Oaks facility contains 200 acres of woods, lagoons, and meadows and includes Stewart Lake. Winding roads lined with weeping willows lead to 600 campsites—450 of which feature electricity. Rowboats, pedal boats, and canoes are available to rent, and there are numerous courts for volleyball and basketball, sports fields, a wading pool, and a children's playground. A covered pavilion with a fireplace is available for casual recreational activities like sitting back and taking in the sights.

Guests at Groveland Oaks tend to favor the three islands on Stewart Lake—Devil's Island, Virgin Island, and Paradise Island—where they find seclusion and extraordinary picnic sites. Another mega-attraction at this park is a thrilling 35-foot roller-coaster-type slide that plunges into the lake.

Independence Oaks

This park in Independence Township was purchased in 1967. It offers 1,062 acres of camping and recreational space in the wooded lands south of springfed Crooked Lake, home of many a pike, many a bass, and more panfish than a family of four would want to consume on a cool Oakland County evening. Positioned near the headwaters of the Clinton River watershed and two miles north of Pine Knob, the park provides protection for the floodplain surrounding the river. Visitors can discover the beauty of nature firsthand on the park's multiuse trails, which lead to marshes, meadows, deciduous forests, and a glacial lake.

In the summer visitors take to 68-acre Crooked Lake,

which is equipped with a boat launch and docks. There are three picnic areas, a concession stand, beaches, and playground equipment for children. Shelter rentals and group camping are also available. The park offers barrier-free accommodations for the handicapped, and a hard-surfaced, All-Visitors trail has been installed.

For cross-country skiers, Independence Oaks has more than nine miles of trails, including the Lakeshore Trail that circles for 2.4 miles and is recommended for novices; experts tackle the 2.7-mile Rockridge Trail or the challenging Springlake Trail—known by experts as the Ted Gray Loop. The trails are groomed and marked, and a nordic ski patrol provides assistance to skiers. When the fun is over, the fun has actually just begun, as Independence Oaks also has the Twin Chimneys Shelter, where skiers can relax in front of—you guessed it—two fireplaces.

There is also a nature center at the park for those seeking

Facing page: The Kensington Petting Farm is a popular spot for family outings and school and summer-camp field trips. Photo by Ann Winder

Below: The Waterford Oaks Wave Pool, Michigan's first Wave-Action swimming pool, with three-foot waves and a giant, two-flume "Slidewinder" waterslide, is an exciting place to cool off. Courtesy, Oakland County Parks and Recreation Commission

the comforts of the indoors. Dedicated in 1985, the 4,000-square-foot center emphasizes nature interpretation. It houses an exhibit room, assembly room, information area, offices, and support facilities. In the exhibit room visitors view life-size scenes of the park; in a special, children's discovery corner, there are scaled-down exhibits. Another space is available to quietly observe wildlife at the nature center's outdoor feeding station.

Year-round naturalist-guided tours are offered, along with workshops and mini-classes for all ages. Tours, lectures, and field trips are also on the agenda, as is an environmental awareness program that attracts school groups from throughout the county. The Sadie and Irwin Cohn Amphitheater is located 100 yards from the nature center and is used year-round by schools, senior citizens, and organizations. The amphitheater offers a reverse screen for slide presentations and a fire circle for group sing-alongs.

Addison Oaks

Purchased in 1969 by Oakland County, this park includes a meeting center and stunning forests in the rolling hill country northeast of Lake Orion. Spanning 700, acres it features more than 12 miles of cross-country trails and offers night skiing on a lighted 1.5-mile trail. Located on Romeo Road, 12 miles north of Rochester, Addison Oaks includes a Tudor-style conference center with formal gardens and two banquet rooms. Given its splendor, the center is a great setting for weddings, receptions, business meetings, seminars, and banquets. Constructed in 1927, the building has a white masonry exterior, an exquisite wood-paneled interior, and 15 fireplaces. Its main dining room seats 200, and catering is available.

Summertime visitors swim, boat, and fish in three small spring-fed ponds on the park grounds. Concessions and boat rentals are available. In the winter Addison Oaks offers 13 miles of groomed snowmobile trails through the

woods and open fields. Ice-skating, fishing, and sledding are also important activities at this fine park. Between seasons natural attractions take top billing—from a unique cedar swamp to strands of willow, oak, pine, and sugar-maple trees, in all stages of growth.

A 15-acre botanical garden is also a top Addison Oaks attraction. It includes an arboretum and residential and sensory gardens. Two pavilions are available for picnickers and groups; each accommodates up to 200 persons. The park also offers 50 modern campsites—complete with electricity, water, and cement camper pads. Wooded sites are available for scouts and camper clubs.

Waterford Oaks

This facility is located immediately behind the Oakland County Service Center in Waterford Township and features a clubhouse, a pool, platform tennis, and an ample number of trails throughout its 145 acres. It serves as headquarters for the Oakland County Parks and Recreation Commission. A 10,000-square-foot activities center also graces this park. It has a kitchen, bar, and small room for meetings. In addition to four lighted, wind-screened platform tennis courts, the Waterford Oaks Court Games Complex offers eight regular tennis courts, sand volleyball courts, numerous shuffleboard courts, and horseshoe pits. Other attractions at the park include Michigan's first Wave-Action swimming pool, with three-foot waves and a giant, two-flume "Slidewinder" waterslide.

The activity center at Waterford Oaks can accommodate up to 400 people and is often used for parties and various recreational classes. Instruction is provided for all the court-related activities, and camps focusing on these specific activities are conducted throughout the year. Senior citizens and young people alike attend special events held in conjunction with the Court Games Complex, from tournaments to clinics.

Glen Oaks Park

Glen Oaks Park in south-central Oakland County focuses on an 18-hole, par 70 golf course. It is located on Thirteen Mile Road, between Orchard Lake and Middlebelt Roads. The setting is enhanced by an outdoor terrace as well as by putting greens which accompany the challenging golf course. The 137-acre site also features a newly renovated clubhouse with banquet facilities and lounge. During the winter months cross-country skiing is also an option.

Orion Oaks Park

This relatively new park is comprised of 927 acres in Orion Township, including a body of water with a somewhat distinctive name—Lake Sixteen. The property was formerly owned by Chrysler Corporation and was part of a 2,400-acre acquisition by the Michigan Department of Natural Resources. Plans are under way to develop winter sports activities and facilities for camping, boating, fishing, and picnicking.

Red Oaks Waterpark

Newer than new is the Red Oaks Waterpark in Madison Heights, with a Wave-Action swimming pool and three-flume waterslide. Three-foot waves are created in the pool, while the slides offer a variety of "directional experiences." For those hesitant to partake in the more daring activities, the waterpark also offers picnic grounds and a large deck for sunbathing.

White Lake Oaks

Located near the geographic center of the county, just beyond the western edge of Waterford Township in fast-growing White Lake Township, this park is a virtual paradise for golfers. Golf—on an attractive 18-hole layout, with watered greens and fairways—is the only activity offered. The clubhouse has locker rooms, a pro shop, pull and electric carts, and a restaurant. A private banquet room is also available.

Kensington Metropolitan Park

One of the most popular parks in southeastern Michigan is the Kensington Metropolitan Park, which stretches out for 4,300 acres immediately north of the I-96 Freeway. The Board of Commissioners of the Huron-Clinton Metropolitan Authority renamed its Kent Lake Project in 1947. Kent Lake had been a 60-acre lake, surrounded by marshland and fed by the Huron River. Shallow and nondescript, "it could hardly be dignified by the word 'lake,'" one writer noted. That reputation changed when officials decided to build a dam on the Huron—on land leased from the State Conservation Department. Stretching 290 feet across the river, the dam was completed in 1947 and created a "new" Kent Lake, with 1,200 acres of prime waters.

Within years Kensington Park had become a major attraction in the five-county area, hosting millions of visitors annually. It remains today one of Oakland County's greatest resources, not only for fishermen, boaters, and swimmers, but also for picnickers, bicyclists, hikers, and all sorts of outdoor enthusiasts. In 1988 Kensington marked its 40th anniversary with a fireworks display and a number of events at its nature center and farm center. Kensington Metropolitan Park is the largest of the Huron-Clinton chain of eight parks throughout the counties of Livingston, Macomb, Oakland, Washtenaw, and Wayne. Other sites in Oakland County include Stoney Creek Metropolitan Park, near Rochester, and Indian Springs Metropark, near Clarkston.

Ultimately Oakland County's greatest recreational strength lies in the nature of the state in which it is located. Michigan, as residents of all nearby states have come to appreciate, is truly the Midwestern leader in campsites, of which there are 14,000 statewide, and in overall recreational opportunities. Additionally, currently under development is a linked recreation trail system that utilizes, in part, abandoned railroad rights-of-way. Providing Oakland County residents with additional access to parklands, the system will be a part of the Discover Michigan Trail—a proposed statewide trail network.

To live in Oakland is to be at the gateway to the entire state, with its 94 parks, thousands of lakes, and infinite recreational playgrounds. In fact there are 19 state parks in southeast Michigan, all within a short drive of Oakland County, and seven of them are actually in the county. Included are parks in Ortonville, Holly, Lake Orion, Pontiac, Rochester, and Milford. Activities range from archery and hiking to swimming and fishing. State parks and recreation areas offer over 200,000 acres of land that are open for hunting, and in southern Michigan parks alone, there are six equestrian campgrounds and 185 miles of bridle trails. For winter sports enthusiasts there are over 200 miles of cross-country ski trails and over 83,000 acres available to snowmobiles.

Add water opportunities and you have a veritable recreational nirvana. Statewide there are over 500 miles of Great Lakes and inland lakes shorelines—in the park system alone! Include an additional 82 designated swimming beaches, and the overall picture becomes clear: there is no excuse for staying dry in Oakland County, or in Michigan.

In total it's enough to wear anyone out . . . just reading about it. Baseball, fishing, golfing, jogging, boating . . . where does it end?

Certainly not in Oakland County.

Most of the more than one million residents have settled here for the same reasons: Oakland County is a pleasant place to live and a promising area for finding employment (and employees); splendid cultural offerings are abundant, and the educational and medical infrastructure is superior; finally, Oakland County has become the working center of Michigan because of its essential quality of life . . . for everyone fortunate enough to be here.

Oakland County's Enterprises

The Standard Federal bank headquarters is located in Troy, home to more than a dozen industrial parks. Photo by Balthazar Korab

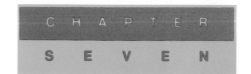
Manufacturing

Producing goods for individuals and industry, manufacturing firms provide employment for many Oakland County area residents

Photo by Gary Quesada/Korab Ltd.

IBM

IBM Corporation began operations in Michigan in 1915 with a handful of employees working out of a small office on Jefferson Avenue in Detroit. The company originated one year before in New York as the Computing-Tabulating-Recording Company (CTR). CTR manufactured tabulating machines, scales, and time recorders. In 1924 the company changed its name to International Business Machines Corporation.

Today the company employs 1,800 men and women in southeastern Michigan and more than 2,500 people throughout the state. Southfield is headquarters for IBM's Great Lakes Area, which encompasses marketing and service operations in Michigan, Ohio, Kentucky, West Virginia, and western Pennsylvania.

"Locating IBM's five-state area headquarters in southeastern Michigan makes good business sense," explains Robin W. Sternbergh, vice president and area general manager for IBM. "We are conveniently located to cover both our Michigan customers and our customers located throughout the area."

IBM's Great Lakes area is headquartered in the Galleria Officentre complex on Northwestern Highway in Southfield. The company's facility on Nine Mile Road in Southfield is the showcase of an ultramodern, energy-efficient office building.

In addition to the Southfield buildings, IBM has 11 major facilities across Michigan, including sites in Ann Arbor, Detroit, Flint, Grand Rapids, Kalamazoo, Lansing, Midland, and Traverse City. IBM occupies about 700,000 square feet of office space in Michigan.

Throughout its history, IBM has enjoyed its greatest suc-

cess in the marketplace by transforming advanced information technologies into products and services that provide customers with innovative solutions to their varied needs. IBM's customers can be found in business, government, science, space exploration, defense, education, medicine, and other areas of human activity around the world.

The company has more than 380,000 employees worldwide and provides solutions to its customers through its marketing organizations as well as through business partners, including authorized dealers and remarketers.

IBM's personnel practices make the company a leading employer. IBM has not laid off a regular employee for economic reasons in more than 50 years. Instead, the company retrains its work force when necessary to meet changing business condi-

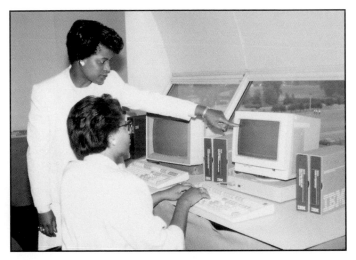

Facing Top: Evelyn Evenson (left) and Audrey Cooper at work in the IBM Customer Center in Southfield. Photo by Charles Maniaci

Facing Bottom: IBM's area headquarters are in the Galleria Officentre complex in Southfield. Photo by Charles Maniaci

Below Left: IBM's Southfield Centre on Nine Mile Road is home to several IBM marketing and service branches. Photo by Charles Maniaci

Below Right: IBM and Oakland Community College are partners in teaching computer integrated manufacturing to area employees and students. Here, Don Golonka (left) of IBM and Bob Harsha of OCC team up on a computer design at OCC's Advanced Technology Center at the Auburn Hills campus. Photo by Charles Maniaci

tions. IBM offers a full range of employee benefits, including health benefits and a number of newer programs such as the IBM Child Care Referral Service, IBM Elder Care Referral Service, flexible work hours, extended personal leaves, as well as wellness programs and community service assignments.

In addition to the company's commitment to its employees, IBM has a long-standing commitment to the community. "We work with the communities in which we operate, and we give back to the communities in which we work," says Sternbergh.

The company contributed $159.4 million nationally in 1989 to education, social programs, cultural activities, and charitable causes. From 1983 to 1989, IBM's financial contributions totaled one billion dollars.

IBM had capital investments in Michigan of $65 million in 1988 and a positive economic impact of $232 million, a figure that includes payroll, local taxes, purchases from in-state vendors, and charitable and business contributions. There are about 1,500 IBM shareholders in Michigan.

Through its Fund for Community Service, IBM provides assistance to charitable and civic organizations in which employees, retirees, and their spouses are involved. IBM has provided $43 million in grants to 27,000 projects nationally since the fund was created in 1972. In Michigan more than $52,000 was provided in Fund for Community Service grants to 23 projects in 1989. Several southeastern Michigan organizations benefited.

Through a unique partnership program at the Auburn Hills campus of Oakland Community College, IBM and OCC are offering a new curriculum in computer integrated manufacturing (CIM). CIM is the process by which manufacturers link their various departments—from business planning and design to engineering and marketing—by computer.

IBM's commitment to OCC includes hardware, software, and technical assistance worth an estimated $3 million. Two kinds of students are enrolled in the college's CIM curriculum: general students looking for skills that will help them find jobs in industry, and employees from industry seeking state-of-the-art training.

The IBM and OCC partnership is one of 75 similar alliances IBM has formed with colleges and universities throughout the country as part of its CIM in Higher Education Alliance. "The CIM in Higher Education program is designed to be the catalyst to help colleges and universities develop training programs and the instructional materials necessary to establish a national base of skills in computer integrated manufacturing," Sternbergh says.

IBM Corporation makes other contributions to southeastern Michigan. The company supports many local organizations. IBM employees also are involved in a host of community activities. Many volunteer their time, money, and talents to organizations that work toward improving the quality of life throughout Michigan.

"IBM has enjoyed a long tradition of business in Michigan, and we expect to maintain that tradition," Sternbergh says.

ITT Automotive, Inc.

ITT Automotive, Inc., is a young company born from a rich heritage and with an already abundant manufacturing base. The global supplier of components and system-oriented products to the automotive industry was formed in 1987 by the ITT Corporation through the consolidation of its worldwide units into one corporation, established in Bloomfield Hills. In 1990 it moved to a 36-acre headquarters and research and development site in Auburn Hills.

Today ITT Automotive has operations in the United States, Canada, Mexico, South America, and Europe with 73 plants and facilities in 12 countries employing about 30,000 people.

With an estimated 50 percent of its manufacturing base in Europe and about 95 percent of its business in passenger cars and light trucks, ITT Automotive products can be found in almost every vehicle made in the western world. Although the product list is extensive, ITT Automotive is divided into three primary manufacturing groups: braking and suspension, electrical and mechanical, and an aftermarket division.

The "flagship" of the braking group is the ITT Alfred Teves GmbH company in Germany. This world's largest independent manufacturer of brake systems and components has 17 plants in Germany, Belgium, France, Italy, the United Kingdom, and the United States. ITT Teves manufactures complete braking systems from brake pads to the sophisticated ABS—an electronic, four-wheel-controlled, fully integrated antilock braking system that allows drivers to maintain full control of their vehicles.

The suspension group consists of ITT Way Assauto (Italy) and ITT Koni (Netherlands) who is an industry leader in high-performance shock absorbers.

ITT Automotive's mechanical systems and components group's North American operations consist of four companies. ITT Higbie Baylock is a specialist in tubular products such as

Below Left and Right: ITT Automotive's Hancock and the electrical systems group have developed custom seating systems that will redefine luxury car seating for the next decade. ITT Automotive's single-arm windshield wiper system is produced by its SWF operation, which is a leading producer of electromechanical automotive products.

Facing Top: An entire family of front brake calipers are produced by ITT Teves, the world's largest independent manufacturer of complete braking systems and components.

Facing Bottom: ITT Automotive World Headquarters and Technology Center.

brake lines, fuel lines, and emission-control components. It has 13 plants in the United States and Canada. ITT Hancock, with five locations, specializes in seating systems, safety engineering systems, door and hood hinges and latches, and parking-brake assemblies. ITT Milrod, with two plants in Canada, provides automotive metal-stamping assemblies while ITT Lester, a quality producer of high-pressure die castings, has three facilities in Ohio.

In Europe, the ITT mechanical group is represented by ITT Bergneustadt (Germany) and Fispa Ulma (Italy), whose products include shock absorbers, window regulators, fuel pumps, exhaust systems, welded assemblies, and an automatic deployable roll-bar.

The ITT Automotive electrical group is made up of ITT SWF Auto-Electric and Altissimo (Italy). SWF is one of Europe's leading producers of electromechanical components and systems, including windshield washer-wiper systems, motors, lights, relays, flashers, switches, and sensors for all types of vehicles. It has 18 plants in Germany, Spain, Canada, the United States, and Mexico. They also produce wire harnesses, electrical components, and connectors for major North American car makers.

The aftermarket group, ITT Parts Supply Division, was formed to provide greater customer service and support through parts and products such as the comprehensive Aimco brake line of Teves and Koni products.

ITT Automotive is an offspring of ITT Corp., which dates back to the early 1900s when it was called International Telephone and Telegraph Corp. Today ITT Corp. is a $20-billion company with 120,000 employees in 100 countries. ITT Automotive is one of nine operating corporations under the ITT Corp. umbrella. In much the same way that ITT Automotive has products in most cars, ITT Corp. touches everyday life in numerous ways through ITT Hartford (insurance), ITT Sheraton, ITT Fluid Technology, ITT Defense, ITT Financial, ITT Rayonier, ITT Electronic Components, and ITT Educational Services.

ITT Automotive started with well-established manufacturing operations. The technology center in Auburn Hills is part of the company's continuing efforts to remain a leader in the world market of automotive components and systems. This world headquarters consolidates engineering, technology, and designing operations from throughout the Detroit area.

Jack Holland, ITT Automotive's director of facilities, says the center is ITT Automotive's attempt to not only develop component parts for cars and trucks but also entire systems. Instead of just making a wiper blade, ITT Automotive is involved in producing entire arms and blade systems. Instead of just seat covers, ITT Automotive, Inc., produces entire car seats.

About 50 percent of the center is dedicated to research and development and is located at North University Drive, near Interstate 75. The site is on the edge of the Oakland Technological Park, within walking distance of Oakland University, which the ITT Automotive group uses for educational and cultural activities. The four-story, 300,000-square-foot building is designed to blend into the heavily wooded site. Dark stone and glass skylights throughout the building accentuate the site's natural beauty. A 9,000-square-foot commons area houses conference rooms, an auditorium, and a cafeteria for the 650 employees who were brought together from sites in Bloomfield Hills, Troy, Southfield, Rochester, and Jackson.

"We are in the business to grow and to develop better products and systems," says Charles Peters, president of the Mechanical Systems and Components Group. "We intend to grow in the automotive supply business, and the research and development capabilities at the Auburn Hills center is a major step in that direction."

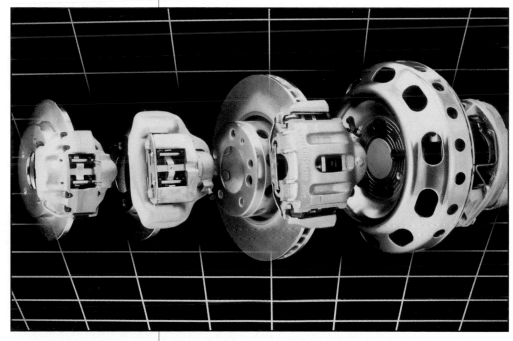

The Budd Company

The Budd Company's commitment to Oakland County and southeastern Michigan is strong and obvious. Not only are its world headquarters based in Troy, but the company's three major divisions are also located in Oakland County communities.

The stamping and frame division is based in Rochester. The wheel and brake division has its offices in Farmington Hills, and the plastics division is headquartered in Madison Heights. In addition, Budd's Technical Center is in Auburn Hills.

An international corporation, The Budd Company has 11,000 employees worldwide and 2,500 in the Detroit metropolitan area. It produces both sheet metal and plastic composite auto components. Budd products include stamped-metal body panels and assemblies, vehicle frames and chassis products, fiberglass-reinforced composite body panels, structural components, steel-disc truck wheels, drum and brake parts, engine block heaters, and other cold-weather starting devices.

The stamping and frame division makes hundreds of designed and engineered parts and pieces for cars and trucks. These include doors, quarter panels, hoods, floor pans, and roofs. The plastics division offers products such as doors, deck lids, grille opening panels, and tailgates. It also produces water skis and other recreational products. In the wheel and brake division, the product mix includes a wide range of steel disc wheels for commercial vehicles, demountable rims, and disc brake components for trucks.

Budd has eight major subsidiaries, including prototype-builder Milford Fabricating Company in Detroit; castings-maker Waupaca Foundry Inc. in Waupaca, Wisconsin; Phillips Temro of Eden Prairie, Minnesota; and Temro Division of Budd Canada Inc., in Winnipeg, Manitoba.

Budd's Technical Center serves Budd operations and customers with product and process development, manufacturing research, materials studies, product improvement, technical consultation, forecasting, and applications of

Bottom Left: Siegfried Buschmann, chairman and chief executive officer.

Bottom Right: Engineers at Budd's wheel and brake division use CAD/CAM capabilities to design and evaluate new products.

computer sciences.

The company was started in 1912 in Philadelphia and even then was formed to work with the auto industry. Its primary first product was an all-steel touring car body developed by company founder Edward G. Budd. In 1972 Budd moved its world headquarters to Troy to be closer to the major automotive companies.

In 1978 the billion-dollar, multi-industry, globally structured Thyssen Company of West Germany purchased The Budd Company. Thyssen produces capital goods, manufactured products, steel, and specialty steels as well as holdings in mining and other industries. A large multipurpose corporation, Thyssen is also a high-technology automotive supplier that produces metal body stampings, vehicle bodies, and vehicle chassis, among a wealth of other vehicle parts.

Siegfried Buschmann, who is president of Thyssen Holding Corporation, served on the Budd board of directors for seven years before being named chairman of the board and chief executive officer in 1989. He succeeded James H. McNeal, Jr., who retired December 1, 1989.

A spokesman for Budd noted that Oakland County gives the company the ability to hire excellent, well-educated people as well as having a good road system that offers quick access to Budd customers. "Our faith in Oakland County is self-evident, based on what we've done here. It is definitely the center of the Budd system."

Mold-A-Matic

Mold-A-Matic, based in Madison Heights, entered the plastic-mold industry as pioneer in its field and has more than kept pace with technology.

"Basically, we've just gotten better at what we do," says Frank Prasatek, president of the firm. Mold-A-Matic makes production molds for the plastics industry. The molds are basically steel tools that make plastic parts for autos and appliances.

Prasatek says the company deals particularly in the larger molds that are used for making such things as auto bumpers, instrument-panel retainers, and door panels. The firm handles molds for both interior and exterior parts.

One of the larger shops of its kind, Mold-A-Matic employs about 70 workers in a facility of about 35,000 square feet. Staff professionals can both design and build molds to the specifications of a client. "We try to do everything in house," says Prasatek. "We have designing and building facilities."

In a high-technology world, Mold-A-Matic's CAD/CAM system is credited with helping the company stay on top of the industry. Under the Mold-A-Matic computer-aided design (CAD) system, designers use state-of-the-art technology to produce a complete range of mold designs. The CAD system is also said to allow the firm to simplify the process of designing and building molds to a client's exact design standards. On the other side of the coin, the computer-aided machining (CAM) equipment allows the firm to build the expertly designed molds.

The CAD/CAM systems are particularly important, notes Prasatek, in helping the company satisfy the changing demands of its clients. Originally plastic-mold manufacturing companies only had to build the molds or tools for a client. Today they are expected to build prototypes, assist in product design, build models or patterns, and other such functions.

Prasatek says that while his firm makes plastic molds for many industries, such as appliance producers, its main business is with auto companies, including not only the Big Three of GM, Ford, and Chrysler but also some Japanese car makers.

Mold-A-Matic's management changes have been particularly smooth over the years, even though the company has not been passed down from generation to generation in one family, a common tradition in this industry.

The firm was incorporated in 1952 by Mike Herzina, who started out with a small staff of just four or five people. Don Gilbert took over in 1971, when Herzina retired, and Gilbert subsequently has turned the management reins over to Prasatek and Dave Truczynski.

"Despite the management changes, the name has always been Mold-A-Matic, and we've always enjoyed a good reputation in the industry," says Prasatek. "We've been here a long time, and we think we do a crackerjack job of what we're supposed to do. We've earned our pats on the back."

Pepsi-Cola Company

When Oakland County and southeastern Michigan residents are thirsty, odds are they reach for a Pepsi-Cola. In fact, the entire Midwest is Pepsi heartland—Pepsi is the number-one soft drink in Michigan and the best-selling product in local grocery stores.

Pepsi-Cola's U.S. operations are divided into four regional divisions: Pepsi East, Pepsi Central, Pepsi South, and Pepsi West. The southeastern Michigan office of Pepsi-Cola is based in Troy, serving an area that includes Detroit, Flint, Oakland, Wayne, and Macomb counties. Pepsi Central, headed by division president Mauricio Pages, comprises 11 midwestern states and seven local marketing areas. Bottling operations throughout the division are either corporate owned or managed by franchise bottling operations.

Pepsi's worldwide bottling operations are headquartered in Somers, New York. Worldwide, Pepsi employs more than 26,000 employees, with total retail sales of more than $14 billion.

Pepsi's roots are based in New Bern, North Carolina. In 1902 a 31-year-old pharmacist named Caleb Bradham created the first Pepsi for his customers, using a combination of spices, juices, and syrup. The concoction was so popular that customers called it "Brad's Drink." Bradham renamed it Pepsi-Cola and its popularity skyrocketed. The business grew steadily until the 1920s, when rising sugar prices dramatically increased operating costs. Bradham was eventually forced to sell the Pepsi trademark in 1923 and returned to his drugstore in New Bern, North Carolina.

Pepsi-Cola, however, began to grow. In the 1930s, despite the Depression, the company boomed. A tremendous increase in sales resulted from a simple idea. Pepsi-Cola began selling 12-ounce bottles of Pepsi for just a nickel—12 ounces was twice as much as other soft drinks offered for the same price. This marketing innovation led to a famous musical radio jingle: "Twice as much for a nickel."

In the 1940s and 1950s the company began an aggressive expansion into international markets. Today Pepsi is sold in more than 145 countries, including the Soviet Union and Eastern Europe.

In 1965 Pepsi-Cola Company merged with snack food manufacturer Frito-Lay, Inc., of Dallas, Texas, to form PepsiCo, Inc. Today Pepsi-Cola remains the soft-drink manufacturing unit of PepsiCo. PepsiCo, employing approximately 235,000 people, is a worldwide consumer products corporation that owns not only Pepsi-Cola and Frito-Lay, but also such restaurants as Kentucky Fried Chicken, Pizza Hut, and Taco Bell. Worldwide retail sales of PepsiCo products total more than $40 billion annually.

Pepsi has a strong bottler network, contributing to numerous community programs. Recent programs include a $4.5-million dropout reduction program called "The Pepsi School Challenge." Detroit's Southwestern High School and Dallas' Pinkston High School were selected to participate in the pilot program, designed to encourage students to pursue college or vocational training after graduation from high school. Each school receives a $2-million grant. Under the terms of this financial award, students who maintain at least a "C" average and avoid substance abuse are eligible for scholarships of up to $2,000 toward higher education. Pepsi-Cola's grant also includes money for teachers who act as mentors, tutoring and counseling students.

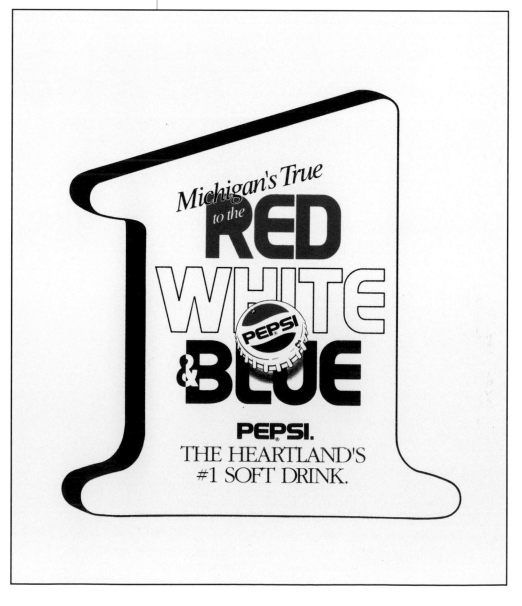

Michigan's True to the RED WHITE & BLUE

PEPSI.
THE HEARTLAND'S
#1 SOFT DRINK.

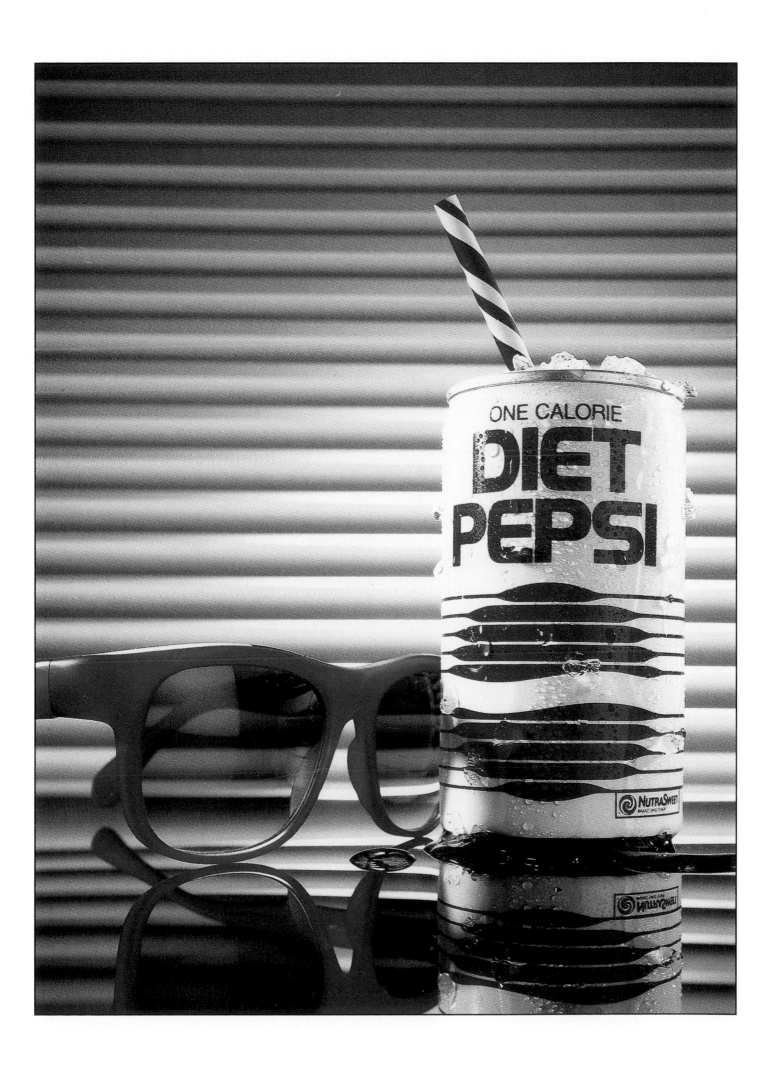

Inter-Lakes Steel Products Company

Inter-Lakes Steel Products Company in White Lake Township has not changed its name since being organized in 1951. Nor has the firm been at any other location than its Highland Road site, about eight miles west of Pontiac. But the company has been far from stagnant during the past 40 years.

"We adapted to the market changes and requirements and changed with the times," explains Otto E. Sohn, president and chief financial officer.

Sohn says the company started out dealing with the major auto firms and has continued to do so, updating its technology until today it is a producer of high-quality, automated robotic welding systems.

Inter-Lakes designs and builds applications of automotive components, from the floor pan to seating. Other specialized areas include automatic transfer systems, drilling, tapping, assembly devices, weld guns, and related components. It can design and build jigs and fixtures, special machines, resistance, arc and MIG welders, automated equipment assembly devices, fabrications, and machining.

"Everything we make is specialized and unique for the auto industry," says Sohn. "The programs we are into now are quite large, and that limits our activity in other manufacturing areas."

Inter-Lakes employs about 60 people at its 65,400-square-foot facility. For special projects, the number of workers has reached as many as 100.

"Every system we build is different and customized for a particular project," Sohn says. Inter-Lakes was involved in the underbody welding system for the Ford Aerostar van.

The company was organized by four men—Al Stanker, Basil Thompson, Don Wolverton, and Joe Venticinque. At that time the company supplied sheet-metal parts to the auto industry. Changing with the times, the company concentrated on jigs and fixtures in the 1960s and switched to the more automated robotic welding systems in the 1970s and 1980s.

The original founders of Inter-Lakes are now retired, although they still live in Oakland County. Six partners, three of whom are sons of the original organizers, hold equal stock in the company. In addition to Sohn, the stockholders are: Larry J. Thompson, vice president/engineering; Richard Stanker, vice

president/purchasing; Gary Wolverton, vice president/manufacturing; Leo B. Rickman, vice president/manufacturing; and Barry Carter, vice president/estimating.

Sohn notes that the reason Inter-Lakes started in Oakland County and will remain there is that most of the principals in the company live in the Oakland County area, and Oakland County and southeastern Michigan is where the auto industry is centered.

Steady, planned change has been a watchword for Inter-Lakes Steel Products Company, and Sohn says there is no reason to believe it will change in the future.

"We're looking to possibly add another assembly bay in the near future for auto-industry work," Sohn says. "The auto industry is projecting that the next four to five programs are going to be quite large, because a lot of new models and changes are planned in the next few years to keep up with the world market. We're looking forward to growing with the automotive market."

Gresham Driving Aids, Inc.

Below Left: Gresham can manufacture and install special hand-controlled driving aids as part of its modification process.

Bottom: Gresham performs complete modifications for the handicapped on vehicles such as this one, parked before the company's new, 19,000-square-foot production and service facility.

Gresham Driving Aids, Inc., in Wixom, was basically started out of necessity and has turned into one of the most successful family businesses in Oakland County that caters to the handicapped. As the name implies, the business produces and manufactures special hand controls used as driving aids by paraplegic and quadriplegic individuals. In addition to making the devices, the company also installs them in vehicles.

The business recently expanded to a total of 19,000 square feet of production/service facilities across the street and in the facility that has served as home for the company since 1964.

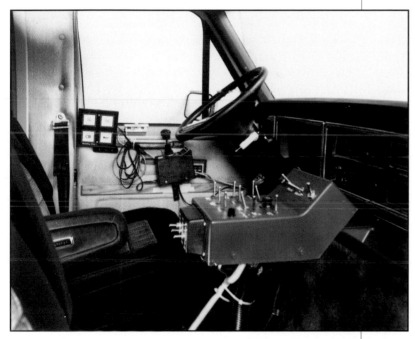

who became a quadriplegic after a swimming accident in 1952. The elder Gresham struck a rock while diving.

The IRS auditor who was studying law and delivered new trucks as a moonlighting job obviously had to completely revamp his life. He tried selling insurance for a couple years. In 1958 Lee Gresham met Ken Wainman, described by Jerry as a "natural mechanic," and started his own business selling hand controls for the handicapped. The business got its first break in 1962 when it contracted with Oldsmobile to build hand-controlled driving aids. In 1964 the business moved from Detroit to Wixom. In 1974 the company began van conversions.

"We started from scratch, and we now do complete vehicle modifications for the handicapped," says Jerry Gresham. Among Gresham Driving Aids' credits is being the first to have its hand controls tested and approved by the Veterans Administration.

Jerry Gresham says he plans to continue to foster growth in the company. "We're going to extend our range of services to both sales and service, trying to become an auto dealership for the handicapped," he says.

Proud of his staff, Gresham says most of his business comes from referrals. The firm also offers some nonfinancial benefits. "I get an immense amount of satisfaction from my job," he says. "When you make a delivery and see the beam on people's faces, you know you've given them a new lease on life."

Employing more than 30 workers, the business has continued to grow over the years, taking referrals from the major auto industries and doing business internationally.

In 1979 the company had sales of about $650,000 and was converting about 100 to 150 vans per year. Today annual sales top $2 million and between 300 to 350 vans are converted per year for the handicapped. This work has included about 30 vans per year shipped to Israel for General Motors.

"We do all kinds of specialty conversions because we have the ability to adapt," says Jerry Gresham, president and owner of the company. Although its mainstay is vans, the business also does specialty work, such as customizing the Detroit Library's bookmobile or revamping mobile medical units for X rays and mammograms.

It was not by accident but because of an accident that the business was born. It was started by Gresham's father, Lee,

Lear Seating Corp.

The Lear Seating Corp. does not take a back seat to anyone, unless the company made the back seat. With its world headquarters in Southfield, the international company is a leading supplier of automobile and light-truck seating systems and interior trim products, services, and components. One of the fastest-growing companies in the automotive industry, Lear accounts for about 40 percent of the total North American automotive seating-systems market. Fiscal year 1989 sales were expected to top one billion dollars.

Lear is a world leader in the manufacture and the in-sequence just-in-time (JIT) delivery of fully trimmed seats. The company's financial, technological, and human resources have been committed to establishing dedicated JIT manufacturing facilities in close proximity to customers' assembly plants worldwide. The facilities produce more than 3 million seats annually.

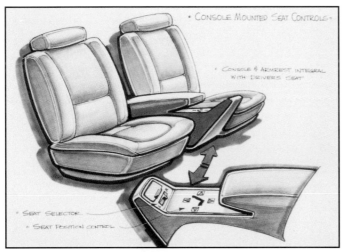

Below Left: Lear designs complete ergonomic seating systems for the ultimate in driving ease and convenience.

Bottom: Lear's innovative engineers are committed to surpassing the industry standard.

Facing Top: Even on the racetrack, drivers trust Lear seating systems for safety and comfort.

Facing Bottom: Computer-aided design and production help create perfect models, manufactured with efficiency.

"At Lear Seating Corp., we accept total responsibility for providing seating systems that meet the highest standards in the industry," says Bob Rossiter, company president. "We prepare for a time in the near future when we will be called upon to provide total interiors—seats, door panels, headliners, console, visors, carpeting, and plastic components."

The global company has 2.5 million square feet of manufacturing and technical facilities at more than 30 locations. The world headquarters also is the site of Lear Automotive Technical Center, which was completed in 1988. The $7-million facility represents a management commitment to product excellence. The center, company officials note, provides the unique, simultaneous link between idea generation, prototype development, and product tooling and manufacturing to pave the way to tomorrow's product innovation.

With more than 10,000 employees worldwide, Lear builds more than 2,500 different option level seat sets in its JIT plants and can adjust production by quickly adding or removing module cells. In addition to its U.S. plants, Lear has facilities in Canada, Mexico, and Europe.

Company officials stress that the JIT program is not just a warehousing or delivery operation. They say it is a complete ma-

and were used in Chevrolet Camaros.

Although advancements have been great since these first trimmed seats, the company has kept the high-performance tag and continued to be leaders in sport and specialty seat applications. These have included vehicles for media presentation, competitive racing, and work on the U.S. Olympic bobsled.

Officials say because of the success of the trimmed seat business and the perceived desire of customers, Lear aids the high-performance seating division. Ideally, the intent is to offer customers accessibility to specialty seating experts. The focus can be aimed at a seat that is styled and engineered similar to a competitive racing seat for a sports car application or for performance criteria for a family sedan.

Lear Seating Corp. strives to continue to be a leader in the seat systems industry, using its computer-aided design and computer-aided manufacturing skills to constantly update and improve its technological abilities.

"Only those companies who have the

terials and facilities management process. Just-in-time delivery is technological expertise, innovative engineering, and teamwork—all moving in unison to provide superior services and products when and where customer assembly facilities need them.

The company was founded in 1917 and has provided the automotive industry with a number of important advances in seating technology, including the first aluminum and plastic structured seating systems, advanced manual and power-activated seat comfort adjustments, proprietary pour-in-place foam processes, and molded seat manufacturing processes.

One of the latest advances that has received international attention is the SurcBond process. It uniquely combines existing mechanical processes and space-age adhesive technology in bonding a wide variety of materials to foam. This eliminates imperfections such as bagging and sagging. A constantly evolving process, SureBond allows automotive interior-design engineers the freedom to design complicated stitching patterns and comfort-enhancing contours that until recently were either too costly or impossibly labor intensive to produce in quantity. Thanks to SureBond, designers are limited only by their imagination and artistic talent, not by the mechanics or archaic production techniques.

Officials say the new freedom has translated into an ability to target and rapidly respond to specific market niches. They point out that just as the consumer now has the freedom to choose from minivans, pickup trucks, high-performance cars, top-of-the-line luxury vehicles, or small, compact economy cars, design engineers now pave the freedom to design interiors that reflect the personality of the vehicles, as well as those of their prospective owners.

One of the newer areas of Lear is its high-performance seating division. Its roots date back to 1980, when Lear began work in the trimmed seat business. The first trimmed seats that rolled off the line were called the Lear high-performance seats

resources to pursue global markets, who can compete by intelligently allocating resources internationally, who can meet both automotive manufacturers' and consumers' demands, who have the commitment to continually work in partnership with secondary suppliers, and who form the strategic alliances with leading-edge experts on ergonomically sound interiors can hope to be an industry leader in the future," says Rossiter.

"Only if we continuously research and identify those market niches that will be economically feasible and provide automakers with seating and interior systems at the lowest possible costs that will meet those specific demands without even the slightest sacrifice in quality can we hope to remain competitive in the future."

Federal-Mogul Corporation

Federal-Mogul Corporation is a worldwide manufacturing and distribution company with its roots buried deeply in the Detroit area. The company produces and distributes precision component parts and is a leader in many of the industries it serves. Officials note with pride that the company's businesses span the globe serving the transportation, farm equipment, construction, and manufacturing industries.

Federal-Mogul's principal products—vehicle and machinery components—are sold to five major markets. They are aftermarket or replacement parts; heavy truck, farm, and construction; auto and light truck; industrial; and aerospace.

Specific products include ball bearings, engine and transmission products, sealing devices, fuel systems, lighting and electrical components, and air bearing spindles. Fastening systems consist of fasteners, installation tools, and power sources.

Federal-Mogul has 37 manufacturing plants in 12 countries, four major research facilities, and more than 70 distribution centers serving 90 countries. The company employs about 12,600 people worldwide.

Officials of the *Fortune* 500 company, which has more than

one billion dollars in sales yearly, stress that Federal-Mogul holds leadership positions as both a manufacturer and distributor—a factor that gives the company a unique competitive advantage. From its distribution center in Jacksonville, Alabama, the firm services markets worldwide. The center, considered one of the most modern, highly computerized material-handling and order-processing operations in the industry, supports a vast network of service centers worldwide. It has 50 million pounds of storage capacity, 27,000 total pallet locations, and two miles of conveyors. In addition, Federal-Mogul has a Free Trade Zone warehouse in Port Everglades, Florida, and export centers in Antwerp, Belgium, and Singapore. Among the company's facilities are 43 service centers in North America and 24 warehouses in 16 countries.

With a constant eye to the future, the company has four major technical centers: two in Ann Arbor, Michigan, one in Irvine, California, and one in St. Louis, Missouri. In addition, it maintains research, development, and quality-control programs at each of its facilities.

Federal-Mogul's history dates back to 1899, when J. Howard Muzzy and Edward F. Lyon formed a Detroit-based firm called Muzzy-Lyon Company, which specialized in the sale of mill and factory supplies. In 1924 the company merged

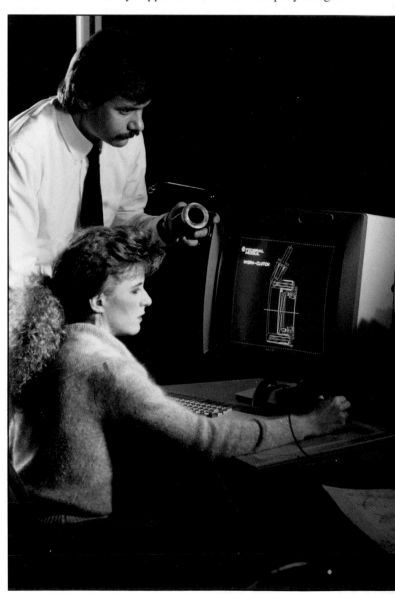

with Federal Bearing and Bushing Company to form Federal-Mogul. The company grew along with the auto industry and the nation. Its world headquarters were moved to Southfield in 1966. Its present-day status includes a number of acquisitions that took place in the 1980s. They included Huck Manufacturing Company (aerospace and industrial fastening systems), Mather Seals (oil seals), Signal-Stat (lighting and safety components), Switches Inc. (electrical components), and Carter Automotive (fuel systems).

The company is focused on five guiding principles that drive its business. One principle is quality—complete customer satisfaction in products and services. The company believes this is crucial to its continued survival in a global environment.

Another principle is customer response. "Our customers are our reason for being. All of our efforts must be directed toward providing them with the best products, services, and value," according to a company spokesman. Other principles are continuous product improvement, respect for all individuals, and ethical conduct in the marketplace.

Federal-Mogul officials are particularly proud of their team concept of management. Employees at all levels not only participate in the day-to-day manufacture and distribution of products, but also make problem-solving decisions. Workers as well as management have a say in the decision-making process.

In addition to the team concept, Federal-Mogul stresses community involvement. The firm donates generously to local and national charities. Also, employees are encouraged to volunteer their services to community civic and service groups.

In keeping with the international scope of the company, Federal-Mogul officials see the firm's global role in business continuing to expand. They note that one-third of the company's business is international and say that the figure will increase significantly in the coming years.

"We want to enhance our worldwide position," says D.J. Gormley, chairman and chief executive officer. "We will have a growing presence around the world."

While the company expects to expand internationally, officials still see it as maintaining a strong presence in Oakland County and southeast Michigan. Presently there are about 800 employees working in the Detroit metropolitan area and a total of 2,200 in Michigan.

Gormley says Oakland County and the City of Southfield are particularly supportive of business, boasting a good road system and fostering excellent business relationships.

"Oakland County is an attractive place to do business," says Gormley. "We're a worldwide company, but our world headquarters is in Southfield and we're proud of our Detroit roots."

Sanyo Machine America Corp.

Sanyo Machine America Corp. has a simple philosophy and goal—it strives to produce the world's best assembly-line equipment. The firm makes production systems for the auto industry and has been at its present Rochester Hills location at Rochester and Avon roads since 1986.

The rationale for the philosophy, officials say, is that if the company produces the best equipment, then its customers can make better products. And consequently, if customers are completely satisfied, then they will remain customers for life.

Sanyo Machine prides itself on being able to design, manufacture, and maintain assembly-line systems from concept to final product. The range of automated systems it has produced is extensive. The systems include engine assemblies for four- and six-cylinder autos, assemblies for motorcycles and lawn mowers, as well as assembly systems for both front and rear axles, steering gear, transmissions, clutches, brakes, and shock absorbers.

Included among the present product lines are friction roller conveyors, electric fastening equipment, robots, precision automatic measurement and inspection equipment, automated welding systems, and jigs.

Generally customers come to the company with a problem that automation and proper design may rectify. For example, Sanyo Machine recently worked with the Pontiac Motor Division to develop and install an automation line that increased space efficiency and reduced the work force. To facilitate the process, Sanyo shared its patents with Pontiac. In addition to designing, manufacturing, and installing a system, Sanyo also does periodic inspections to make sure the line is operating properly.

The company's reputation rests on its ability to provide an original service to customers; all assembly systems are unique. In addition, Sanyo officials point with pride to the fact that their firm has the ability to produce systems capable of assembling an entire automoble.

Below Right: Engineering and design personnel discuss a new project.

Bottom: Sanyo Machine America Corp. headquarters in Rochester Hills.

Facing Top Left and Right: Highly capable systems utilizing flexible automatic and manual tasks, based on a versatile transfer system, solve customer problems.

Facing Bottom: The technological advancements that Sanyo continually seeks are used internally as well as with its own systems. Sanyo strives to challenge tomorrow. Pictured are high tech CAD engineers using the computer to aid in drafting and design.

In addition to assembly-line systems, Sanyo also produces several special machines at its Rochester Hills plant. Chief among them are the Nutrunner and the Programmable Slide.

The Nutrunner is a programmable fastening system used to fasten bolts and tighten screws during the manufacturing process. The Programmable Slide assists in the positioning function of various assembly-system components. Both machines

are offered to the consumer independently or as a component of a multifaceted system.

Sanyo Machine of Rochester Hills originates from Japan, where a similar facility has been long established in the assembly-line systems business. In Japan the company's plant is the leading assembly-line systems manufacturer. In addition, Sanyo owns and operates an assembly plant in Elmira, Canada. The Rochester Hills facility employs about 100 workers while its Canadian counterpart has about 60. The Japanese facility is by far the largest, employing a staff of more than 300.

Sanyo officials stress that the American plant works pri-

marily with American auto companies and is quite independent, but it does have the ability to draw on the home office's technology and expertise.

Along with the company's ability to produce unique assembly-line systems, officials point out that it also has great versatility in its operation. Sanyo is rapidly becoming known as a leading force in its field in the U.S. automotive industry. A credit to the company's professionalism and confidence is its ability to work satisfactorily and efficiently with two competing auto producers simultaneously. An example of this situation could be Ford and General Motor's Saturn Division in the United States, and Toyota and Nissan in Japan.

At the U.S. plant, at least 75 percent of the employees are American and all design and manufacturing teams are led by two individuals, one Japanese and one American. Officials also state that any profits from the U.S. facility are reinvested in North America.

Sanyo Machine attempts to create what it calls a "family feeling" among its workers. It strives to reproduce in the United States the strong sentiment that employees in Japan have for Sanyo. The Japanese have a strong emotional trust and sense of belonging to their employer. Such a beneficial atmosphere helps promote more satisfied workers, who in turn produce better products.

In building a family feeling, company officials say they attempt to stretch resources to ensure that workers are happily producing quality products. The firm strives to meet its employees' needs in the same fashion that it strives to satisfy its customers. One practice that seems to assist both the employee and the customer is the practice of sending employees out to do research so that they can help Sanyo stay on the leading edge of technology.

Sanyo is pleased with the results of its philosophy and accomplishments. From the customer's standpoint, the company feels successful, largely due to the fact that most of its business contracts come from previously satisfied customers.

From the employee standpoint, results also appear to be quite impressive. In Japan, the employee turnover rate is only about 3 percent. In America and Canada, the rate is close to zero, although officials admit that their North American facilities are still relatively new.

"A company is a family," explains Takeshi Horiba, chief operating officer for Sanyo Machine. "We will not sell our company. We are looking for an eternal relationship with our customers."

Although operating relatively independently, the Rochester Hills plant is visited often by Horiba and various other Sanyo officials. To facilitate the smooth interaction between American and Japanese workers, two translators are employed at the plant full time.

Sanyo is pleased with its choice of Oakland County as the site for its U.S. plant. In fact, it presently is expanding the 178,000-square-foot facility by another 20,000 square feet to meet its ever-expanding needs.

The Oakland County Sanyo Machine America Corp. facility is centrally located for the benefit of its automotive customers, officials note. It also offers employees excellent communities to live in with exemplary schools, good commercial transportation, and an experienced technical labor force.

Su-Dan Company

A dedication to quality and customer satisfaction coupled with the excellent teamwork of its employees has made the Su-Dan Company in Rochester Hills a successful stamping and assemblies manufacturer. The company makes products for both the auto and appliance industries. Through its computer-aided design/computer-aided manufacturing (CAD/CAM) capabilities, Su-Dan can take a project from the design concept stage to the finished product.

Its stampings are used in the auto industry for such basic products as armrests, headrests, and ashtrays. In the appliance

Below Left: Su-Dan's various stamping products are used, for example, as door hinges and wheel roller assemblies as well as in automobile armrests, headrests, and ashtrays.

Bottom: Su-Dan's main facility in Rochester Hills.

field, the stampings go for door hinges and wheel roller assemblies. Secondary operations include resistance, spot and projection welding, automatic bolt staking, and riveting. The company's assembly process includes welding, riveting, staking, and other labor-intensive assembly operations.

Su-Dan was founded in 1966 by its current president, Richard Dryden. It has grown from a two-man shop serving a small community to an organization that meets needs worldwide.

Named after Dryden's first two children, Susan and Daniel, the company's main facility in Rochester Hills employs 70 people; however, it still holds the same family atmosphere of its early days. In addition, Su-Dan recently established a second facility in Belton, South Carolina. Together both plants have the capacity to distribute custom production stampings to domestic and world markets

Dennis J. Keat, vice president of Su-Dan, notes the company is proud that most of its business comes from repeat customers who have been more than pleased with the firm's work. The company uses a zero-defects philosophy and makes sure all materials, components, and tooling are of the appropriate quality before the job begins.

"We encourage employee involvement, and I feel that Su-Dan has a definite competitive edge because we use the team approach to management, and we produce quality products," says Dryden. Keat notes that Oakland County is a perfect choice as the Su-Dan Company's base of operations because the firm is close to its customers and its vendors, and the area also offers a quality, skilled work force.

Dryden's objectives for the company are simple and clear. "My goal is to continue with strong, controlled growth and provide a working atmosphere for our employees. We go that extra mile to make sure the job is done right and delivered on time."

Hubert Distributors

Hubert Distributors in Pontiac not only sets industry standards in the beverage-distribution business but also can boast of being a leader in community service. Under the expert leadership of Alice Shotwell Gustafson, president and chief operating officer, the distributorship has earned the Ambassador ranking from the Anheuser-Busch Co. The rating is based on the quality of how a distributorship conducts business and is the highest industry award presented by Anheuser-Busch Co.

"I see our business as one of the most highly automated and functional distributorships in the United States," says Shotwell Gustafson. "We have some of the finest employees anywhere." As a beer and wine wholesaler, she points out that her company has about 50 percent of the market share in its selling area of Oakland County.

Helping keep the distributorship among the best in the industry is the recently completed $6-million warehousing and administrative complex located at Auburn and Opdyke roads in Pontiac. The facility was opened in 1986 and can store 500,000 cases of beer and 8,000 half and quarter barrels in its 118,000-square-foot environmentally controlled warehouse.

Shotwell Gustafson, through both personal involvement and through her company, has made Hubert Distributors one of the largest supporters of community groups and projects. Personal funds from Floyd J. Shotwell and Alice Shotwell Gustafson along with company funds helped convert the former Meadow Brook Farm Riding Ring at Oakland University into the college's Shotwell Gustafson Pavilion. The pavilion is a popular gathering place for business forums and can hold 1,000 people for any type of function. The pavilion also houses the Oakland University Health Enhancement Center. In Pontiac the business is responsible for establishing the Floyd J. Shotwell Recreational Park for the handicapped.

On a personal level, Shotwell Gustafson purchased the Howard Shelly wildlife film collection, which was shown on Mort Neff's "Michigan Outdoors," and donated it to Oakland University. She also was a founding member of the African Heritage Cultural Center.

Hubert Distributors supports an extensive list of local chari-

Below Right: Under the leadership of Alice Shotwell Gustafson, president and chief operating officer, Hubert Distributors has earned Anheuser-Busch Co.'s highest rating.

Bottom: The recently completed $6-million warehousing and administrative complex in Pontiac helps to keep the distributorship among the best in the industry.

ties, including Big Brothers/Big Sisters, Boy Scouts of America, Oakland County R.E.A.C.T., Pontiac Area Urban League, Pontiac Oakland Symphony, Pontiac Lighthouse, United Way of Pontiac/North Oakland, and many others.

The late Floyd J. Shotwell started the distributorship in 1937. Shotwell Gustafson joined the business in 1947 as a file clerk and worked her way up the corporate ladder. She was vice president of the company until 1985, when Shotwell died and she took over the top position.

Although already a well established and recognized business and community leader, Shotwell Gustafson says she will not let Hubert Distributors stand still. "We are already expanding offices and have plans to expand the warehouse in the 1990s to continue our high level of customer service and commitment to the community in Oakland County," she says. "I feel very fortunate that I've had the time and resources to involve myself and the company in extensive community activities, and we will continue to do so."

Numatics Incorporated

William Carls built a better air valve and paved the way for one of the most successful businesses based in Oakland County. Numatics Incorporated, headquartered in Highland Township, started operations in a garage in 1945, and through Carls' persistence and hard work, it has become an international company.

As founder and chief executive officer, Carls has seen Numatics become a company that employs about 700 people worldwide. Numatics has five facilities in Michigan; one in Angola, Indiana; one in Nashville, Tennessee; one in London, Ontario, Canada; one in Bonn, Germany; and Numatics Ltd., north of London, England.

In addition to earning a reputation as an astute businessman and industrialist, Carls has been described as a man of compassion and caring, not just for his employees but for the community as a whole.

"He has always looked at this company as his family," says John Welker, company president. Carls has been associated with Oakland County Children's Village and Children's Hospital of Michigan for many years. Carls says that those who benefit from a free society have an obligation to support that society.

"He is one of our largest benefactors for Children's Hospital in recent times," says Robert A. Jones, vice president/development and public relations for the Detroit hospital. Jones says that Carls, through the William and Marie Carls Foundation, has

Below: The company, headquartered in Highland Township, is now an international operation employing 700 people worldwide.

Facing Top: As founder and chairman of the board, William Carls has guided Numatics to become one of the most successful businesses in Oakland County.

Facing Bottom: Numatics Incorporated began operations in a garage in 1945.

helped the hospital financially since 1985. Jones credits the foundation with providing the initial grant that helped relocate and equip its hearing and speech facility, named the Marie Carls Communication Disorders Center in honor of the late Marie Carls, who suffered from a hearing loss in her later years.

Speaking from a business standpoint, Carls is described as an American who saw the opportunities the country offered an individual and took advantage of them. Born in Germany, Carls immigrated to the United States in 1924 at age 21. He used his four years of experience as an apprentice toolmaker in Germany to work his way up through a series of die shops, including 11 years as a die engineer for Chrysler Corporation. In 1939 he went to Midwest Hydro-Pierce, a precision-machining shop. He managed the company until branching out to become a partner in a contract engineering firm known as B&M Engineering.

In 1944 Carls and two men from Milford, Michigan (Fred Brussels and Roy McLeod), joined forces to form Numatics

Operating Valve Company. They established the first Numatics facility in a three-car garage in Milford in 1945. But it was 1949 when Numatics established itself as the modern company it is today. It was then that Carls invented and patented the lapped spool and floating-sleeve air valve.

The valve, according to Welker, is a device that controls and directs the flow pressure to perform work. Its design was considered a totally new concept that is still used today. It launched Numatics on the growth pattern that led to its present-day size.

In 1951 Carls became the sole owner of the company. The firm moved to its present building in 1956, although the structure has doubled in size five times through expansion since then.

Today the valve is used in many different industries. Numatics services not only the three major auto companies of Ford, General Motors, and Chrysler, but also has customers in the petrochemical, packaging, food processing, plastics, rubber, and transportation industries.

Carls is credited with not only having the genius to invent a product that is so widely in demand, but also with having the ability to market and manufacture the item. "He [Carls] is a rare individual," says Welker. "His success comes through his persistence. His competitors thought his invention would not work—even some of his friends had doubts."

Friends and associates note that hard work was definitely a part of the businessman's life, especially during the early years. They tell the story of how Carls and his first wife, Marie, would personally drive to Detroit-area foundries, sometimes as late as midnight, to pick up castings for the next day's work. Marie, who died in 1981, worked side by side with her husband to make the business a success. William Carls is still active in the company.

The company president notes that technology has, in many respects, made things easier for the company. But he says one thing has not changed.

"Everything he [Carls] did came from the standpoint of quality," says Welker. "We will continue to operate with that in mind."

Although many areas in metropolitan Detroit could have been locations for his business, Carls is known to have a special fondness for the lakes area of Oakland County. In fact, Carls' current home is located near the same lake where he built his first home. The reason for locating Numatics Incorporated in Highland Township is rather simple to explain, friends say: He loved Oakland County, and he wanted to work where he lived.

Digital Equipment Corporation

Oakland County and southeastern Michigan play a major role in the worldwide operations of Digital Equipment Corporation. In addition to serving as the headquarters for the computer company's regional area, much of the company's development and research in Oakland County is the basis for many products used throughout the United States and the world.

"We have an outstanding relationship with such major universities as Lawrence Tech, University of Michigan, Michigan State University, and Oakland University," explains Pamela Cunningham, Digital spokesperson. "Many advancements in technology are being done in southeast Michigan."

The company's presence and commitment to Michigan is strong, with about 850 employees in Oakland County alone, as well as at other facilities in Michigan.

Nationally and internationally, Digital is impressive. A company that was started more than 30 years ago by Kenneth H. Olsen, president, Digital has grown since 1957 to include more than 1,000 sales, service, engineering, administrative, and manufacturing installations in 64 countries. It has about 33.6 million square feet of manufacturing facilities and employs 124,500 people worldwide.

Digital, headquartered in Maynard, Massachusetts, is one of the world's leading manufacturer of network computer systems and services. Its worldwide customer-support services, including customer service, software support, network management,

education and training, and special systems, are consistently rated among the best in the industry, according to independent surveys. "We can design and develop a total turnkey system for a customer," notes Cunningham. "We don't just sell computers—we sell solutions to informational and data problems."

Among the industries to which Digital provides total computing solutions, one of the largest is discrete manufacturing, which includes automotive, electronics, aerospace, plastics, consumer durable goods, and furniture manufacturers. The Digital Customer Center, located in Farmington Hills, is a focal point for customer visits and training activities. It is also one of the corporation's primary facilities used for the development and testing of

Facing Top: The VAX 6000-460.

Facing Bottom: The Printserver 20 is one of the products that has helped Digital to become one of the world's leading manufacturers of network computer systems.

Below: The DECstation 2100.

key Digital products for the discrete manufacturing market. The Digital facility in Farmington Hills complements the district headquarters on Orchard Hill Place. The building is located off Interstate 275 and Haggerty Road in Novi.

Through its employees and modern facilities, Digital is able to service a variety of customers. Those in the discrete manufacturing industry include GM/EDS, Ford, Chrysler, Eaton, Rockwell, and TRW. Customers in the process industry include Dow Chemical, Du Pont, and Borg-Warner. Digital has financial services and insurance customers such as Bank One, National Bank of Detroit, Comerica, Nationwide Insurance, and Alexander Hamilton. In the general business sector, it serves K mart, Kroger, Compuware, and numerous regional accounting firms.

Digital also services customers in government, including U.S. Department of Defense affiliate groups such as Wright-Patterson Air Force Base, Fort Knox, NASA, and the Veterans Administration.

Digital's community involvement extends beyond the business sector. The company has been involved in supporting organizations such as the United Way, Detroit Urban League, and the Girl Scouts. Recently Digital sponsored a Computer Discovery series in Farmington Hills aimed at providing Girl Scouts with insights into the world of computers and to pro-

vide opportunities for them to see that science, mathematics, and computer technology are exciting and fun.

Digital also is a strong supporter of the National Association for the Advancement of Colored People. It has been particularly active in participating in the NAACP's annual convention, which was in Detroit in 1989. Digital has been active in the NAACP's Afro-academic, cultural, technological, and scientific Olympics program since the early 1980s.

The program honors talented high school minority youths for academic achievement. Competition for awards begins at the local level and progresses to national contests. Local competitions are held in a number of categories, including humanities, science, performing arts, and visual arts. Top winners can proceed to compete with youths from nationwide in finals held during the NAACP's national convention. The program is rooted in the conviction that blacks can succeed in the classroom at the same superior levels of achievement they consistently display in the athletic arena.

Olsen, Digital's founder, is considered one of the most successful entrepreneurs in American history. He started the company with about $70,000 and in 30 years turned it into a company with $7.6 billion in annual revenues. Today Digital Equipment Corporation is looking for continued growth in Oakland County and southeastern Michigan as a key factor.

"We attribute growth to the willingness to make investments in people and dollars," says Cunningham. "We like Oakland County because it's centrally located on major thoroughfares and close to major airports. So we can easily service Oakland and Wayne County customers. Oakland County is a hub for Digital in this area. There's a lot of growth and development in Oakland County that is very attractive to a company like Digital. I see us maintaining a strong presence here."

General Motors

General Motors' presence in Oakland County is strong, and the contributions of its local facilities are impressive. Together the county operations perform many vital functions for the world-renowned automaker.

GM's Oakland County facilities include the world headquarters for the Truck and Bus Group, the Buick-Oldsmobile-Cadillac (B-O-C) Group's Orion plant, the Pontiac operations of the Chevrolet-Pontiac-General Motors of Canada (C-P-C) Group, the Pontiac Division, and the GM Service Parts Operations plants in Pontiac and Drayton Plains.

The Truck and Bus Group has become one of the largest and most important parts of GM's worldwide business. Two office buildings in the Phoenix Center in downtown Pontiac house the administrative activities of the group.

The group, with its 43,000 employees, is responsible for the engineering and manufacturing of GM trucks. The group operates 12 manufacturing and assembly plants in nine U.S cities.

The facilities produce light- and medium-duty trucks, school-bus chassis, and special-vehicle chassis. Six of the plants are in Michigan, including Pontiac, Flint, and Detroit. The Pontiac facilities assemble Chevrolet C/K and GMC Sierra full-size pickups, Chevrolet S-10 Blazer and GMC S-15 Jimmy sport utility vehicles, Chevrolet S-10 and GMC Sonoma compact pickups, and commercial and special-vehicle chassis.

The GMC Truck Division, which is also part of the group, handles sales and service of GMC Truck products, primarily through a dealer network. It coordinates light-duty marketing with Chevrolet and handles medium-duty marketing for Chev-

rolet dealers. The Truck and Bus Group itself, without the balance of GM operations, would rank in the top 25 of the *Fortune* 500 companies in America.

It is no mystery why GM has established its truck world headquarters in Pontiac. The area has been a truck manufacturing center for GM since the early 1900s. Its truck-building roots stretch back to 1900 and two part-time Detroit inventors, Max and Morris Grabowsky. The brothers designed and built a chain-driven truck powered by a horizontal gasoline engine capable of speeds up to 10 miles per hour at a time when hauling generally was done in horse-drawn wagons.

The success of the truck prompted the Grabowskys to form the Rapid Motor Vehicle Company and build a new plant in Pontiac. Sales boomed and the facility prospered. In 1909 it was one of the 22 companies that William Durant formed into the General Motors Corporation.

GM and its truck facilities in Pontiac grew and changed with the times. In mid-1981 the GM Truck and Bus Group was formed to consolidate and strengthen GM Truck and Bus operations worldwide. In September 1982 GMC Truck and Coach manufacturing and assembly operations were combined with several GM Assembly Division and Chevrolet Motor Division truck plants into a single new division—the Truck and Bus Manufacturing Division, now called Truck and Bus Operations.

Through the 1980s the Truck and Bus Group continued to spearhead advancements in truck engineering and production. In 1985 a versatile mid-size van was introduced. Marketed as the GMC Safari and the Chevrolet Astro, it is smaller than conventional full-size vans, but has more room than a typical compact van. In 1987 Truck and Bus introduced an all-new full-size pickup truck, marketed as the GMC Sierra and Chevrolet C/K pickup.

Facing: General Motors' Truck and Bus Group world headquarters are located in Pontiac, Michigan.

Below Left: The Truck and Bus Group, with its 43,000 employees, is responsible for the engineering and manufacturing of GM trucks in 12 plants in nine U.S. cities.

Top Right: The GMC S-15 Jimmy Sport Utility is engineered and built by the GM Truck and Bus Group.

Bottom Right: The beautiful 1991 Pontiac Grand Prix STE is manufactured at the company's operations facility in Oakland County.

The divisional marketing and administration responsibilities for GMC Truck and Chevrolet medium-duty trucks were consolidated within GMC Truck Division in 1987. In 1989 a redesigned medium-duty truck was introduced and marketed as the GMC TopKick and the Chevrolet Kodiak. The 1980s saw truck production skyrocket. Sales doubled as customers switched from passenger cars to trucks.

Another GM facility in the county that is a showpiece of high-tech, quality production is the B-O-C Orion Township plant. It produces Cadillac Fleetwoods, Sedan DeVilles, and Coupe DeVilles as well as the Oldsmobile 98 Regency and the Oldsmobile Touring Sedan.

The plant is impressive in many ways. From a statistical standpoint the numbers are awesome. It is one of the largest manufacturing assembly facilities in the world, with 3.7 million square feet (or 77 acres of space) under one roof. The plant's 6,400 employees work two shifts that produce about 230,000 automobiles a year.

Ground was broken for the plant in 1980, with the first car

rolling off the line in 1983. The high-tech plant features 157 robots plus 150 operations that are performed by fixed automated equipment. The difference, officials note, is that robots can be reprogrammed to perform different functions fairly quickly and easily. However the fixed automation processes must be modified, or even redesigned, when changes to the cars are made.

But people also play a critical role in the plant's operation. To fulfill the company's goal of commitment to quality and customer satisfaction, the Orion plant uses a special team concept in its operations. Employees meet in groups of 10 to 15 to discuss quality and production problems.

Public tours of the impressive facility guide 50,000 people each year through the plant. These visitors range from local officials and residents to state legislators, congressmen, and business executives from all over the world. Probably the most prominent visitor to the plant was President Ronald Reagan, who came for special dedication ceremonies in July 1984.

Turning to another GM facility in the county, the Pontiac manufacturing operations in Oakland have changed extensively over the years. But its role as a key part of the company has remained constant. The 450-acre facility in Pontiac is now part of the C-P-C Group and is called C-P-C Pontiac Manufacturing Operations. Originally it was a complete manufacturing complex that included foundry work and auto assembly operations.

Today C-P-C Pontiac Manufacturing Operations employs 4,980 people. Operations now include the manufacturing of components and final assembly of the 2.5-liter and 2.0-liter engines. The 2.5-liter engine is used in several GM vehicles including the Pontiac Grand Am, Oldsmobile Cutlass Calais, Buick Somerset Regal, as well as specific small-truck applications such as the Chevy S-10 and GMC Sonoma compact pickup trucks, Chevrolet Astro, and GMC Safari vans. The 2.0-liter engine is used in the Pontiac Sunbird.

The pressed-metal operation at the site produces major metal panels such as hoods and fenders for the Oldsmobile Toronado, Cadillac Seville, Buick Riviera, Pontiac Bonneville, and Pontiac Firebird. It also manufactures metal for bumper and suspension systems, plastic applications of various interior and exterior trim components used in a multitude of GM vehicles, and trailing axles for GM's front-wheel-drive automobiles.

The C-P-C Engineering North Building on the site includes Advanced Vehicle Development. Together with the Advanced Engine Development group, located on Brown Road, C-P-C Engineering North and its 1,200 workers are expected to take GM into the twenty-first century.

Also part of the C-P-C Group is the Pontiac Division. Pontiac Division's primary responsibility, as the name implies, is to market and sell Pontiac nameplate vehicles. The administration building, located in Pontiac, is the world headquarters for the GM's Pontiac Division. In addition to its Oakland County site, various marketing offices throughout the United States work with Pontiac dealers.

The division is responsible for the Pontiac LeMans, Sunbird, Grand Am, Grand Prix, Bonneville, Trans Sport van, Firebird, and the Pontiac 6000. About 800 employees analyze the auto market and determine what area's efforts will be made to promote the Pontiac models. A sales staff in the division works with dealerships on various sales techniques.

Pontiac Division officials also deal with advertising agencies and research marketing firms in promoting Pontiac. There are division representatives who consult with dealership service departments to improve customer service and satisfaction. Further enhancing this objective is a special Customer

Assistance Center that is part of Pontiac. The center allows people who buy Pontiacs to contact the division directly if they have any questions or problems.

An integral part of any automaker's business is producing and supplying spare parts for the cars it makes. To fulfill this purpose, GM has Service Parts Operations, which includes two major plants in Oakland County—one in Pontiac and the other one in Drayton Plains.

These plants act as a master warehouse, distributing parts to Parts Distribution Centers throughout the United States. These centers then supply GM dealers with parts. The sprawling, 1.8-million-square-foot plant in Pontiac does not manufacture the parts, but packages and distributes them.

However, the plant does more than just ship to GM parts centers. GM uses the Pontiac facility to conduct its Target Program, whereby dealers buy parts in volume directly from the SPO center, allowing the dealer and GM to be more competitive in the parts market.

Also, since 1985, the Pontiac plant has been responsible for distributing many AC Delco parts. These include spark plugs, oil filters, and air filters that go not only to GM dealers but also to retail auto-parts outlets that sell directly to the public. As an example, every AC spark plug, at some time, comes out of the Pontiac plant.

The Drayton Plains plant has a more basic function than its Pontiac counterpart. It is a basic service parts operation. The plant packages parts and ships them throughout the United States. The 1.28-million-square-foot Drayton Plains plant ships an average of 2,600 dealer orders a day. The parts include bigger items, such as front end panels, grilles, and plastic parts, as well as small parts used throughout the vehicle.

The community involvement of the plant's 800 employees is exceptional, and many are active as volunteers. The General Motors Drayton Plains facility views itself as a solid, integral part of Oakland County as it contributes not only as a business but also to the welfare of the community.

UAW-GM Human Resource Center

As the twenty-first century grows near, the United Auto Workers and General Motors Corporation are continuing to forge a much-improved labor-management relationship. Gone are the days of the old adversarial approach and cantankerous confrontations. In place is a new commitment toward working together to develop joint solutions to common problems.

This new relationship has been prompted by demands for greater job security for workers and unprecedented competition in the global economy. Today the UAW and General Motors enjoy one of the most harmonious relationships in their often-tumultuous history—from the contract bargaining table to the plant floor.

The UAW, America's largest industrial trade union, and General Motors, the world's largest manufacturer, are jointly creating a variety of unique and innovative programs that are often the model for how American industry relates to its workers.

Unlike ever before, workers are receiving greater recognition for their contributions. In fact, UAW-represented GM workers now enjoy the most lucrative job and income protection plan found in American industry.

Furthermore, UAW-GM workers are being given a stronger voice in quality decisions, leading to substantial improvements in the quality of GM cars and trucks and, consequently, in a higher level of customer satisfaction by American consumers.

For many years the cornerstone of the UAW-GM relationship has been the numerous joint education and training programs that have helped make UAW-GM workers more productive, both on and off the job. Virtually all of the current 300,000 UAW-represented GM workers, as well as the company, have benefited.

"Keeping pace with technology in today's workplace isn't enough," says Don Davis, UAW administrative assistant. "We must provide workers with the support they need to reach their full potential. We need to help develop the total person of all our workers."

Rich McMillan, GM general director of joint education activities, agrees. "Training must be responsive to current and future work needs, as well as personal development

Bottom Left: The United Auto Workers and General Motors Corporation work together to develop solutions to common problems.

Bottom Right: In 1986 the UAW-GM Human Resources Center was established in Auburn Hills to develop and administer joint education and training programs.

goals," says McMillan. "We must form the basis for a competitive organization."

To achieve these goals, the UAW-GM Human Resource Center was established in 1986 to develop and administer joint education and training programs. Located in the Oakland County community of Auburn Hills, the jointly funded Human Resource Center has become an integral part of the UAW-GM system, providing job-related technical training, basic-education enhancement and interpersonal skills training.

Since 1984, the UAW and General Motors have jointly committed more than $1.2 billion to the training, development, and retraining of its work force.

Understanding that education doesn't stop at the schoolhouse door, the UAW and General Motors have recognized the need for work-based competency training, and they are expanding it to include every person who is a part of the corporation.

In addition, the UAW and GM continue to develop new partnerships with public education, striving to improve educational opportunities for today's youths—America's work force of the future.

Historically, American industry's greatest competitive advantage in the worldwide marketplace has been its creativity, individuality, and sheer enterprise. With the understanding that the joint spirit between the United Auto Workers and General Motors recognizes people as their most valuable resource, it is clear that the new cooperative relationship will ensure a future in which these virtues can flourish.

Universal Flow Monitors, Inc.

Universal Flow Monitors, Inc., is a business that has grown and changed over the years in transitional stages that have been basically smooth and fluid. The company, based in Hazel Park, makes devices that measure the flow of liquids and gases.

"Our devices are basically safety devices—making sure machinery is getting the lubricants or coolants they need," explains Erik J. Rosaen, secretary/treasurer of the company.

Erik Rosaen, and his cousin, Lars Rosaen, who is president of the company, are the present owners. But the firm and its products can be traced back to Oscar Rosaen, grandfather of the present owners. As the business changed hands from different family members, the product itself has evolved in a logical order.

Oscar Rosaen and his sons, Borje and Nils, started a hydraulic-pump design and manufacturing business. Borje is Erik's father, and Nils is Lars' father. In the 1960s, when the cousins began to learn the business, the factory switched from making pumps to making filters for industrial customers. In the 1970s the firm began manufacturing flow meters.

"We have a typical small-business structure," says Erik Rosaen. "Lars does the books and makes the flow devices, and I sell them. It's awfully hard to transfer a business from one generation to another," he adds. "If you do it successfully, it's because there are clear lines of responsibility."

Bottom Left: Eric J. Rosaen, secretary and treasurer (left), and Lars Rosaen, president.

Bottom Right: Each flow meter is carefully calibrated.

Universal Flow was incorporated by Borje and Nils Rosaen in 1963. Their sons took over in the late 1970s. The business has remained in Hazel Park, but it has been expanded over the years. Today there are more than 50 employees in a facility of about 45,000 square feet. Expansion has usually come through the acquisition of adjacent buildings, Erik Rosaen notes.

The company started out with a basic flow meter design, a safety-switch type device, he says. "Now the meters are updated, state-of-the-art devices that can interface with computers."

Dealing completely with industrial clients, Universal Flow's customers include those in the automotive industry, as well as rubber and steel industries. Erik says there are also some power companies and mining firms that use the flow devices.

Some of the recent changes at the factory, notes Lars, include computerizing the facility and modernizing machinery. He says the company will soon produce different types of flow meters.

Erik Rosaen says he is very pleased with Universal Flow's location, both from a city and county standpoint. "Oakland County has the availability of people and resources the factory needs and is close to customers," he says. "And Hazel Park is a good place to do business. There's a sense of community, partly because many employees live nearby."

The owner says he also likes making flow devices. "It's a nice business to be in because the more people automate, the more they want monitoring equipment like ours. The market is always expanding."

Hegenscheidt Corporation

Hegenscheidt Corporation in Troy is a modern machine-tool facility with a proud history. It is associated with an international company, but it succeeds as an independent business.

"We design and manufacture," explains Werner Wodtke, vice president and general manager of the Troy factory. "We have to stand on our own two feet."

The company, which sells in the United States, Canada, and Mexico, deals predominantly with the automotive, railroad, and transit industries. It is involved in providing machines to maintain train wheels that have been worn down from use. The company also produces machinery used in the production of automotive crankshafts and transmissions. The 12,500-square-foot facility with its 33 employees produced revenues of $9.5 million for the 1988-1989 fiscal year.

"We are essentially problem solvers," says Wodtke. "We don't get involved unless a company has a fatigue or strength requirement in its crankshaft production or specialized needs for its transmission manufacturing."

The Michigan company was incorporated in 1966 and rented facilities in Oak Park until constructing and moving into its Troy building in 1969.

The affiliate company is Hegenscheidt GmbH, based in West Germany. It does business in more than 90 countries worldwide, with the Troy facility serving as its North American branch. It began in what was East Germany in 1889 as the Hegenscheidt Company and produced metal items. Over the years the company evolved into a special machine-tool manufacturer for the production of wheel lathes. By 1939 it had three factories and employed about 3,000 people. After World War II, the company relocated to West Germany and resumed making wheel lathes.

About 60 percent of the Troy factory's business comes from the automotive industry, including the Big Three auto manufacturers of GM, Ford, and Chrysler. Another 30 percent comes from the railroad and transit industry, with the balance involving miscellaneous industries.

"We needed to be and wanted to be close to product design facilities such as the GM Tech. Center," says Wodtke. "All of what we need in the way of parts, supplies, and other resources are made for us by companies in the Detroit area. It's a very basic reason why we decided to locate in Oakland County. And Oakland County is a good location from the standpoint of having major expressways and being close to major airports."

Wodtke says expansion is definitely in the future for the Troy plant, but it may not come quickly, as it depends on the economy. "Our counterparts in West Germany are working on a variety of products that will be beneficial here."

Also, Wodtke notes, although Detroit may have lost some of its dominance in the world auto market, Hegenscheidt will still play an important role in the development of machinery for the world cars of the future. "For that reason," he says, "we need to have a presence here to be in the forefront of things to come."

Quality of Life

Medical, educational, and service institutions contribute to the quality of life of Oakland County area residents.

Photo by Balthazar Korab

Economic Development Division

The Economic Development Division (EDD) of Oakland County was established in 1983 with the mission of fostering the creation of jobs by assisting in new business start-ups, business retention, and business relocation. Jobs remain an important goal of EDD, in addition to continuing prosperity and improving the quality of life in Oakland County.

"We're in the business of promoting Oakland County for the purpose of creating jobs," explains Marlys Vickers, supervisor of marketing and research for EDD. "But also we assist businesses in making investment decisions in Oakland County, whether the investments are to finance development projects, expand existing businesses, or help a new business move into the county."

Jeffrey A. Kaczmarek, manager of EDD, heads a staff of 13 people. The EDD is part of the county's Department of Community and Economic Development, directed by Joseph D. Joachim, under the county executive Daniel T. Murphy.

The EDD fulfills its mission of creating jobs through work in six major program areas: area development, community assistance, small-business development, financing, research and analysis, and marketing.

Area development representatives respond to requests from businesses for assistance or information and work with prospective county companies. The EDD helps manufacturing businesses that want to locate or relocate in Oakland County with industrial building and site searches. With a list of sites or buildings that meet their criteria, businesses then seek the

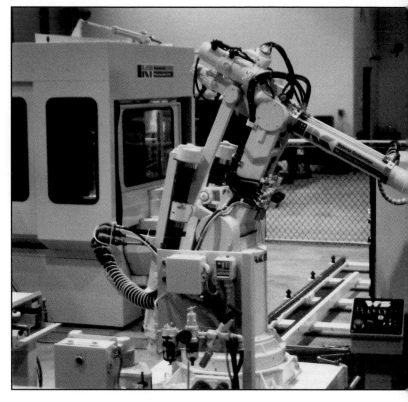

appropriate real estate broker.

"We do not engage in any negotiations for property," explains Vickers. "Rather we provide services for companies who do not want to commit to a specific broker."

The area development representatives also make retention calls. Existing businesses are visited by EDD staff members in conjunction with local communities and are provided with economic data and business information. Staff members also make presentations to business groups such as rotary clubs and chambers of commerce.

Community assistance programs help individual communities by providing marketing support and supplying financial information or advice on economic development projects. For example, the EDD provided project guidance and technical support to the Interstate 696 coordinating committee and helped the city of Rochester in planning its retail recruitment program. Oxford also received assistance in financing the infrastructure of an industrial park. The EDD small-business development program provides professional counseling to small-business owners and start-up businesses.

Administrative and technical support is provided by staff to the county's development finance company—the Local Development Company. The LDC is responsible for packaging small-business loans through the SBA 504 loan program. The loan portfolio has grown since 1983 to a total of 52 loans in 1990. The value has risen to $12.7 million.

Research conducted by EDD contributes to understanding the county economy and improves the quality of county-wide economic, demo-

Facing Top: The Computer Integrated Manufacturing (CIM) laboratory at Oakland Community College in Auburn Hills was developed and is operated in partnership with private industry.

Facing Bottom: The county labor pool is skilled and technically sophisticated, and training occurs continually to keep pace with the changing demands of industry.

Below Right: Galleria Office Park is typical of the quality space constructed for corporate office buildings during the 1980s.

Bottom: Since there are more than 450 lakes in the county, lake living and year-round recreation are part of Oakland County's life-style.

graphic, and physical data available to businesses. Econometric forecasts of county employment and generic and customized business information and research are available for clients. Between 1,500 and 1,600 inquiries are received each year from companies who want to make a financial investment or locate in the county. Community profiles on each municipality in the county and a comprehensive county profile are produced by EDD.

The Oakland Focus, a quarterly newsletter published by the EDD, is widely distributed to county business people. Workshops for businesses and municipal officials are cosponsored with utilities and agencies that provide economic development services. Topics vary from marketing and finance to economic development and communications.

Overseeing the EDD programs is the Oakland County Community Growth Alliance (CGA). Certified by the governor in 1986, the CGA is an advisory organization of public- and private-sector representatives appointed by the county executive. The CGA coordinates activities of the more than 165 agencies in the county that provide economic development services. Staffed by EDD, the CGA provides guidance on economic de-

velopment issues to the county as well as to local communities and economic development agencies throughout the county.

The purposes of the CGA are to recommend the scope of economic development services to be rendered available by county and local service providers, serve as a link between local agencies and the state, and distribute information to businesses about services available through local, state, and federal programs.

Economic Development Division staffers are pleased with their divisional accomplishments and are confident about the future. "We will continue to do the outstanding job we have done in the past for businesses and communities," says Vickers. "We will continue to be the business advocates for jobs but will take steps to enhance the quality of life in Oakland County through helping businesses and communities."

The City of Southfield

The City of Southfield, Oakland County's largest, offers life's best to those living and doing business in the area.

The community was incorporated in 1958 and, during the past 32 years, has earned a reputation as the state's office capital, serving as home to more than 6,000 businesses and 86 *Fortune* 500 corporations. Because of its office industry base, the residential population of 85,000 swells to more than 250,000 each day.

"As the hub of southeastern Michigan and the heart of the metropolitan area, Southfield has it all," states Mayor Donald F. Fracassi, adding that the city offers easy access via major state and interstate expressways, simplifying travel to places far and near; is Michigan's premier business center; has sophisticated city living, as well as lush, tree-lined neighborhoods, the most exciting retail shopping, the finest in dining and entertainment, and a nationally recognized educational system that draws families seeking only the best for their children.

Southfield's business community continues to grow. "If you're in Southfield, you're in business," says Fracassi. "We are recognized as Michigan's office center and offer an unparalleled business climate. Our easy accessibility to every major Michigan expressway is a primary asset, and we are only 20 minutes from downtown or the airport. Southfield is the choice of Michigan's leading enterprises, and we are proud to lead Oakland County in foreign investment firms. In addition to our strong business environment, gracious living is our hallmark. We offer the rural seclusion of peaceful neighborhoods nestled beside country streams in wooded settings."

The city boasts of a generous mix of living facilities, from traditional single-family homes in subdivisions to modern condominiums, town houses, and high-rise apartments.

Officials say Southfield combines the convenience of a modern, thriving city with the charm of gracious living. Hous-

ing values range from $65,000 to $250,000.

Fracassi also boasts that Southfield has varied cultural, educational, and entertainment facilities, as well as nearly 50 churches and synagogues for spiritual fulfillment. For the gourmet palate, the restaurant offerings range from continental to deli. Specialty shops tempt with imported wines, cheeses, chocolates, fruits, pastries, and other delicacies. Many of the shops are located in sophisticated shopping centers, which also

Facing Top: The Prudential Town Center has become the city's signature landmark office complex.

Facing Bottom: Victor Center, one of the community's many new office buildings, features unique architectural design and houses the offices for Plante & Moran, a national CPA firm.

Below Left: Southfield features nearly 100 different neighborhoods that provide housing in all styles and price ranges. Pictured is a typical home in the Stonycroft area of central Southfield.

Below Right: Chanticleer, one of Southfield's outstanding condominium complexes, offers pastoral living in the heart of the city.

feature the latest in fashion, from designer originals to quality merchandise at a variety of prices.

"Southfield's municipal services are unparalleled and are another key reason why discerning residents select the city as their home," Fracassi explains.

The Southfield Public Library features more than 200,000 volumes and 1,000 videocassettes. In addition, it has computers and software for public use; a computerized business reference service interfacing with international data bases; and is one of Michigan's official census information centers.

The city's parks and recreation programs and facilities include two municipal golf courses, baseball diamonds, tennis courts, an ice arena, two municipal swimming pools, a water slide, and neighborhood playgrounds. Private tennis, golf, and swimming clubs also are located within or near neighborhoods.

Southfield's emergency medical services serve as a national model for communities throughout the country, and residents benefit from superior police and fire services. The city also offers a full schedule of leisure-time activities for all ages. Annual programs include the International Folk Dance Festival, the Original Old World Market, Michigan the Bountiful (an afternoon of gourmet delights from Michigan), an annual ice show, Fourth of July celebration, and other special programs.

There are numerous day-care centers and preschools, and the public school system ranks among the best in the nation in

student achievement, per-pupil expenditures, and pupil/teacher ratio. About 84 percent of Southfield's graduates continue their studies at the university level. Several private schools and institutions also are located in Southfield, including Lawrence Technological University, Michigan's largest private college.

"Our children are our most precious asset, and if you're looking for a good community in which to raise a family, Southfield is the place," comments Fracassi. "Since some of the biggest reasons for moving to a community are the little ones, make your move to Southfield—you and your children will be glad you did."

For information about Southfield's housing opportunities, the City's Housing and Neighborhood Center offers personalized service to answer questions on housing, schools, shopping, and recreation, all available free of charge. The City's Economic Development Division and the Planning Department also provide business development or relocation information. City offices are located at 26000 Evergreen Road.

"Ultimately, Southfield is about families," Fracassi summarizes. "We are dedicated to families, neighborhoods, shared values, and a wholesome quality of life. This city's foundation was built on desirable family housing, and it remains one of our most important values. We're a community in the truest and warmest sense of the word."

Oakland Community College

Oakland Community College received a mandate in 1964 from the people of Oakland County to provide higher education classes to local residents. OCC has more than lived up to its obligation, and today it is not only one of the finest community colleges in Michigan, but is receiving national recognition.

Its varied curriculum and programs annually serve 70,000 students attending five campuses strategically located throughout the county. Because it is accredited by the North Central Association of Colleges and Schools, credits earned at OCC can be transferred to any major university in the United States. More than 40 percent of the students plan to transfer to four-year colleges. The other 60 percent are in career training and enhancement programs or have undeclared majors.

While the credits can be used anywhere in the United States, surveys indicate OCC students usually stay close to home, attending such local major universities as Michigan State, the

Below Left: Students can earn credits in core science courses such as biology at four of OCC's campuses.

Bottom: OCC's Auburn Hills campus is home to the Advanced Technology Center.

Facing Top: Oakland Community College offers health science programs in such fields as dental hygiene, nursing, emergency medical technology, and medical laboratory technology. These students are participating in the nursing program at the Highland Lakes campus.

Facing Bottom: The stylish library is a showpiece building on OCC's beautiful Orchard Ridge campus in Farmington Hills.

University of Michigan, Wayne State, Oakland University, or Eastern, Central, and Western Michigan universities.

OCC offers two types of degrees. The preprofessional associate degree is earned by students who plan to transfer to four-year universities. They enter the major college as juniors. Studies have shown that those students earn a higher grade point average at major universities than students who have attended the school since they were freshmen. Preprofessional degrees are available at OCC in six general areas: business administration, pre-international commerce, liberal arts, fine arts (visual), science, and pre-engineering.

Also, OCC offers career associate degrees primarily designed to give students the credentials needed for work in more than 100 technical and semiprofessional occupations. The four major categories of career programs include business and office programs such as accounting, data processing, and food-service management; health science programs in such fields as dental hygiene, nursing, emergency medical technology, and medical laboratory technology; industrial and technology programs such as automotive technology, computer-aided design, and electronics; and public service programs such as mental health/social work, criminal justice, and gerontology.

In addition, certificates are available in most career programs showing a student completed certain courses. Also offered is an associate degree in general studies that allows students flexibility in class selection.

OCC's business programs have proven particularly popular. Also, officials note that the school's nursing program has earned special recognition because 90 percent of its graduates pass the state exams on the first try, and the other 10 percent pass the exam on their second try.

Of particular interest is OCC's computer-integrated manufacturing (CIM) program. The program involves computer manufacturing and has a complete, functioning assembly line used for educational purposes. Located at the Auburn Hills campus, which is near the rapidly growing Oakland Technology Park, CIM was developed in a partnership with the IBM, Cross & Trecker, and Kennametal corporations. The companies supply OCC with the latest high-technology equipment. In return, OCC uses the equipment to train not only those businesses' employees but other students interested in high-tech manufacturing. The program has become a model for similar ones throughout the nation.

In addition to Auburn Hills, OCC's campuses include Highland Lakes, situated in the rolling countryside of Union Lake, west of Pontiac; Orchard Ridge in Farmington Hills; Royal Oak in the downtown Royal Oak business district; and the Southfield campus, located near many of the county's major health and office facilities.

Also part of OCC is the Pontiac Center, established to work with the Pontiac community. In addition, OCC has numerous extension centers established in local high schools. OCC covers 540 acres, has 54 major buildings, 350 classrooms and laboratories, and about 760 employees, including 275 faculty members.

OCC is an open-door institution where admission to classes is available to all high school graduates, transfer students, and people over 18 years old. A selection process is necessary in some specialized programs.

Oakland County residents approved establishment of OCC in 1964 and authorized the levying of a mill property tax to support the college. Despite inflation over the past 25 years, the original one mill tax continues to financially support the college. Tuition at OCC is among the lowest in the state.

OCC is governed by a volunteer board of trustees elected by the voters. Seven people serve staggered six-year terms.

OCC's interim chancellor, Richard Thompson, says the college is at capacity, and he does not expect that to change soon. "Oakland County is going to grow, and so there will be more need for our services," he says.

Thompson also says he expects the average age of OCC's student population to continue to be older than four-year colleges because many of those taking classes at OCC are doing so to either update their professional skills or enhance their general education.

"Learning for professional and personal reasons is a lifetime proposition," says Thompson. "We are here to satisfy that need."

Lawrence Technological University

Lawrence Technological University is widely recognized for providing a quality education to its students and also working comprehensively with local business and industry. One of Michigan's largest independent universities, Lawrence Tech enrolls 5,500 students. It was named after its founders and first presidents, Russell E. and E. George Lawrence.

Both engineers, the Lawrence brothers were determined to make a university education accessible and affordable. The program they and the faculty developed in 1932 was one of the first in the nation to offer both day programs as well as a fully scheduled evening college for students who held jobs concurrent with academic studies. For student convenience, most programs are still available day or night or in some combination of the two. Classes begin as early as 8 a.m. and run as late as 11 p.m. The university has four student bodies, according to its extended hours. There is the day baccalaureate session, the evening baccalaureate program, evening associate, and evening graduate courses.

Originally specializing only in engineering, Lawrence Tech has gradually broadened its range of classes. Today it offers more than 30 degree programs and course concentrations through the College of Architecture and Design, College of Arts and Science, College of Engineering, and College of Management. Degrees are granted at the associate, baccalaureate, and graduate levels.

The university is accredited by the North Central Association of Colleges and Schools, and some programs have additional professional accreditation. Evening master of business administration and master of engineering in manufacturing systems programs have been added within the last two years.

Below Left: The Wayne H. Buell Management Building, Lawrence Tech's newest academic facility, reflects the university's growth in recent years.

Below Right: Students and faculty interact in an information-sharing environment.

Facing Top: All students have access to the university's outstanding computer facilities.

Facing Bottom Left: Lawrence Tech's experienced faculty teach practical courses that focus on real-world solutions.

Facing Bottom Right: In the past decade the number of laboratories and technological facilities on campus has more than doubled.

Lawrence Tech's 100-acre campus in Southfield includes eight major buildings that offer classrooms and laboratories as well as a University Housing Center, Campus Affairs and Activities Center, library, and recreational field house. All buildings on campus have been built since the university moved to Southfield from Highland Park in 1955. Construction projects totaling more than $20 million have taken place since 1981.

Lawrence Tech's location, on Ten Mile Road and the Lodge Freeway, just south of Interstate 696, makes travel to campus particularly convenient from throughout southeastern Michigan. Considered more important is that the university is surrounded by some of the world's leading technological industries. This proximity to the latest advancements in technology, management, manufacturing, engineering, and architecture enhances student exposure to current professional activity and increases the immediate value the university's graduates offer employers.

The university's Edward Donley Computer Center is continually enhanced and upgraded, providing students and staff superlative resources for academic, administrative, and communication support. All students, faculty, and staff are electronically linked through the university's mainframe VAX cluster. Students use the computer to receive and send homework assignments, compose essays, do research, and contact other students, faculty, and staff

directly, up to and including the president of the university. There are several hundred open terminals scattered throughout the campus. In addition, students have "dial up" access through modems at home or at work.

Lawrence Tech's faculty members are widely recognized for their professional achievement and experience in commerce, science, and industry. In addition to possessing outstanding academic credentials, most faculty have ongoing professional experience in actual work situations. This attribute provides students with the unique educational perspective that is embodied in the university motto "Theory and Practice."

Nearly 40 student clubs and professional organizations provide campus leadership, social, and career-preparation opportunities. The university's new Don Ridler Field House offers a variety of recreational facilities, including a 1,500-seat gym, weight and conditioning room, running track, and ball courts. More than half of Lawrence Tech's students participate in intramural sports programs.

Most of the students commute and come primarily from the greater Detroit area. However, there are students attending from most states and about 40 nations. There are housing options available for both on-campus living and living in the surrounding area.

About $5.5 million in financial aid is provided yearly to students from federal, state, and private sources, benefiting about 75 percent of the student body.

Currently, there are about 19,000 Lawrence Tech alumni. More than 800 students graduate yearly. The university's graduates enjoy an enviable record of success. More than 90 percent of the job seekers in each graduating class find career positions appropriate to their level of education within six months of graduating. Many other graduates advance with employers they worked with while attending the university.

Although Lawrence Tech graduates live throughout the world, most remain in the Midwest and, in particular, continue to stay in Michigan, contributing to the state's growth and the region's economy. About 40 percent of the graduate engineers each year in the three-county metro area are supplied by Lawrence Tech.

Dr. Richard E. Marburger, president of the university, is very optimistic about its future. "Looking ahead, the future appears bright for Lawrence Technological University. As Michigan and Oakland County increasingly turn to high-tech industries to sustain economic growth and employment, the university is well positioned to help attract new companies to the area. In addition, beyond providing highly qualified graduates, Lawrence Tech seeks to expand its service in providing the region's industries with continuing education and cooperative educational opportunities as well as applied research assistance and development."

White Chapel

White Chapel Memorial Cemetery today is unique among cemeteries not simply for its physical beauty but for its concept of unsurpassed service. The private, nonsectarian cemetery was conceived by its founders more than 60 years ago as a place where "Memory Lives in Beauty." It is designed to help families and friends of loved ones find solace and understanding. The loveliness of its sculptured gardens and the serenity of its stately structures in enduring marble and bronze inspire feelings of reverence and peace.

White Chapel's extraordinary facilities provide for earth interments, mausoleum entombment, cremation, and inurnment, as well as a most complete range of services in the lovely private chapels. The magnificent Temple of Memories contains many sanctuaries, with full provision for masoleum entombment in private compartments. White Chapel's crematorium is unrivaled for the completeness and dignity of its appointments, while bronze memorial urns may be selected for permanent placement in the columbaria.

The stately grandeur of the Temple of Memories is an unsurpassed example of classic architecture, a sanctuary of snow-white marble and bronze, and is built to endure through the ages. The temple is a treasure-house of priceless sculpture, exquisite stained-glass windows, mosaics, paintings, pediments, and carved relief panels.

Entering its Great Hall, one is dazzled by the magnificence of its architecture and the breathtaking beauty of its appointments. Also in the Temple of Memories is the Allen digital computer organ, believed by many authorities to equal or surpass the tonal performance of traditional pipe organs.

Three lovely chapels are available in the Temple of Memories, designed for those who prefer to have services indoors, avoiding possible inclement weather. The chapels are available during daylight hours for meditation, while memorial services are conducted regularly by the chapel staff. There also, provision is made for mausoleum entombment in private compartments.

White Chapel's lovely memorial gardens have attracted nationwide attention. The approximately 220 acres are the result of a master-planned development. Designed in a series of memorial gardens, each with its own distinctive sculpture in marble or

Below Center: The magnificence of the Chapel of Memories is matched by the beauty and richness of its appointments.

Below Right: The Great Hall of the Temple of Memories is distinguished by impressive architecture that features marble, bronze, and crystal.

Bottom Left: The esplanade approach to White Chapel's Temple of Memories overlooks the placid waters of Mirror Lake.

Bottom Right: The touching bronze statue of Saint Francis of Assisi stands in the center of the Garden of Love, one of many theme gardens at White Chapel.

bronze, they portray in chronological order the history of the Christian faith, beginning with the prophets of the Old Testament and continuing through the centuries to the present day.

The gardens, already numbering three dozen, express a variety of themes. Among them are the Gardens of Religious Liberty, the Garden of the Resurrection, and the Garden of Brotherhood. The Garden of Love features a bronze sculpture of Saint Francis of Assisi, and one may also view such special pieces as the famous Polar Bear Memorial, the Four Freedoms Memorial, and the Korean and Vietnam Memorial on the White Chapel grounds. The White Chapel master plan continues to evolve, with new memorial gardens in various stages of planning.

White Chapel's lush lawns and gardens, as well as its beautiful buildings and statuary, are maintained by a large staff of gardeners, stonemasons, and carpenters.

Noteworthy is White Chapel's pioneering efforts in preplanning of interments, allowing families to make decisions without haste. Visits are encouraged, while guided tours of White Chapel are also accommodated by the staff. The grounds are located on Long Lake Road at Crooks Road in Troy.

Pontiac Osteopathic Hospital

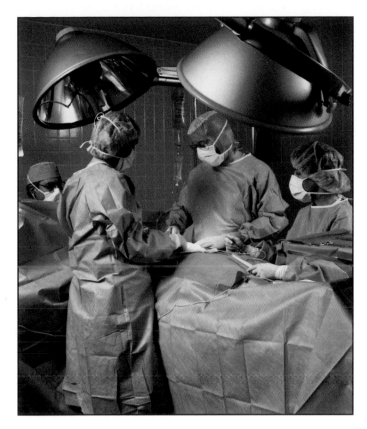

Left and Bottom: The Pontiac Osteopathic Hospital is well known for its 24-hour Emergency Trauma Center and offers a variety of specialty and subspecialty services.

Pontiac Osteopathic Hospital (POH) is well known for its 24-hour Emergency Trauma Center. However, the hospital also prides itself on its high-quality medical staff. In addition, the hospital offers a network of Family Practice and other medical specialists located throughout the greater Pontiac and northern Oakland County area.

The 308-bed hospital boasts the latest capabilities in diagnostic testing through its laboratory and medical imaging departments. These capabilities befit POH, which is the eighth-largest teaching facility accredited by the American Osteopathic Association in the United States and the fourth-largest osteopathic hospital in Michigan.

POH is ideally situated to service the health care needs of northern Oakland County communities now and in the future. Its Community Health Care Center in Oxford provides, in addition to Family Practice and Urgent Care, a variety of services. Cardiology, dermatology, gastroenterology, rehabilitative medicine, a hearing-aid center, substance-abuse counseling, and occupational health are a part of this progressive ambulatory-care setting. In addition, the hospital recently received approval to build a satellite hospital in Independence Township, adjacent to Interstate 75, between Pontiac and Flint. It expects to complete this new construction project in the near future.

POH is particularly proud of its Occupational Health Program. "We are excited about it because we feel we've put together a total package of health care services that any one business can pick and choose from according to its particular needs," says Jack Whitlow, POH's executive director.

The total program includes two traditional occupational health clinics. It also boasts of a mobile health van, which provides on-site screening, testing, and educational programs. This unit, especially created for POH, also includes a sound-proof hearing room and EKG. A final component to the program is Workwise. Located near the hospital campus in downtown Pontiac, this modern rehabilitation center simulates work environments to help patients readjust to their work situations before actually returning to their jobs.

Since its establishment in 1953, POH has continually updated and expanded its facilities and services. It owns and operates its own print shop, biomedical engineering services, home health and medical equipment company, and the Lake Orion Nursing Center. In addition, the hospital recently opened a child-care center and a fitness center for its employees.

The hospital has the potential for use by a much larger audience than just Oakland County. Given the reputation of its Emergency Trauma Center and considering its close proximity to I 75, the Palace of Auburn Hills, the Oakland Technological Center, the Pontiac Silverdome, and the beautiful northern Oakland County lakes and parks, POH can include virtually any visitor to Michigan as a potential patient.

Pontiac Osteopathic Hospital is as dynamic as the county it serves. As Whitlow states, "We have taken the steps necessary to guarantee our survival in today's changing health care marketplace. We have initiated activities and programs that will ensure not only survival but also prosperity and better service to our clientele today and in the years to come."

St. Joseph Mercy Hospital

St. Joseph Mercy Hospital in Pontiac combines its state-of-the-art equipment and facilities with its highly trained professional staff for one basic goal—quality patient care. The hospital has just completed a $12.5-million expansion project—work that complements its continuing efforts to update and expand its specialty medical departments.

"In our enthusiasm about our growth we haven't lost sight of our primary goal of quality patient care," says John P. Cullen, president and chief executive officer of the 531-bed hospital. "And quality patient care encompasses more than new buildings, advanced medical equipment, and greater technical skills. It's a way of thinking—a sensitivity toward the needs of others."

The Pontiac hospital employs about 2,000 people and is part of the Sisters of Mercy Health Corporation, a subsidiary of Mercy Health Services. The system owns 18 hospitals and numerous ambulatory care facilities in Iowa, Indiana, and Michigan. Through management contract, SMHC operates 12 additional hospitals in Iowa, Illinois, Nebraska, and New York.

St. Joseph Mercy Hospital sponsors a variety of programs that brings its services closer to communities throughout Oakland County. The hospital operates five Family Medical Centers serving the Farmington, Union Lake, Rochester Hills, Birmingham, and Waterford areas.

Many of St. Joseph Mercy's medical staff members have practices in office buildings located in Clarkston and Bloomfield Township. These convenient locations provide easy access to specialty care for community residents.

In the fall of 1989, St. Joseph Mercy, along with sister hospitals in southeastern Michigan, introduced ASK-A-NURSE. ASK-A-NURSE is a 24-hour health information service. Specially trained registered nurses provide accurate answers to a wide range of health care questions on a confidential basis. They also work with callers to help them find a physician in their area if needed.

St. Joseph medical services are extensive and varied. It has

Below Left: St. Joseph Mercy Hospital, a health leader in Oakland County, is a 531-bed, acute-care, community-based hospital serving more than a million people in Oakland County and the surrounding area.

Below Right: Nearly 600 physicians in every specialty and subspecialty work with the skilled nurses and technicians at St. Joseph Mercy's modern facilities. Whether one needs open-heart surgery, emergency care, or maternity and pediatric services, St. Joseph Mercy Hospital can care for the entire family.

Facing Top: More than 2,000 babies are born each year at St. Joseph Mercy's Birthing Center. The center offers a vast array of programs and services for the entire expectant family, including birthing rooms, private labor rooms, a neonatal intensive care level II nursery, childbirth classes, and a low-impact aerobics program for pregnant or new moms.

Facing Bottom: St. Joseph Mercy's wide range of pediatric services include a Pediatric After Hours Center. The Pediatric Intensive Care Unit (PICU) medical team provides care 24 hours a day, seven days a week.

a full range of cardiac services, from open-heart surgery to outpatient education. The hospital offers the newest technology in medical and surgical intervention, a recently expanded intensive care unit, complete catheterization facilities, and a cardiac rehabilitation center. There are two cardiac surgery teams on the medical staff.

In addition to comprehensive cardiac care, St. Joseph is proud of its laser surgery center, which was the first established in Oakland County. Several different lasers are used for a variety of procedures, including cataract removal, tumors of internal organs, and some types of cancer treatment.

In the research center of the hospital, a highly talented,

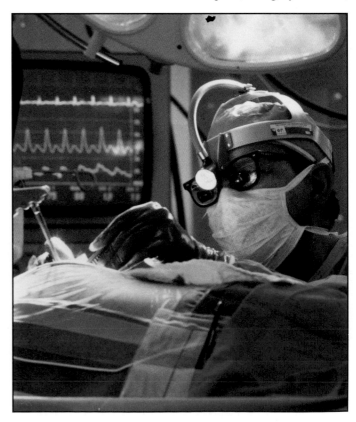

multidisciplinary research team studies a wide range of areas from coronary heart disease and cancer to hypertension. The center utilizes the skills and knowledge of more than 570 physicians on its staff and collaborates with centers at the major state universities, including Oakland University, University of Michigan, Michigan State University, and Wayne State University.

The Pediatric Intensive Care Unit (PICU) is composed of a dedicated team of pediatric critical care specialists. The unit manages complex life-support systems, including mechanical ventilation, and monitors neuro-intensive care, intracranial pressure, cerebral blood flow, and metabolism.

The Department of Psychiatry's Harold E. Fox Center, located next to the hospital, is a leader in Oakland County in the treatment of substance abuse. The center provides comprehensive mental health services in-

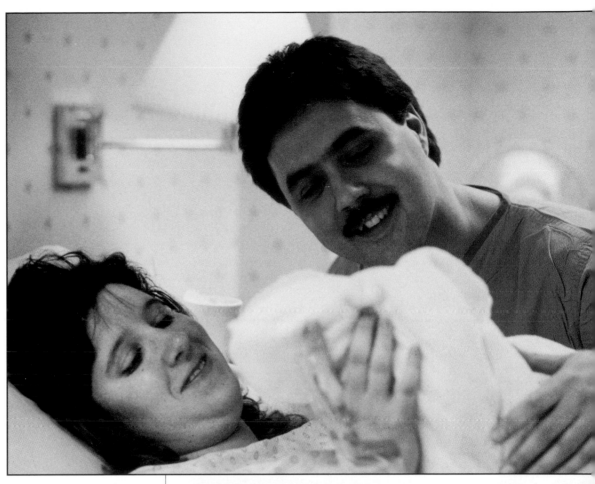

cluding a child and adolescent psychiatric unit, an adult psychiatric unit, a day hospital, an inpatient substance abuse unit, and an outpatient psychiatric/substance abuse unit. The department also has an intensive, three-week alternative treatment program for substance abuse, a program for children with attention deficit disorders, a psychiatric service focusing on geriatric problems, and an adolescent day hospital.

Proud of its nursing staff, the hospital strives to create an environment where nurses can continue to use their knowledge and skills to benefit patients. For example, to promote professionalism and job satisfaction, a competency-based clinical advancement system rewards superior performance in nursing care.

Since its opening in 1927, expansion and modernization have been the hospital's watchword. Most recently, its $12.5-million project included construction of the Mercy Medical Building, an 85,000-square-foot, five-story structure that features custom-designed medical office suites and ancillary programs and services. The building can accommodate about 40 physician offices. Also part of the project was the construction/renovation of the main lobby and parking structure. The new look for the front of the hospital includes a covered patient drop-off area and glass-encased lobby. Also, two levels were added to the hospital's parking structure providing increased parking area and easy access to the facility for patients and visitors.

Cullen expresses pride and optimism in St. Joseph Mercy Hospital. "Today I see St. Joseph's as an institution going through a significant amount of change to adapt to what the community will need in the future," he says. "We think the St. Joseph of tomorrow will see us focusing on areas of cardiac,

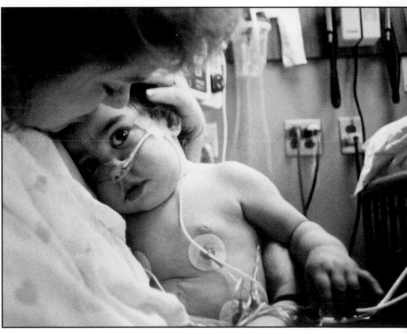

pediatric, obstetric, and mental health services."

He says St. Joseph Mercy Hospital's reputation of providing quality care through the most up-to-date equipment and personalized care where patients are seen as individuals will definitely continue.

"St. Joseph Mercy Hospital is an institution that brings together personalized care and the latest medical technology," Cullen says. "We are excited about being part of a growing, dynamic Oakland County."

Oakland University

Oakland University is a comprehensive, state-supported educational institution that has a multifaceted service role including high-quality academic and continuing education programs; the advancement of knowledge and promotion of the arts through research, scholarship, and creative activities; and a multitude of programs to render public service by applying the expertise of the university to issues of society.

OU was recently rated by the education editor of the *New York Times* as one of the best buys in American higher education. The final report of the 1989 North Central Association review committee granted full accreditation for 10 years and characterized OU as a model university for the twenty-first century.

OU offers its 12,000 students a broad range of rigorous educational programs, including 70 undergraduate areas, 30 master's programs, and 5 Ph.D. concentrations. Anchored by a strong liberal arts program, OU is organized into the College of Arts and Sciences; schools of Business Administration, Engineering and Computer Science, Health Sciences, Human and Education Services, and Nursing; a program of Continuing Education; and the Office of Graduate Study.

OU is predominantly a commuter college, with about 1,500 students living in its residence halls. It employs more than 1,400 faculty and staff and operates on an annual budget of

Below: Meadow Brook Hall, the former home of OU benefactors Alfred and Matilda Wilson.

Facing: Oakland University's residence halls house more than 1,500 students annually.

nearly $90 million.

Aiding minorities is always a goal at OU for which there are a number of programs at the university. Project Challenge is conducted in cooperation with the Pontiac School District. Seventh graders, through this program, are brought to campus to involve them in a unique educational experience. The program follows the students through high school and then helps obtain scholarships for them to go to college.

One special program coordinated through the Office of Student Affairs offers parents in the program a contract that promises a grant for their child at OU if they encourage their child to finish high school with an acceptable level of achievement.

Another university-based program is the Martin Luther King, Jr./Cesar Chavez/Rosa Parks program. This brings thousands of economically disadvantaged middle school and high school students to campus each year to participate in programs geared to encourage them to consider attending college.

OU takes pride in being a research and scholarship institution with such programs of research excellence as the Center for Robotics and Advanced Automation, the Eye Research Institute, and its Institution for Biochemistry and Biotechnology. OU staff

and faculty work closely in these areas with firms and medical facilities in the region.

The Center for International Programs coordinates studies and services in the area of world civilizations and cultures. For example, the center has Japanese and Chinese study programs that help Americans understand Far Eastern cultures. One of the goals is to help Americans doing business in or touring those countries to understand cultural-based differences. The center also works with foreign visitors and business people to help them learn about the United States.

The Division of Continuing Education offers staff development programs to business and industry for job training and updating such as applied statistics, engineering, and computer science; diploma, certificate, and relicensure programs such as plastics technology, legal assistant, and personal financial planning; and a variety of special topic conferences, such as for writing, productivity improvement, and the prevention of coronary heart disease. The division strives to meet the current and ever-changing educational needs of the general public and professional workers in our society.

The Continuum Center serves adults of all ages in personal exploration and planning by offering workshops on supervisory skills, assertiveness training, communication effectiveness, and many other topics as appropriate. Other programs include services for displaced workers and the elderly.

The Adult Career Counseling Center aids community adults who need assistance in reviewing educational and training opportunities as well as career decision making. Computer-assisted career guidance and individual counseling services are available.

Through a variety of outreach programs, the university is fulfilling its mission of public service geared to the needs of area citizens and organizations both private and public.

The Center for Business and Corporate Services coordinates various consulting agreements to assist the small-business owners in the community while the Center for Economic Development and Corporate Services serves as the liaison with the Oakland Technology Park.

Another multipurpose program is the Ken Morris Center for the Study of Labor and Work, which offers state-supported programs for members of labor organizations and holds seminars for workers and management.

The Meadow Brook Health Enhancement Institute offers wellness programs, including health screening and specific programs for cardiac rehabilitation, industrial health, and movement reeducation. The major thrust of the institute is improving a person's health through life-style management, nutrition, and stress reduction. Participants in the program are often referred by their physicians.

The university offers professional cultural events at the Meadow Brook Art Gallery, the Meadow Brook Hall, the summer Meadow Brook Music Festival, and the Meadow Brook Theatre. In addition, the Center for the Arts coordinates student performances in art history, dance, art, mime, music, and theater.

The university is continually evolving and improving. It recently dedicated a new addition to Kresge Library, and plans are under way for a $36-million science and technology center.

"Oakland University sees its mission as helping the community grow—academically, culturally, and economically," says an OU spokesperson.

Networks

Oakland County's energy and communication providers keep products, information, and power circulating inside and outside the area

Photo by Balthazar Korab

WWJ/WJOI

Between radio station WWJ's all-news-and-sports format and WJOI's easy-listening music, the two form the top radio combination in the Detroit area.

"WWJ is number one in Michigan for news and sports and reaching affluent Oakland County," says Rod Zimmerman, vice president and general manager. "Sister station WJOI is Detroit's easy-listening station." Both radio stations, based in Southfield, were purchased by CBS in 1989.

WWJ, 95 on the AM radio dial, is an information station, broadcasting at 5,000 watts 24 hours per day, seven days a week. Its world and national news includes hourly reports from the CBS Radio Network. With more local reporters than any

Below Left: Don Patrick (left) and Joe Donovan, WWJ's morning team, have developed a rapport with early risers throughout Oakland County.

Bottom: WJOI's music director and on-air talent Ben Hooker programs a popular mix of easy-listening favorites.

by Charles Osgood and "Dan Rather Reporting."

WWJ's history dates back to 1920, boasting the first radio broadcast in the United States. The station has earned both Associated Press and United Press International honors for features, spot news, investigative reporting, documentaries, and public services and was named 1989 UPI Station of the Year.

Complementing WWJ is WJOI's 97.1 FM easy-listening music broadcasts. In addition to the music, the station also provides newscasts on the hour and half-hour during the morning rush hour and reports every other hour from 2 p.m. to 10 p.m. Weather reports are scheduled every hour on the half-hour, with local and national sports updates within regularly scheduled newscasts. The 12,000-watt station also provides stock market updates during its newscasts.

The two radio stations have exclusive formats in the Detroit market and have had very consistent programming during the past 10 years, notes Zimmerman.

"WWJ is the station people turn to for news and sports," he says. "And WJOI is the station the market turns to for relaxation. We reach a very up-scale, professional market in Oakland County. The radio stations reach the county very effectively. It would make sense that Oakland is the geographic area where we do most of our business."

other Michigan radio station, WWJ excels at local and statewide coverage. Sports reports are offered at 15 before and 15 minutes after each hour, and the station broadcasts the Detroit Lions, University of Michigan football and basketball games, as well as play-by-play coverage of the Detroit Pistons.

Traffic reports and weather forecasts are broadcast together, every 10 minutes. WWJ also provides business reports twice per hour from before the markets open until late into the night.

Special broadcasts include "Your Health" by Pat Sweeting, "Automotive Insights" with Robb Mahr, and "Your Business" hosted by Murray Feldman. WWJ also has been designated the official radio station of the Michigan State Lottery. The radio station also offers a variety of CBS-produced features, including "The Osgood File"

The Observer & Eccentric Newspaper, Inc.

Recognized as Birmingham's oldest continuing business, *The Eccentric* began in 1875, when George H. Mitchell and Almeron Whitehead, fellow members of The Eccentric Club, decided that their village needed a printing office—a business establishment to provide the community with small printing needs. They ordered and received a Novelty press from Boston along with a few fonts of type. Total cash outlay was $90.

Early in 1878 they made a second, significant decision: The village of Birmingham and the surrounding area needed a newspaper, and so *The Eccentric,* named after their men's organization, began to serve the growing turn-of-the-century village. With few setbacks and a dedicated march forward, *The Eccentric* grew, operating from second floors, storefronts, and various buildings throughout the community.

In March 1974, The Eccentric Newspapers group and The Observer Newspapers group, both owned and published by Philip H. Power, were merged into a 12-newspaper group, The Observer & Eccentric Newspapers. Growth has continued with an added 13th edition, *The Lakes Eccentric,* rolling off the press in 1989. Construction of a new building was completed in the spring of 1989.

The 10,000 square feet of office space in the new building in downtown Birmingham houses editorial, circulation, advertising, and creative services departments.

While each Eccentric newspaper is part of a larger newspaper group, all are individually edited and as devoted to community coverage as the first two-cent issues printed by Whitehead and Mitchell.

Published twice each week at its parent company, Surburban Communications Corporation in Livonia, *The Birmingham Eccentric, The Farmington Observer, The Southfield Eccentric, The Rochester Eccentric, The Troy Eccentric, The West Bloomfield Eccentric,* and *The Lakes Eccentric* are circulated to 80,000 households in Oakland County. Throughout their history, the newspapers have received many awards from

Below Right: An area resident grabs a copy of The Eccentric *to find out what is happening in his community.*

Bottom Left and Right: Each issue of The Eccentric *is as individually edited and as devoted to community coverage as the first, two-cent copy was in 1878. Throughout their history, the newspapers have received many awards for excellence in content and appearance.*

Michigan and national press associations for excellence in content and appearance.

Because hometown news continues to be primary focus of *The Eccentric,* photos of the local sports scene, coverage of city hall, and news of neighborhood and community-wide activities dominate the pages of each Eccentric newspaper.

Advertisers in these community newspapers enjoy a rich, expanding market and an upscale, enthusiastic audience for their messages. With environmental concerns dominating the immediate and foreseeable future, The Eccentric newspapers are currently printed on 50 percent recycled newsprint, and the organization has an internal office-paper recycling program solidly in place. On a recent public service page, The Eccentric newspapers told its readers, "We don't cover world news, but we care about the world."

It has been said by those involved in metropolitan, national, and international press that suburban coverage is difficult—too many jurisdictions, school districts, meetings, and police calls.

And they are right—it is difficult. However, anything that serves a community, holds a mirror to its strengths and weaknesses, records its history, and gives its readers a sense of their hometown is worth continuing for at least another century.

Consumers Power Company

Consumers Power Company has been dedicated to powering Michigan's progress for more than 100 years. The company is the principal subsidiary of CMS Energy Corporation, a diversified energy firm with operations in electricity generation and distribution, natural-gas distribution and storage, oil and gas exploration and production, independent power generation, and utility services.

As Michigan's largest utility and the nation's fourth-largest combination electric and natural-gas utility, Consumers Power is committed to serving the growing energy demands of nearly 6 million of Michigan's 9 million residents in all lower peninsula counties except Berrien.

Consumers Power Company, based in Jackson, Michigan, divides its service area into regions. It provides Oakland County's 1.1 million residents with natural-gas service. Oakland and parts of Macomb, Wayne, Washtenaw, and Livingston counties compose the utility's metropolitan region. The region is Consumers Power's only all-gas region.

"Meeting the diverse energy needs of nearly 720,000 industrial, commercial, residential, and agricultural customers is an ongoing challenge," says Edgar L. Doss, metro region general manager. "We are working with all our customers to help them use energy in a wise, safe, and efficient manner."

Doss points out that Consumers Power energy consultants are available to help commercial and industrial customers apply new technologies and reduce their operating expenses by minimizing overall energy costs.

Heating and cooling systems powered by natural gas provide Consumers Power customers in Oakland County with both energy-efficient and cost-efficient applications. A few of these new technologies

Below Left: John Roberts is part of an 80-person department that each month provides direct service to more than 85,000 customers.

Below Right: Gas distribution lines that serve Consumers Power industrial, commercial, and residential customers in Oakland County are installed and maintained by gas-lines workers such as Diann Urbaniak.

Facing Top: Consumers Power natural-gas customers share the advantages of reliable supplies at low rates because of the utility's underground storage capabilities and purchasing practices.

Facing Bottom: Consumers Power energy consultant Robert L. Gregersen (right) discusses energy efficiency with Gary Sabo, an Oakland County home builder and contractor.

include: energy pump systems for residential and commercial customers; gas engine-driven water chillers to provide effective, reliable commercial space cooling; desiccant dehumidification systems to cause more efficient air conditioning of supermarkets and ice-skating arenas; infrared natural-gas heating systems to prevent water from freezing in boat-slip areas in winter; and cogeneration to produce electricity, hot water, and steam for commercial and industrial operations.

for the state and the general public. From its air- and water-quality programs to wildlife habitat protection and enhancement activities, the utility works closely with state and federal agencies, environmental associations, and sports and recreational groups.

Education is another area in which the company provides commitment and leadership. Consumers Power Company is in its third decade of offering its Educational Services Program (ESP) to state educators. ESP provides students in kindergarten through 12th grade with educational materials such as videotapes, booklets, posters, films, multimedia kits, and other curriculum aids for teachers to use in the classroom.

Consumers Power Company over the past few years has been

While Consumers Power customers benefit from the new technologies of today, they also will share the advantages of future supplies and low rates because of the utility's natural-gas purchasing policies and underground storage capabilities.

Consumers Power's history as a reliable supplier of natural gas in Oakland County parallels the county's development into a strong and vibrant economy. At the turn of the century, some Oakland County home owners drilled their own little natural-gas wells in their backyards to use the gas for cooking. Manufactured natural gas and supplies piped into and stored in Michigan from the southwestern United States helped Consumers Power become an important partner in the economic growth and development of Oakland County.

The relationship that Consumers Power has with Oakland County is one in which the utility welcomes its ongoing commitment to powering its progress as the strongest urban economy in the state. The utility is heavily involved in county economic development activities to attract new business to the area, expand current businesses, and create job opportunities.

Consumers Power annually pays more than $7 million in taxes to cities, towns, and townships in Oakland County. The utility is active in and supportive of many civic, business, and service organizations through the participation by employees in a wide range of community activities throughout the county.

Long recognized for its care and concern for the environment, Consumers Power is active in a number of environmental enhancement programs. It also provides recreational properties

growing stronger financially, along with its parent company, CMS Energy. Under the progressive and firm leadership of William T. McCormick, Jr., chairman of the board and chief executive officer, CMS has been improving its weak financial condition. The Dearborn-based firm's program in the late 1980s included financial restructuring, operating cost reductions, productivity improvements, asset value increases, and positioning for future competition.

As the 1990s unfold, Oakland County's healthy economy and sustained economic growth will depend on long-term, reliable energy supplies provided at competitive prices by a healthy utility. Consumers Power Company will meet the energy requirements of its customers in the future, just as it has

The Marketplace

Oakland County's retail establishments and accommodations are enjoyed by residents and visitors alike

Photo by Balthazar Korab

Crissman Cadillac

L. Keith Crissman, father of Crissman Cadillac president Charles Crissman, established himself as an auto dealer about 40 years ago. The Crissman name, which Charles Crissman credits as at least part of the reason for the success of his present-day Birmingham business, has been firmly rooted in Oakland County with the establishment of the family farm 150 years ago.

Charles Crissman joined the family business about 20 years ago and has been president for the past six. "We keep the Crissman name on each dealership. We really strive for service," he says.

Crissman considers the mainstay of Crissman Cadillac the dealership located on Woodward Avenue in Birmingham. However, the company also owns Crissman Lincoln-Mercury in Rochester, which was acquired in 1988 and is located in Lakewood, a suburb of Denver.

The three dealerships employ 120 workers. Crissman proudly notes that his Birmingham dealership is the largest Cadillac retailer in Oakland County. He also is proud that his dealership ranks 14th in the nation out of 2,500 Cadillac dealers, according to the Cadillac-conducted customer-service index of factory-rated dealerships.

Crissman offers limousine service for customers who must

Below Left: Crissman Lincoln-Mercury in Rochester was acquired in 1988.

Bottom: One Crissman Cadillac dealership is located in Lakewood, a suburb of Denver, Colorado.

leave their vehicles at the dealership, and company employees provide vehicle pickup and delivery. There is a 24-hour emergency service.

"We match in service the affluent area we are in," says Crissman. "We learned to do this over the years because people expected it, and we do it at other dealerships because it works well."

Crissman family roots are firmly entrenched in Oakland County. About 150 years ago the family started a land-grant farm. L. Keith Crissman had a General Motors truck dealership with another Oakland County man, Ed Wilson, in the 1940s and early 1950s. In 1953 he broke away from Wilson and purchased Crissman Chevrolet in Rochester. In 1967 he sold that dealership and went back into business with Wilson operating Wilson-Crissman Cadillac in Birmingham, the site of the present dealership. Wilson died in the early 1980s, leaving L. Keith Crissman the sole owner. L. Keith Crissman died in 1985, a year after Charles took over as president.

Charles' wife, Penny, is mayor pro tempore on the Birmingham City Council; she is a fourth-generation Crissman in the city's politics. Charles Crissman has been active in the National Cadillac Dealers Council, a past president of the Detroit Cadillac Dealers Association, and president of the Denver Dealers' Association. Crissman is on the board of directors of Crittenton Hospital and on the Oakland University School of Nursing board of directors. L. Keith Crissman was on the original board of directors for Oakland University.

Charles Crissman believes that Oakland County is not only a great place to do business, but also to live. "Our family roots are in Oakland County," he says. "If you're going to be in the auto business, you can't be any better place than in Detroit—and if you're going to be in the Detroit area, you can't be in any better place than in Oakland County."

Arbor Drugs, Inc.

With its continued emphasis on the pharmacy, Arbor Drugs, Inc., is one of the nation's fastest-growing and most successful retail drugstore chains.

Arbor today is the 22nd-largest drugstore chain in the United States, with more than 100 stores and 3,500 employees. Company offficials expect the firm's rapid growth to continue and anticipate 150 stores in Michigan by 1993. Supporting this goal is the chain's Novi, Michigan, distribution center, which has the capacity to supply merchandise to 175 stores.

Arbor is a drugstore industry leader with average store sales of $3.5 million and sales per square foot of $380. This performance exceeds the industry average by about 70 percent. Sales in fiscal 1989 were $300.2 million; sales increased at an average annual compounded rate of 26.1 percent for the previous five years.

Arbor's market share in its primary trading area of south eastern Michigan is 21.4 percent of total drugstore sales. According to its founder, Eugene Applebaum, the chain's chairman of the board, president, and chief executive officer, the company's short-, intermediate-, and long-term goals share the same objective: meaningful and profitable growth achieved through a professionally managed, highly disciplined chain drugstore operation. As an organization, Arbor is committed to improving sales and profits annually. Management is also dedicated to exceeding drugstore industry averages in both operating efficiency and financial performance, while maintaining high standards of integrity and fairness to customers, employees, suppliers, and shareholders.

Applebaum is particularly proud his company has attracted and retained a dedicated and results-focused organization. This feeling is expressed as "Come for a job and stay for a career" in the firm's new-employee package.

Founded in 1963 by Applebaum, Arbor is the second-largest drugstore chain in Michigan. Management continues to stress the pharmacy area, where 40 percent of the company's total sales are generated, as the chain's core operation. Health and beauty aids are 22 percent of sales, photo finishing and film make up 7.4 percent, and general merchandise, such as soft drinks, snacks, beer, wine, cigarettes, and seasonal merchandise comprise the balance.

With its corporate headquarters in Troy and its distribution center in Novi, Arbor Drugs, Inc., is firmly established as a major leader in Oakland County. Applebaum is optimistic about the future of the drugstore industry in general and Arbor Drugs in particular.

"We believe that the chain drugstore concept, built on a strong pharmacy foundation, will continue to have a very promising but competitive future," he says. "From our vantage point, we are confident that Arbor has the financial resources, a dedicated and determined organization, and unique strengths to manage the opportunities and challenges ahead."

Holiday Inn of Southfield

The Holiday Inn hotel chain is noted for its quality facilities and service. And among the more outstanding hotels in the chain is the Holiday Inn of Southfield. The local hotel can boast of all the amenities offered by its counterparts throughout Oakland County and the nation. In addition, the local hotel has some facilities that others may lack.

The 417-room hotel is among more than 1,500 Holiday Inns nationwide. It offers free in-room movies, cable television, a gift shop, and car-rental services. It also has the Holidome, a family recreational area that includes an indoor swimming

Below Left: The Holiday Inn of Southfield's sports bar, Tailgates, is a gathering place for local residents and hotel guests alike.

Bottom: The Holiday Inn of Southfield features the Holidome, a family recreational area that includes an indoor swimming pool and whirlpool among its many attractions.

The Southfield hotel also has recently remodeled its sports bar, Tailgates, which has a large-screen television and four smaller monitors. The bar, along with its South Street Grille, are two gathering places that Finley says are aimed at attracting local residents as well as hotel guests.

He notes that community appeal and involvement are important to the hotel. The Sunshine Club allows local residents to use the hotel's recreational facilities. The hotel has also been used as a telephone center for Muscular Dystrophy telethons and supports local community projects such as youth hockey and basketball programs.

The hotel was originally constructed in the early 1960s and was added onto three different times. It started out as a two-story, L-shape hotel with 100 rooms. A five-story building with 100 rooms and then the 200-room tower were added next. In the 1980s the Holidome was constructed.

Finley notes that in addition to having an edge over the competition because of the well-established reputation of the Holiday Inn chain, the Southfield hotel has another advantage with its convenient location. Built on Telegraph Road near Interstate 696, the hotel is in a bustling city and near excellent road systems.

"Because of our excellent location, excellent facilities, and top professional staff, we have an edge over other hotels in the area," says Finley.

pool, whirlpool, electronic game room, weight room, billiards and table tennis, and play equipment for children. The hotel's meeting and banquet facilities can accommodate up to 450 people. In its 16-story tower section, the Southfield Holiday Inn also has 200 deluxe rooms with queen-size beds designed for the corporate traveler.

General manager Reggie Finley notes that the Southfield hotel takes the Holiday Inn hospitality promise very seriously. It states, "We will do everything we can to ensure you are satisfied with your stay. If there is anything we can do to make your stay a more pleasant one, please call our management on duty or front-desk staff anytime, day or night." Finley says to help keep this promise, he makes sure all guests receive courtesy calls to see if they need anything.

The Townsend Hotel

Luxury accommodations, outstanding personal service, and attention to every detail just begin to describe The Townsend Hotel. Built and designed with a European flair, the intimate Townsend is within walking distance of enchanting downtown Birmingham and its more than 200 shops, boutiques, art galleries, parks, restaurants, and theaters.

With its 87 luxury accommodations, more than half of them suites, the Townsend offers a quiet, relaxing elegance that makes it one of the finest hotels in the world. Opened in June 1988, the Townsend has already earned the elite Preferred Hotel Worldwide status, making it one of only 90 properties worldwide to carry this designation.

"The Townsend has a unique mix of service and quality that is evident through recognition from our peers in the preferred status," says Bonnie LePage, Townsend managing director. "Our goal was to bring a luxury property to Oakland County to cater to the needs of this community in a way not provided before."

The Townsend's quality shines through at the Rugby Grille, known for its "power breakfasts" and memorable after-theater dinners. From Angus beef and fresh seafood flown in daily to organically grown vegetables, the Rugby Grille is

Below: The lobby of the Townsend Hotel is decorated in rich mahogany woods, Italian Carrara marble, and traditional English furnishings.

considered to be a premier gourmet dining establishment.

The hotel accommodates a variety of events from business meetings to banquets in its elegant Regency Room, which can serve more than 200 reception guests. The adaptable Hunter Room provides a perfect venue for corporate meetings and educational seminars. It can also be converted for a banquet of up to 140 guests.

To highlight its European atmosphere, the Townsend offers an authentic English afternoon tea featuring loose leaf tea and a wealth of tea sandwiches, canapes, scones, cheese straws, and pastries. Tea has become so popular that several requests a month are made for private tea parties, including tea bridal and baby showers, birthday celebrations, and entertainment for out-of-town guests.

Pride in the Townsend is apparent from the doorman who greets guests by name to the maid who leaves treats at turndown. "The dedication and friendliness of the staff make the Townsend an oasis from the pressures of everyday life," says LePage. "We make guests feel at home in our home by paying attention to every detail in an unobtrusive way."

CHAPTER

ELEVEN

Professions

Oakland County's professional community brings a wealth of ability and insight to the area

McEndarffer, Hoke & Bernhard, P.C.
168

Parry and Associates, Inc.
170

Freedman, Krochmal, and Goldin, P.C.
171

Harley Ellington Pierce Yee Associates, Inc.
172

Ellis/Naeyaert/Genheimer Associates, Inc.
174

Hubbell, Roth & Clark, Inc.
176

Ralph Manuel Realtors
177

Photo by Balthazar Korab

McEndarffer, Hoke & Bernhard, P.C.

Doing business in Oakland County is generally an excellent experience, as the people from the other organizations described in this book will say—there are friendly people, a healthy economy, and pleasant surroundings. On the other hand, anyone who has visited southeastern Michigan in the dead of winter knows certain days can make getting around somewhat of a challenge.

On one of those days last year, Maree Mulvoy, a tax partner at McEndarffer, Hoke & Bernhard, drove to the home of a client in Bloomfield Hills. The husband of the woman who welcomed her at the door had run a business and worked with McEndarffer, Hoke & Bernhard for several years before he passed away. Maree Mulvoy's mission was to help the widow prepare her tax returns. In this particular case, that meant more than adding the numbers. She literally went through the desk and file cabinet of this longtime client to find bills that had been paid and records of income generated. The result was more than fact gathering. It was also a way to build the client's confidence that her personal financial situation was under control.

Maybe sending a staff person would have been a more efficient way to gather the required information than a personal visit from a partner with years of experience and a law degree. But the comfort in the eyes of the client made the effort more than worthwhile. And it is that kind of effort that makes client service a reality and not just an abstract concept.

Paul Bernhard, the managing partner of the firm and

also a lawyer and CPA, would certainly call Maree Mulvoy's effort an example of client service personified. He would probably also cite another example that had a much broader impact. It happened when the tax laws changed in 1986.

One of the more confusing aspects of the new law was the treatment of regular versus subchapter S corporations. The relevant provisions were supposed to go into effect as of January 1, 1987. As the fall progressed, no one knew exactly what the law meant or how to interpret it—not MHB, not the Big Eight, not even the IRS, and certainly not clients. Finally, the service provided additional clarification—the bottom line was that those who were or could become sub S corporations by the

Facing Top: Research and study continues to be the foundation that enables the firm to be creative in its problem solving.

Facing Bottom: MHB considers teamwork to be a high priority for its client service teams. Professionals are cross-trained in the audit, tax, and consulting disciplines and work together to respond to client needs.

Right Top: The firm's professional staff attends numerous seminars during the year. This enables MHB to provide clients with first-rate professional advice.

Right Bottom: Internal computer classes enable firm members to enhance their skills. An in-house computer network helps MHB to keep up with the latest technologies.

new year could save substantial tax dollars. Paul Bernhard and the other five partners went through their client lists and found almost 200 different situations where a change should be considered. Given the late notification from the IRS, only about 30 days were left before January 1, and it was the middle of the holiday season and year-end planning—an MHB client-service challenge.

The challenge was met with typical MHB commitment. Partners and staff alike worked together to communicate the situation to clients. They explained what needed to be done and made the necessary changes at a rate of about six or seven clients per day.

Of course, not all examples of client service come from the tax area. MHB provides a wide range of services from audits to computer assistance to general business advice. One of the founding fathers of the firm, Dick McEndarffer, has long been viewed by his clients as the man to talk to before making major business decisions. The reason for this reputation is well demonstrated by a recent example involving a new client of the firm.

The client came to MHB through a referral from a banking executive who had worked with McEndarffer before. The client had come to the banker for financing to buy a business in a highly leveraged deal.

Dick McEndarffer and the client sat down and went over the whole transaction. The client really wanted to buy the company and was hungry to do the deal. MHB set up a computer model to see if changes in the operation of the business could generate the dollars necessary to handle the substantial debt that would exist. Assumptions were changed, various options examined, but in no way would the business make it at the original purchase price.

The client, armed with computer printouts, met with the seller, who was supposedly uncompromising in his demands. Negotiations continued with hard data that both sides could understand. The end result was a successful transaction at a price of 20 percent or $2 million less than the original deal. No doubt MHB will have a happy client for years to come, and Dick McEndarffer has another business owner out there who tells his friends, "You know, before you make that deal, you really ought to talk to MHB."

Of course, there are other stories about other partners that could be told as additional examples of client service. Tom Degregorio has helped many a bank to interpret the complex

regulations for financial institutions, saving them time and avoiding future problems. John Mach has used his tax expertise literally to save a business from going into bankruptcy by dramatically speeding the delivery of an IRS refund. Doug Toppin has worked with entrepreneurs to take an idea and make it reality by providing financial, data-processing, and marketing advice.

These stories are all indicative not only of McEndarffer, Hoke & Bernhard's style of client service but also of the way people do business in Oakland County. Maybe it is the grassroots sense of self-reliance that came from those who first settled there hundreds of years ago. Or maybe it is the let's-get-the-job-done attitude that was an integral part of the area's industrial success of the past 100 years. Whatever the cause, people in Oakland County know what it takes to achieve goals, and they thrive on the commitment and effort necessary to make it happen. That is probably why the partners of MHB would not want to hang their shingle anyplace else. The firm has dramatically grown since it started in 1978. Oakland County is home, and that is just the way the professionals at MHB want it.

Parry and Associates, Inc.

Michael W. Parry is confident of himself and his company, Parry and Associates, Inc. The business consulting firm, whose original office is in Davisburg, also has facilities in the Renaissance Center in Detroit and in Ann Arbor. Started in 1988, the company has six staff members on call to clients 24 hours a day.

Parry, as president of the company, explains his firm's early success: "Consultants generally are very good at giving advice. However, putting that advice to work is another matter. Parry and Associates differs from other consultants in that it gives recommendations; then we all roll up our sleeves and make things happen. We are bottom-line oriented."

The company specializes in profit enhancement, crisis management, turnaround management, strategic planning, organizational development, and problem identification and solving.

Parry, of British nationality who grew up in South Africa, says his international business experience belies his age of 38. Graduating from a Brother Rice high school in 1970, Parry spent five years with a large accounting firm, mostly as a manager. After playing a leading role in turning around two under-performing companies, he joined Durr GMBH, a West German firm. At its African subsidiary he helped halt a 10-year string of losses and then, as part of a turnaround team, came to the United States to help save another Durr subsidiary that also faced financial woes.

Parry speaks highly of his two company vice presidents, Charles W. Drouillard and Susan E. Wallace. "This is an old cliché, but it is very rele-

Below Right: Mike Parry, founder, strives to ensure that clients have access to him or his staff 24 hours a day.

Bottom: Vice president Susan Wallace meets with clients regularly to review strategy and to ensure that assignments are on track.

vant: You're only as good as the people working for you," says Parry. "I've got to make sure I've got people working for me who can work 40 hours straight when there's a problem."

Although he has several offices in the Detroit metropolitan area, Parry says he considers Oakland County his base of operations. He speaks highly of the county, from both a business

and a personal standpoint.

"For a community to be economically strong, it needs to create opportunities for its residents to earn a decent living and then to provide services to improve the quality of life. Oakland County has done an admirable job of both," says Parry.

He says his wife and their two daughters love living in Davisburg. He notes that he moved his family to an area just west of Detroit when they first came to Michigan, but "I love a rural setting, and we just fell in love with Davisburg."

Looking to the future, Parry says he sees continued growth of Parry and Associates, Inc., but wants to limit its maximum size to about 20 employees. "This way, I can stay in touch with all my clients," he says.

Parry says that starting a consulting firm for ailing businesses during strong economic times was a good test for his company and that he will do even better during economic downturns. "You can't always succeed at everything," he says. "But at this point, I'm batting 1.000, and I intend to keep it that way."

Freedman, Krochmal, and Goldin, P.C.

For the firm of Freedman, Krochmal, and Goldin, P.C., the practice of law is more than just attorneys representing clients. "We look at our practice as a team effort composed of the client and the attorney as well as support personnel," says Gary A. Krochmal, one of the three principal attorneys in the company. He notes that support also comes in the form of computer data and thorough research.

"We're a young and growing firm whose idea is to provide a service to our clients," says Krochmal. "We spend a lot of time with our clients making sure we understand the facts and explaining how the law affects them."

This general-service civil law firm represents plaintiffs and defendants in personal-injury cases. Its professional services include insurance, workers' compensation, and corporate defense work, as well as municipal litigation and counseling. The firm represents companies, individuals, and municipalities.

From a firm of just three people, the company has grown to 13 staff members, including the three principal attorneys. In addition to the Southfield office, there are three other offices used to serve the Detroit metropolitan area and other parts of Michigan. Detroit-area offices are in South Lyon in Oakland County, Westland in Wayne County, and Davison in Genesee County.

One of the principals is Marvin A. Freedman, who has more than 25 years of legal experience. A graduate of Michigan State University and the Detroit College of Law, he is a member of the State Bar of Michigan, the American Trial Lawyers Association, and the Michigan Trial Lawyers Association. He also is a member of the Detroit and Oakland County bar associations and the Michigan Defense Trial Counsel Association. Freedman also is an arbitrator with the American Arbitration Association.

Krochmal is a graduate of the University of Michigan and Wayne State University law school. He is a member of the State Bar of Michigan, the American and Michigan trial lawyers associations, and the Detroit and Oakland County bars. He has

been an arbitrator with the American Arbitration Association, has been appointed to serve as a district and circuit court mediator, and is a member of the Oakland County Bar Association Medical/Legal Committee.

Gary A. Goldin, a graduate of Wayne State and the Thomas M. Cooley Law School, also is a member of the local trial lawyers and bar associations. He has practiced law in the district, circuit, and appellate courts of Michigan, as well as in the federal court system. He is an arbitrator with the American Arbitration Association.

Freedman, Krochmal, and Goldin's clients are not only local but national and international as well, extending as far away as Belgium. Krochmal says the firm is proud that it does not have to advertise to get business. "All of our business comes from referrals from our clients and other attorneys," says Krochmal. "We're a growing firm, and as we service more clients, our referral list keeps growing. Every day is more demanding and calls for more creativity than the day before."

Harley Ellington Pierce Yee Associates, Inc.

"The greatness of so many structures throughout history seems to rest upon that subtle balance between inspired architectural design and engineering genius," says Ralph Pierce, P.E., president of one of Oakland County's premier architecture, engineering, and planning firms, Harley Ellington Pierce Yee Associates, Inc. (HEPY).

A host of significant projects for such prominent clients as Chrysler Corporation, Ford Motor Company, GMF Robotics, and ITT Automotive is evidence that this firm is striving with success to achieve that balance and, along the way, make history for Oakland County. With such impressive projects coming off its drawing boards as the interior of the 3.3-million-square-foot Chrysler Technology Center, GMF Robotics World Headquarters and Technology Development Center, and ITT Automotive Headquarters, it comes as no surprise that the firm has more than doubled its staff and volume of work in the Southfield office over the past 10 years and that its revenues have ranked it the fourth-largest architectural and engineering firm in Michigan.

Established in 1908, the 200-person firm credits its growth and longevity to strong management and the personal responsibility of its 30 principals for the successful completion of each and every project that HEPY undertakes.

Long-term relationships with clients, some dating back 60 years and more, have fostered stability. HEPY attributes its high rate of repeat business to the benefits clients gain from the wealth of experience the firm has to draw from and build upon, established procedures to successfully guide projects, a long tradition of excellence, and the assurance that quality design

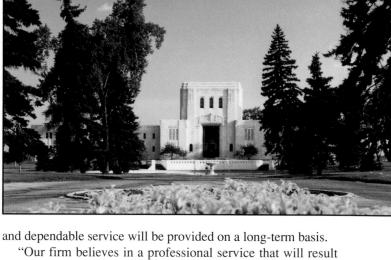

and dependable service will be provided on a long-term basis.

"Our firm believes in a professional service that will result in long, enduring client relationships throughout the years," says Pierce. "Some of our most fruitful relationships have evolved from small projects. We believe small projects are the acorns from which large projects grow, therefore all projects are important to us," he adds.

In fact, the fast-growing Oakland Technology Park owes some of its success to the well-established team of HEPY and Comerica. A client for over 25 years, Comerica asked HEPY to assist in the selection of a site for its proposed Operations Center. Based on the qualities of the site selected in Auburn Hills and the award-winning facility HEPY designed, the Operations Center became the cornerstone of the Oakland Technology Park, now one of the state's leading centers for high-tech and automotive research and development.

HEPY subsequently guided the selection of specific sites for GMF Robotics World Headquarters and Technology Center and ITT Automotive Headquarters in the park, designed both facilities, and is currently providing architectural, engineering, and planning services for the interior of the Chrysler Technology Center, one of the largest interior architecture programs in the world.

Other major projects in Oakland County include

Facing Top: White Chapel Cemetery
Temple of Memories Mausoleum
Troy, Michigan.

Facing Bottom Left: GMF Robotics
World Headquarters and Technology Development Center
Rochester Hills, Michigan

Facing Bottom Right: ITT Automotive, Inc.
Headquarters and Technical Development Center
Auburn Hills, Michigan

Below Left: Comerica Incorporated
Operations Center
Auburn Hills, Michigan

Below Right: FNMC/Northwestern Development Co., Ltd.
First Center Office Plaza
Southfield, Michigan

HEPY's own headquarters, the First Center Office Plaza in Southfield; Space Needs Studies and Master Plans for the Southfield Civic Center and Oakland County Service Center; Oakland Community College's Community Activities Building in Farmington Hills; Oakland University's Science and Technology Center in Rochester; the Rochester Hills Public Safety Building; and White Chapel Memorial Cemetery and Mausoleum in Troy.

Other significant projects state and nationwide include the Corning Federal Credit Union in Corning, New York; the University of Indiana Chemistry Building Addition and Renovation in Bloomington, Indiana; and the Ford Scientific Research Laboratory in Dearborn, Michigan.

The firm works as a team, drawing upon the creative talent and technical expertise of planners, programmers, architects, mechanical and electrical engineers, civil and structural engineers, site development and landscape architects, interior designers, graphics and signage specialists, and construction specialists. With all of these services under one roof, the firm has the luxury of being able to talk with one another a great deal about all of a project's requirements. As a result, they can produce better architectural and engineering designs, fully considering the environmental and social impact of their work.

Although its concentration of projects are high-tech, industrial, and health care facilities, the company uses its expertise in many different areas. HEPY is the nation's foremost designer of cemeteries and mausoleums. The firm offers comprehensive site planning and interior architecture services. In its efforts to diversify its market base, HEPY founded the national network of firms known as The HEPY Group. In addition to the Southfield headquarters, The HEPY Group has offices throughout North America.

HEPY's quality work and innovative designs have not gone unrecognized. The firm has received numerous awards for design excellence over the years from both peers in the architecture, engineering, and planning fields and from organizations representing the owners and users of their facilities. HEPY was recently recognized as one of the country's 1990 Interior Design Top 100 Giants.

"Good design is client responsive and function responsive. We don't ever want to lose sight of the fact that it is people that buildings are designed for—that buildings are for people to work in, to live in, and to play in," says Harry VanDine, FAIA, senior vice president for architecture and design.

"Clients are an integral part of every project, and we discuss their project goals and user needs extensively before the first line touches paper," VanDine explains. "Our solutions are based on clarity and simplicity. They balance form with function. We don't design something that works and then make it look good. The visual solution is inherent in the functional solution. By treating both as one, we achieve balance. The architecture is never a veneer; the engineering is never an afterthought."

Ellis/Naeyaert/Genheimer Associates, Inc.

In the complex world of building construction and renovation, summarizing what the firm of Ellis/Naeyaert/Genheimer Associates, Inc., does is rather simple. "We're a full-service architectural and engineering firm," says James W. Page, P.E., vice president/new business development for the Troy-based company. "Our stock-in-trade is the design of buildings."

But while its purpose may be stated simply, the expertise of the firm's professionals and the quality of its work ranks among the top in today's technologically advanced field of building design.

The company has about 140 employees with approximately 100 working out of the main headquarters in Troy and another 40 stationed at an office in Asheville, North Carolina. Although priding themselves on having clients from coast to coast, officials of the firm say that the majority of work comes from the upper Midwest, predominantly Michigan and Ohio. Projects can include new buildings or building renovation. Its client list is varied.

The company began in 1962, and for the first few years it concentrated on work in the automotive industry. Today 60 percent of the company's projects still involve industrial work with about 45 percent coming from automotive and supplier firms and the other 15 percent in such industries as food, pharmaceuticals, and plastics. However, the other 40 percent of the projects are for a variety of commercial, educational, governmental, and health care clients. The list of projects that Ellis/Naeyaert/Genheimer has been involved in is extensive.

Recent projects have included a 450,000-square-foot central office complex for General Dynamics, a 380,000-square-foot office and corporate learning center for The Upjohn Company, major facility improvement programs for General Motors' B-O-C Group and Hydra-matic Division, two 350,000-square-foot warehouse expansions for K mart Corp., and wind tunnels for the Boeing Co. and Ford Motor Co.

Also among Ellis/Naeyaert/Genheimer Associates' projects are several diverse facilities for foreign-owned companies such as Aisin-Seiki Co., Ltd.; Aisin U.S.A., Inc.; Robert Bosch Corporation; and Immuno-U.S., Inc.

J. Edward Genheimer, P.E., president and chief executive officer of the firm, credits his company's team-approach style of operation with establishing the firm's reputation as a truly client-centered organization.

"It's unique in our profession to be organized this way, and it enables us to be more responsive to our clients' needs," he says. Under the more traditional version, when clients hire an architectural and engineering firm, they are assigned to a project manager, who must work with and draw talent from individual discipline departments of professionals.

However, under the Ellis/Naeyaert/Genheimer system, a client is assigned to a team manager. Within that team are all of the professional and technical personnel—architectural, electrical, mechanical, and structural engineers—needed for the project. The teams are usually composed of about 15 to 20 people and are often seen as small, independent companies.

"The team approach provides close, personal attention and continuing responsiveness to a client's project," says Genheimer. The concept also improves internal communication in the firm and promotes a high level of quality in the design documents.

Facing Top: About 60 percent of Ellis/Naeyaert/Genheimer's work involves industrial projects, such as the Robert Bosch Corporation's automotive office and research center in Farmington Hills.

Facing Center: The Cross Company manufacturing plant in Port Huron is another of the company's designs.

Facing Bottom: Ellis/Naeyaert/Genheimer's list of foreign clients includes Aisin U.S.A., Inc., which commissioned this office and distribution center in Plymouth Township.

Right: Recent projects include this 450,000-square-foot central office complex for General Dynamics in Sterling Heights.

Bottom: Ellis/Naeyaert/Genheimer also completed a 380,000-square-foot office and corporate learning center for The Upjohn Company in Portage.

While the firm originally drew its business from the automotive industry, it was forced to expand into other industrial fields during the 1970s and 1980s, partly to offset occasional economic slumps in the auto industry. As the firm diversified and expanded geographically, it also continued to keep pace with the rapidly changing technology of the 1980s, including computer graphics and computer-aided facility management.

The company was started by cofounders Roger S. Naeyaert, P.E., and William H. Ellis, A.I.A., in Warren, and the offices were moved to Troy in 1977. Genheimer says the move was logical because company officials wanted to be closer to where professionals in the business lived and worked.

Over the years Ellis/Naeyaert/Genheimer has established itself as a firm of integrity that produces quality work. Numerous awards for functional facility design and engineering innovation that have saved clients' money in initial construction as well as day-to-day operations have helped build the firm's reputation. According to Donald C. Brockman, P.E., vice president/operations, the key to Ellis/Naeyaert/Genheimer's success is its ability to offer a broad range of highly specialized services in programming, space planning, architecture, engineering, cost estimating, and construction administration. Officers of the company note with pride that 85 percent of its

projects involve business from previous clients. The company's future plans are as simple as its job description.

"To remain a viable entity in this business, we have to grow," says Page. "Our goals are to continue to grow and expand our presence in the marketplace. We will continue to look for opportunities to expand our services through acquisition or merger. We will take our accomplishments in the architectural design area and build upon them."

For now, Genheimer says Ellis/Naeyaert/Genheimer Associates, Inc., is satisfied with what he feels is the basic image it portrays to clients. "We're recognized as an organization that provides good, basic service to a client, and our clients feel comfortable working with us."

Hubbell, Roth & Clark, Inc.

Much of the work of the engineering firm of Hubbell, Roth & Clark cannot be seen when it is finished. But without it, Oakland County's construction boom would not have happened.

The firm of consulting engineers based in Bloomfield Township provides a wide range of services but concentrates on the planning and building of storm-drainage systems, water-treatment systems, sewers, roads, and municipal facilities. It also serves commercial and industrial clients, working for both municipalities and private industry; many of the projects have led the way for Oakland County's present economic boom.

"We've done a lot of sewer and storm-drainage work that has led to the orderly development of the county," notes Donald R. McCormack, one of the nine principals of HRC.

The well-established local firm has served most communities in Oakland County as well as an extensive list of industrial and commercial clients. HRC provides a wide range of consulting engineering services to municipalities. It prepares master plans to ensure the orderly development of the community's water supply, storm-water control, wastewater collection and treatment, and traffic planning in the community.

Other municipal services include site-plan review, preparation of construction drawings, engineering during construction, construction inspection, surveying, mapping, and special studies and reports.

Hubbell, Roth & Clark, Inc., employs a multidiscipline professional staff of registered engineers, architects, and land surveyors. It provides capabilities in the environmental, structural, mechanical, electrical, architectural, operation and maintenance, computer and instrumentation, transportation, and hazardous-waste management areas.

In addition to municipal consulting services, HRC provides engineering for commercial site developments such as shopping

Bottom Left: Hubbell, Roth & Clark, consulting engineers, has served the Oakland County community from its present location since 1970.

Bottom Right: Water towers and related water supply systems are just one of the specialties of Hubbell, Roth & Clark.

malls and residential subdivisions. Engineering services for industrial clients include studies and designs for industrial wastewater treatment and hazardous-waste management.

HRC was started in 1915 by Clarence W. Hubbell and based in Detroit for many years. It moved to Birmingham in 1954 and then to Bloomfield Township in 1965. It moved into its present building in 1970.

Today the firm employs about 150 professional staff members and support workers. It has a branch in Detroit and has even done some international work for the major auto companies. However, HRC predominantly concentrates on southeastern Michigan.

"We're a conservative, old-line family company that has modernized with the times," says McCormack, who notes there are some third- and fourth-generation employees in the firm. He points out that the company has many repeat clients, some of whom have used the services of Hubbell, Roth & Clark, Inc., for 30 years or more.

"I think our long-term relationships with many of our clients attest to the fact we provide efficient, quality service," he concludes.

Ralph Manuel Realtors

Dennis P. Dickstein has simple yet definitely ambitious goals for Ralph Manuel Realtors. He wants to see it continue to grow and take over a greater percentage of the market.

In the next couple of years, Dickstein says he would like to see another office established. "A lot will depend on how the economy does," he says. "I hope that in the next 10 years we will both double our volume and our number of agents—maybe having seven or eight offices."

If history is any indication, the chairman and chief executive officer of the company should have few problems in seeing his firm reach and surpass his objectives. The Ralph Manuel real estate firm has been in the Birmingham area for more than 30 years, but since 1981, when Dickstein took over, the company's sales skyrocketed from $16 million to more than $170 million in 1989. Today the company consists of four offices. Added to the original office on Maple Road in Birmingham is a second one on Adams Road in Birmingham that now serves as the headquarters for the company. In addition, there are offices in Farmington Hills and Brighton. More than 150 agents and employees work at the four offices. The realty firm deals predominantly in homes sales, although its new commercial division is going very strong. "I don't know anybody who sells more new residential homes and lots than we do," Dickstein says with pride.

The agency specializes in the resale of high-quality new homes in Oakland County, western Wayne County, and Livingston. In addition, Dickstein says his company is now into property management and has recently contracted to handle more than 1,400 condominium units.

As a real estate agency, the company offers a complete range of services, priding itself on its strategically located offices, giving clients personalized attention using the latest in electronic-processing equipment to obtain current real estate information, an in-house advertising program, and a local, national, and international relocation service.

Although Dickstein has only managed the Ralph Manuel firm for a few years, he established his name in the Detroit area as a prestigious builder and realtor. Since 1957 he is credited with personally selling more than 2,700 homes. As a builder and general contractor, Dickstein has been involved in constructing offices, restaurants, and commercial buildings and has built more than 2,000 homes in Wayne, Oakland, and Washtenaw counties.

Dickstein's professional list of credits is impressive. He is a certified residential specialist, a certified real estate appraiser, a graduate of Realtors Institute, and has taught real estate law and construction mathematics for eight years.

Doing business in Oakland County makes sense, says Dickstein. "Oakland County is a vibrant, up-to-date, prestigious community. If we're going to specialize in high-quality homes, what better place than in Oakland County?"

Dickstein also is modest in placing credit for Ralph Manuel Realtors' success. "I'm just plain proud," he says. "Proud of the people that made this company. It's through their efforts that it has grown. I just try to stay out of the way."

Business and Finance

Oakland County's solid financial base has provided a dynamic environment for the economic growth and opportunity of both individuals and businesses in the community

Photo by Gary Quesada/Korab Ltd.

178

Standard Federal Bank

As the area's leading home lender, Standard Federal Bank remains committed to Oakland County as an outstanding place to live and work. Officials of the Troy-based bank credit much of their success as a leading lender to making operations increasingly efficient and to providing basic retail financial services designed to meet the needs of families.

Preeminent among these services is the bank's commitment to single-family mortgage lending. This is the principal business of Standard Federal and one that, year after year, generates more single-family mortgages than any other financial institution in southeast Michigan.

Other popular services of the bank include checking and savings accounts, certificates of deposit, equity line loans, and other consumer lending products. Electronic banking products, such as VISA®, ATM banking, and direct deposit accounts are also significant in the bank's product line.

"As well as offering good service to our customers, our success has largely resulted from staying focused on the basics of our business," says Thomas R. Ricketts, chairman of the board and president.

Below: Located on West Big Beaver Road in Troy, the Standard Federal Financial Center serves as both a bank operations center and corporate headquarters. Photo by Balthazar Korab

Facing Left: Standard Federal Bank service employees begin their banking careers with an intensive training course that emphasizes banking procedures, product knowledge, and customer care. Photo by Balthazar Korab

Facing Right: The first floor of the Standard Federal Financial Center is a "retail" space where a full-service branch office discount brokerage subsidiary, consumer lending area, savings services group, and ATM are located. Photo by Balthazar Korab

Standard Federal began in 1893 in Detroit. It became federally chartered in 1950 and, in 1985, adopted a mutual savings bank charter. The bank moved its headquarters to Birmingham in 1970. Three years later it moved to Troy and began an impressive period of growth and expansion.

Bank assets ballooned from one billion dollars in the early 1970s to approximately $10 billion today. Thirteen mergers have contributed to the bank's expansion into a major regional savings institution with well over 100 branches across southern Michigan and northern Indiana. In spite of its size, the bank's total work force of about 2,500 employees reflects well on its efficient, highly automated operations.

Standard Federal's success can be attributed to three main areas: its strategies; its services, including a strong commitment to community involvement; and its innovations, which include some of the industry's most sophisticated information-management technologies. The bank's strategy is to build a solid foundation for core earnings by controlling interest rate and credit risk and by maintaining low overhead expenses. This involves concentrating on such staples as residential mortgage lending and other family-oriented retail banking products. Utilizing the latest technologies, a number of economy-of-scale efficiencies have made these traditional product lines highly profitable in a rapidly changing industry.

Within the area of retail banking, Standard Federal's services are wide ranging. Passbook and money market savings accounts are offered as well as certificates of deposit. Its home loans range from traditional, fixed-rate mortgages, where interest is the same throughout the life of the loan, to the lifetime adjustable-rate mortgage, where rates annually reprice depending on market rates. With a convertible ARM, borrowers can convert to a fixed-rate mortgage at any time during the lifetime of the loan. Among the bank's consumer lending products, the Equity Line loan allows cus-

tomers to leverage the equity in their homes to secure more favorable rates. In many cases, Equity Line loans may also offer a number of favorable tax advantages as well.

Standard Federal also features a full line of consumer loans, commercial loans, and a number of lending opportunities designed to meet the needs of low- to moderate-income individuals.

Standard Brokerage Services, Inc., a fully owned discount brokerage subsidiary, provides customers with access to up-to-date trading information and the opportunity to execute trades at substantial discounts. Also among the bank's many services are direct deposit accounts for recurring checks, automatic overdraft protection for checking customers, and the convenience of ATM banking for checking and passbook customers.

Being a good corporate citizen is also very important. As an active supporter of many activities that benefit the community, Standard Federal continues to participate in the annual United Way campaign, the annual March of Dimes Walk-a-Thon, and numerous American Red Cross blood drives throughout the year. To support the cause of education, the bank participates in the Detroit Compact program, Junior Achievement's Project Business, and an annual children's book drive called A Gift of Reading. To assist low- to moderate-income individuals become home owners, Standard Federal is an active supporter of the Michigan Housing Trust Fund and the Detroit Neighborhood Housing Services, Inc. The bank is also a frequent sponsor of the Detroit Festival of the Arts, the Detroit Symphony Orchestra, the Detroit Institute of Arts, and many other cultural programs.

Company officers and employees are encouraged to support their local communities and have donated thousands of hours of time to hundreds of volunteer activities. The bank is also an active member of the Michigan Corporate Volunteer Counsel, the sponsor of Paint the Town.

Another special program that the bank supports is called Twelve Together. Developed by the Metropolitan Detroit Youth Foundation, this project helps keep students in school and reduce dropout rates. Meeting once every week at Standard Federal's downtown Detroit Branch office, "at-risk" students receive peer counseling and develop strong support systems as they gain insight into what it takes to be a success in school and in life.

Standard Federal is also the leading financial institution in participation and support of the Michigan Education Trust (MET) program. The bank worked closely with the Office of the State Treasurer to develop the program, which is designed

to help parents afford the high cost of a college education through a one-time investment in a special state-administered trust fund. For 1988 and 1989 Standard Federal financed more MET loans than any other financial institution.

Innovation is also a watchword for Standard Federal Bank. Officials stress how much they are committed to constantly evolving new technologies to provide significant economies of scale and operating efficiencies.

The bank's new, six-story financial center on West Big Beaver Road in Troy serves as an investment in the future. It is a 450,000-square-foot modernist landmark structure featuring a central atrium and uncommon architecture that give the

building its unique appearance. As both a corporate headquarters and a centralized bank operations center that serves the entire corporation, the building's floor plans were designed to maximize human interaction along functional lines. For example, the computer center is located close to the imaging and printing complex, which, in turn, is located next to a paper supply area. The bank's highly automated mail room is also nearby to facilitate processing information within the bank and to outside business associates and customers. Standard Federal's presence in Oakland County is and has been consistently strong.

"Standard Federal Bank is the largest savings institution headquartered in Oakland County," notes Tom Ricketts. "We've also been the leading originator of single-family mortgage loans for 13 out of the past 16 years in southeastern Michigan."

"We will continue to focus on expanding our retail banking franchise throughout the 1990s," says Garry Carley, executive vice president. "That is, we will continually increase our customer base and the number of accounts served while staying dedicated to the best service available in our markets."

First of America Bank— Southeast Michigan

To most people the phrase "community banking" sounds like an anachronism from the American frontier era. But to employees of First of America Bank, these are words to live by.

"Community involvement is second nature to our employees," says David T. Harrison, president of First of America Bank—Southeast Michigan. "Our employees are not only professionally but also personally committed to the communities where they live and work."

Commitment means more than joining the local chapter of the Rotary Club. The bank strongly believes that any Oakland County financial institution must understand the diverse cultures, economics, industries, and life-styles of the region—such as farming, tourism, lumber, and automobiles—in order to serve it properly.

"To understand what our communities want and need in terms of financial services and economic assistance, we need to be involved," says Harrison.

Formed in April 1988 with the merger of four independent First of America affiliates—including Detroit, Wayne/Oakland, Oakland/Macomb, and Rochester—First of America Bank—Southeast Michigan boasts $2.7 billion in assets. The bank has more than 1,300 employees and serves the Detroit metropolitan area with 70 banking offices.

First of America Bank—Southeast Michigan is an affiliate of Kalamazoo-based First of America Bank Corporation, Michigan's second-largest banking company with more than $12.8 billion in assets. The company's 36 affiliate banks provide financial services to more than 350 communities in Illinois, Indiana, and Michigan through 400 banking offices.

Below Right: The bank's 15,000-square-foot operations center under construction in Royal Oak, Michigan, is scheduled to open in 1992.

Bottom: The beautiful, modern Orchard Lake-Maple Road office located in West Bloomfield is First of America Bank's newest Oakland County office.

One of the natural benefits of its community banking policy is a wide array of locally available deposit, investment, and lending services, including several banking industry innovations. With the home improvement loan account, for example, customers can finance home improvements and home-related purchases as they are needed, without having to apply for a new loan each time. This account also services local merchants by providing them with a convenient, affordable financing alternative to offer their customers.

In addition to more traditional loan and deposit products, the bank offers a variety of services that require a high level of specialization and expertise. First of America provides a wide array of international services that facilitate the import and export activity of its domestic customers. The bank's trust

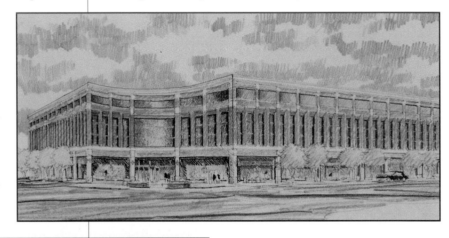

division features professional corporate and individual trust services through all of its branches. Included among these services is investment management. Through the division's own Parkstone family of mutual funds, bank customers have access to investment returns that consistently rank among the top in the nation.

As First of America Bank—Southeast Michigan moves into the 1990s, it will continue its dedication to Oakland County, actively seeking new branch sites in the region. The company is finalizing plans for a new $15-million, 150,000-square-foot operations center adjacent to its present headquarters in Royal Oak.

"We see Oakland County as a dynamic, progressive environment in which to continue our growth," affirms Harrison. "Our commitment to our communities is the cornerstone of our past and future success."

Thompson-Brown

For thousands of their families and businesses, Thompson-Brown is a part of their American dream. One of the area's oldest realtors, Thompson-Brown is active in leasing and sales of office, commercial, and industrial buildings as well as land development, residential home sales, and resort development.

The firm specializes in site search and evaluations for commercial, industrial, and research companies, for offices and for institutions. It also deals in residential relocation services. Thompson-Brown is a member of the national relocation network known as Homes for Living. In five years 15 Thompson-Brown staff members have completed more than 1,000 property transactions.

Hundreds of businesses have found their niche in a Thompson-

The resort has two 18-hole championship golf courses as well as ski slopes, tennis courts, an indoor/outdoor swimming pool, and a clubhouse with formal dining facilities.

When Henry Thompson and Charles Brown formed their partnership in 1924, Detroit's economy, including the real estate business, was excellent. For 67 years the company has continued to buy, develop, and market a mixture of commercial, industrial, office, and residential property.

Thompson-Brown president William W. Bowman joined the firm in 1954, rising to executive vice president by 1965 and to his present position in 1979. He has not only guided the company through vital business moves, but is an active representative, serving as lecturer and panelist for local, state, and national associations. Bowman has been appointed by the governor to serve as a state commissioner on the Construction and Safety Standards Commission. He presently is serving a second term as the commission's chairman.

Thompson-Brown has played a significant role in the development of Oakland County. As a new century approaches, the firm will continue to be a vital factor in local achievements. Much of the county's progress will undoubtedly be entrusted to the experienced sculpting of Thompson-Brown.

Headquartered in the Thompson-Brown Office Center at 32823 Twelve Mile Road in Farmington Hills, the firm also has offices in Novi, at 45650 Grand River Avenue; in Livonia, at 32646 Five Mile Road; and in West Bloomfield, at 7399 Middlebelt Road.

Brown development. In 1965 the company ventured into industrial park and property development in what was known as Farmington Township. Today the 300-acre Farmington Hills Freeway Industrial Park houses more than 100 businesses, including Nabisco, TRW, White Castle Systems, and Holiday Inn. This is the first industrial park development to receive a Class A rating by the State of Michigan.

Thompson-Brown has been involved in developing six other industrial parks. Along with new job opportunities, the parks have increased revenue for whole communities by expanding tax bases. The company has also been developing and marketing single-family home communities since the late 1940s. Now these developments thrive in the Oakland County area.

The firm is presently developing about 3,000 acres of land near Gaylord, Michigan. The year-round recreational community is called Michaywe (MICH-eh-way).

Allstate Insurance Group

With emphasis on the customer and a commitment to being the best in the industry, Allstate Insurance Group has grown into the second-largest property and casualty insurance company in the nation. Top priority of the company is its commitment to the customer, says Ken L. Styles, regional controller for Allstate's Michigan area, which is headquartered in Southfield. The next three commitments are to employees, the community, and quality.

Styles says insurance companies today must provide more than just insurance. "Providing quality customer service, peace of mind, and adapting the product to the needs of the customer are what insurance companies must do today," he says. Key values in this process, Styles adds, are integrity, innovation, caring, and initiative.

Allstate's presence in Oakland County is not restricted to just Southfield. It has two other major claims offices, one in Troy and one in Farmington Hills. There are more than 20 sales offices with one or two agents each. Of the company's 50,000 employees nationally, 1,450 are in Michigan, serving six other claims centers in the state in addition to those in Oakland County.

Allstate has two drive-in claims offices in Oakland County, one in Pontiac and the other at the Southfield headquarters. Although such centers are common today, "The drive-in concept is one we invented and one we're proud of," says Styles. "It's a good example of the innovative service we're able to offer our customers. We're pleased with the relationships we've established in Oakland County and look forward to the

Below: The headquarters for Allstate's Michigan area is located in Southfield.

Facing: Duncan Mitchell writes a damage estimate at Allstate's Southfield drive-in claims office, one of two such centers in Oakland County.

future service we will be providing," he says.

Allstate has more than $300 million in investments in Michigan, from municipal bonds to sewer projects. As company president Ray Keifer points out, "The insurance industry is the glue that holds the financial aspect of society together."

Among the basic insurance services provided by Allstate is its personal property and casualty division, which offers auto, personal liability, and home owner insurance. Also part of this division is Tech-Cor, Inc., an automobile research and claims training center.

Allstate Life Insurance Company offers a wide variety of personal and group life insurance, short- and long-term disability insurance, annuity, and pension products. Subsidiaries of this division include Northbrook Life Insurance Company, Surety Life Insurance Company, Lincoln Benefit Life Company, and Allstate Life Insurance Company of New York.

The business insurance division meets the property and liability needs of small, medium, and large businesses as well as the reinsurance needs of other insurers. Specialized products include workers' compensation, surety bonds, and ocean/marine coverage.

Other Allstate operations include Allstate Enterprises, Inc., which serves as the holding company for Direct Marketing Center Inc., and Allstate Motor Club. The marketing center is a full-service, telemarketing/direct-mail resource. The motor

club, which was the first of its kind in the United States, provides automobile and travel-related services to more than 2.5 million members. Also, the Allstate research and planning center conducts research and provides Allstate businesses with planning information about products, customer service, and operations.

The company also has several operations outside the United States that demonstrate its commitment to serving the global insurance market. These include Allstate Reinsurance Company Limited, which underwrites European reinsurance business from offices in London, England, and Zug, Switzerland.

Allstate of Canada, with headquarters in Toronto, sells and services personal and commercial lines property liability products and personal and group life, health, and annuity insurance products throughout Canada. Seibu Allstate Life Insurance Co. Ltd. in Tokyo is a joint venture between the Seibu Saison Group and Allstate. Through its other joint venture, Allstate Automobile and Fire Insurance Co. Ltd., a full range of property and casualty insurance products are sold in Japan.

Although a large company, Allstate has not forgotten its responsibility to be a good, caring corporate citizen. To demonstrate its commitment to the communities it serves, Allstate has established several public service programs.

Its Allstate Foundation gives about $10 million annually to support education, culture, health, youth, safety, and other worthwhile endeavors. The foundation allows employees to participate actively in grant-making decisions.

Allstate conducts forums on public issues, reflecting the company's belief that business has an obligation to help solve major problems facing society. The forum brings together leaders from diverse sectors of American society who communicate about pressing public issues.

Corporate advocacy efforts show Allstate's concern for promoting government and industry responsibility. As a vigorous advocate of auto safety, the company championed mandatory seat-belt use, lobbied for bumper reform and passive passenger-restraint systems, fought to eliminate drunk driving, and promoted driver education.

Allstate also supports its employees who may wish to perform public service on their own. The company encourages workers to participate in the United Way and other charitable programs.

Allstate was started in late 1930 and, despite the Depression, managed to remain in business and grow. The company came to Michigan in the 1950s and opened an office in Detroit. It moved to offices near Northland, then to Southfield in the mid-1960s, and opened its present offices in Southfield in 1968.

"We have been in Oakland County for more than 20 years and it has served Allstate well," says Styles. "We see Oakland County as a very profitable market for us to do business in. We expect to continue to be a part of the county and its development."

NBD Bank, N.A.

Since its establishment in 1933 as National Bank of Detroit. NBD Bank has had as its goal to provide quality banking services to both individuals and businesses. Begun in Detroit during the Depression, NBD has a history of expansion that includes drawing upon and enhancing the expertise of such local facilities as the former National Bank of Rochester and the former Pontiac State Bank.

NBD provides consumers with the full array of banking services, including checking and savings accounts, mortgages, consumer loans, and installment loans for such items as autos or home improvement.

NBD also provides trust services to individual customers. For corporate customers NBD acts as an investment adviser, administrator, shareholder record keeper, and dividend disbursing agent for trusts. The company is one of the nation's largest providers of Master Trust services. This is a specialized custodial service that is used by employee benefit, institutional, and foundation accounts. Home Equity loans allow people to borrow money for many different purposes using the equity in their homes as collateral.

The bank also is a leader in offering a wide range of technology-based services. In 1989 NBD installed several drive-up automatic teller machines to supplement its ATM network. The drive-up machines allow customers to bank any time of the day or night from the safety of their own cars. NBD also has a telephone banking center that allows customers to open an account or borrow money by simply making a telephone call.

But complete consumer services are only a part of NBD. "We are a commercial bank that provides numerous services to both small and large businesses," notes Andrew Creamer, first vice president and director of NBD's Pontiac-North Oakland Regional Banking Center.

Creamer notes that one of NBD's strong points is its corporate cash-management program for businesses. Bank experts

instruct their commercial customers on ways to improve cash flow and invest surplus funds at higher rates of return.

NBD also has established several special lending services over the years, such as the loan placement group. This group arranges long-term permanent financing for commercial real estate projects. The group represents five major life insurance companies and are advisers for a large domestic pension fund. The projects it can finance range from as small as $500 thousand up to $150 million. Loan structures and terms are somewhat flexible. Generally loans have seven-year to 15-year maturities and 25-year to 30-year amortizations, with fixed interest rates priced slightly over treasury bills. In some cases, the pricing can include a participation in cash flow and appreciation if the borrower desires a larger than normal loan amount at a below-market interest rate. The placement group is head-

Facing Top: NBD's loan placement group is headquartered in the NBD Troy Towers.

Facing Bottom: NBD Bank's West Maple-Cranbrook office in Birmingham, Michigan.

Right: NBD's Pontiac-North Oakland regional banking center is located in the Pontiac State Bank Building.

Bottom: NBD's Telegraph West Long Lake Office in Bloomfield Hills.

quartered in Troy, but it works on projects all over Michigan, northern Ohio, northern Indiana, and greater metropolitan Chicago. Over the past three years, this group has averaged one loan closing every 10 days.

NBD also has foreign offices located in London, Tokyo, Frankfurt, Windsor, Toronto, and Nassau. The Tokyo and London branches, which marked their 15th and 20th anniversaries, respectively, have been operating profitably the past few years, providing substantial support to NBD's domestic lending staff in assisting customers' overseas operations, as well as developing new business with foreign companies investing in the Midwest.

Today NBD is a wholly owned subsidiary of NBD Bancorp, which has financial operations in Michigan, Indiana, and Illinois.

In 1933 National Bank of Detroit, NBD Bancorp's predecessor company, was founded by General Motors and the Reconstruction Finance Corporation. The bank prospered and grew until GM sold its stock in the bank and it became a public company in 1945. Coincidentally, in 1945, Pontiac State Bank opened its doors, although it would not be until about 40 years later when it would become part of NBD.

In 1955 NBD merged with the Oakland County-based Rochester National Bank, and in 1973 NBD formed a bank holding company, which would become known as NBD Bancorp. The bank made its largest Oakland County acquisition in 1984, when it took over the 20 offices and $600 million in assets of the Pontiac State Bank.

NBD is the largest bank in Michigan and one of the top 20 in the nation. It has 150 branches in southeast Michigan and 46 branches in Oakland County. Of its $12 billion in deposits, $2.3 billion are in Oakland County.

In its continuing efforts to remain a leading financial institution, NBD Bancorp plans are under way to build a Technology Center near Interstate 94 and Interstate 275 in Van Buren Township. The building will consolidate operational activities for greater efficiency and service to customers. The project, being constructed on a 52-acre site at the northwest corner of Haggerty and Tyler roads, is expected to be finished in the early 1990s.

Creamer credits much of the success of NBD Bank to its 6,000 employees. "We like to think we're providing our customers with quality services because we have people who care," says Creamer.

He notes the bank's objectives are simple: to be the financial service provider of choice in southeast Michigan. "You have to be sensitive to the consumers' needs and to the market," Creamer says. "NBD is a quality organization from its loan portfolio to its employees."

Biltmore Properties

The impressive list of development and construction projects that Biltmore Properties has completed literally touches thousands of lives in the Detroit metropolitan area.

Over its 35-year history, the corporation and its affiliated companies have developed thousands of acres of land in Oakland, Macomb, and Wayne counties. More than 20,000 residential lots have been developed in more than 100 subdivisions. Biltmore has constructed more than 10,000 single-family homes and condominiums, as well as about 5,000 apartment units.

"We believe that Biltmore Properties may be the largest developer of residential properties in Michigan," says Bernard H. Stollman, secretary/treasurer.

One of the firm's major achievements was the development and construction of the Somerset Park project in Troy. This included 2,226 rental apartment units, a nine-hole golf course, a 21,000-square-foot office building, and the fashionable Somerset Mall, which includes such stores as Saks Fifth Avenue and Bonwit Teller.

Also among its accomplishments is the construction of the Cherry Hill, Carriage Hill, and Carriage Park complexes in Dearborn Heights. The 395-unit Thornberry Apartments were recently completed in West Bloomfield, and the 300-unit Birchcrest Apartments are under construction in Sterling Heights. Office and industrial developments are under way at I-275 and Ford Road in Canton Township and in the Sterling Technology Park in Sterling Heights.

Stollman's father, Max, and his uncle, Phillip, started the company in the 1930s. They concentrated mainly on construction and, by the 1950s, had become one of the largest home-construction companies in Michigan. Gradually, however, the firm began to move into land development, which is its predominant activity today.

In addition to Bernard Stollman, the two other partners in the firm are Norman J. Cohen, president, and Abraham Ran, vice president. Cohen's responsibilities are primarily land acquisition, de-velopment, and marketing. Ran is in charge of construction of homes, condominiums, apartments, and office buildings. Stollman's duties include finance and property management. Max and Phillip Stollman are still associated with the firm in consulting capacities.

Recently the company has started two projects in Orlando, Florida. The Williamsburg Development is a mixed-use project that will contain 1,150 homes, 3 hotels, more than 400,000 square feet of office/industrial space, and 750 apartments. Renaissance is a downtown, five-story, luxury condominium project.

Looking ahead for Biltmore Properties, which started in Oak Park and moved to Troy in 1967, Stollman says, "We would like to increase both our land development and construction activities in Michigan and Florida, and we are exploring new markets as well."

Patrons

The following individuals, companies, and organizations have made a valuable commitment to the quality of this publication. Windsor Publications and the Oakland County Michigan Government gratefully acknowledge their participation in *Oakland County: Making it Work in Michigan.*

Allstate Insurance Group*
Arbor Drugs, Inc.*
Biltmore Properties*
The Budd Company*
The City of Southfield*
Consumers Power Company*
Crissman Cadillac*
Digital Equipment Corporation*
Ellis/Naeyaert/Genheimer
    Associates, Inc.*
Federal-Mogul Corporation*
First of America Bank-Southeast
    Michigan*

Freedman, Krochmal, and Goldin,
    P.C.*
General Motors*
Gresham Driving Aids, Inc.*
Harley Ellington Pierce Yee
    Associates, Inc.*
Hegenscheidt Corporation*
Holiday Inn of Southfield*
Hubbell, Roth & Clark, Inc.*
Hubert Distributors*
IBM*
Inter-Lakes Steel Products
    Company*
ITT Automotive, Inc.*
Lawrence Technological
    University*
Lear Seating Corp.*
McEndarffer, Hoke & Bernhard,
    P.C.*
Ralph Manuel Realtors*
Mold-A-Matic*
NBD Bank, N.A.*
Numatics Incorporated*

Oakland Community College*
Oakland University*
The Observer & Eccentric
    Newspaper, Inc.*
Parry and Associates, Inc.*
Pepsi-Cola Company*
Pontiac Osteopathic Hospital*
St. Joseph Mercy Hospital*
Sanyo Machine America Corp.*
Standard Federal Bank*
Su-Dan Company*
Thompson-Brown*
The Townsend Hotel*
UAW*
Universal Flow Monitors, Inc.*
White Chapel*
WWJ/WJOI*

*Participants in Part Two, *"Oakland County's Enterprises."* The stories of these companies and organizations appear in chapters 7 through 12, beginning on page 106.

Select Bibliography

BOOKS

America's Fascinating Indian Heritage. The Readers Digest Association, Inc., 1978.

Angelo, Frank. *Yesterday's Michigan.* E.A. Seemann Publishing Co., 1975.

Catton, Bruce. *Michigan, a History.* W.W. Norton Company, Inc., 1976.

Dunbar, Willis. *A History of the Wolverine State.* Eerdmans Publishing Co., 1970.

Fox, William A. *Rochester, A Sketch of One of the Best Towns on the Map.* W. A. Fox, 1907.

Hagman, Arthur A. *Oakland County Book of History.* Oakland County Sesqui-Centennial Executive Committee, 1970.

May, George S. *Michigan: An Illustrated History of the Great Lakes State.* Windsor Publications, Inc., 1987.

——————. *Pictorial History of Michigan: The Early Years.* Eerdsmans Publishing Co., 1967.

McMehan, Jervis Bell. *The Book of Birmingham.* The Bicentennial Committee of The Birmingham Historical Board, 1976.

Nelson, George. "A Fountainhead in Michigan." *Signature Magazine.* July 1983.

Peckham, Howard. *Pontiac and the Indian Uprising.* Princeton University Press, 1947.

Pound, Arthur. *The Only Thing Worth Finding.* Wayne State University Press, 1964.

Pray, Evla. *A History of Avon Township.* Nonce Press, 1986.

Seeley, Thaddeus S. *History of Oakland County: A Narrative Account of Its Historical Progress, Its People and Its Principal Interests.* The Lewis Publishing Co., 1912.

Sloan, Alfred P., Jr. *My Years With General Motors.* Fadden-Bartel, 1965.

Waddell, Richard Lee. *Out of Small Beginnings: A Bicentennial Historical Sketch of Oakland County, Michigan 1815-1976.* Oakland County American Revolution Bicentennial Commission, 1976.

Westbrook, Adele, and Anne Yarowsky, eds. *Design in America: The Cranbrook Vision 1925-1950.* Harry N. Abrams Inc., 1983.

NEWSPAPERS

The Detroit Free Press
The Detroit News
The Motor City News
The Oakland Press

MAGAZINES

Michigan Business
The Michigan Historical Review
Oakland Business
Oakland Focus

ADDITIONAL RESOURCES

Baldwin, Augustus C. Paper contributed to the Michigan Pioneer and Historical Collections.

Fulton, George A., and Donald R. Grimes. "The Economic Outlook For Oakland County in 1989-90." The Institute of Labor and Industrial Relations, University of Michigan, April 1989.

McCann, W.H. "A Brief History of the Beginnings of Oakland County." Oakland County Schools social studies project.

Profile, '86, A Compilation of Economic Data on Oakland County. Oakland County Office for Economic Development, 1986.

Index